Praise for
Retire Securely: Insights on Money Management from an Award-Winning Financial Columnist

"Once again, Julie Jason demonstrates an astute understanding of the psyche and motivations that drive investors. She's not here to sell you 'get-rich-quick' schemes, but to provide you with the right resources and education required to make wise, long-term investing decisions that make the most sense for your financial future."

—Don Phillips, managing director, Morningstar

"Outstanding! Out of the hundreds of books on how to navigate retirement, in her newest book, *Retire Securely*, Julie Jason writes from her own experience. Her inside knowledge shines a bright spotlight on the issues that matter most.

If you've ever been confused about how investment advisors work, or which type of advisor you should consider hiring, Julie has laid it all out for you. In chapter five, she clearly points out the potential conflicts of interest and gives readers simple steps to avoid hiring the wrong advisor, such as the importance of reviewing an advisor's disclosure records as the first line of defense. Readers will come away both informed and empowered."

—Pam Krueger, executive producer and cohost of the award-winning TV series *MoneyTrack* on PBS, and founder of Wealthramp.com.

"For two decades, Julie has been sharing her financial and investment expertise in an easy-to-understand manner. Her common-sense guidance on saving, investing and estate planning is both priceless and a must-read by all."

—Charles Rotblut, CFA, vice president, American Association of Individual Investors, author, *Better Good than Lucky*

"Let's face it, investing requires a little homework. Julie Jason's new book, *Retire Securely*, is a good place to start for anyone who wants to plan a more comfortable retirement."

—Howard Brecher, Publisher, The Value Line Investment Survey

"Julie Jason's weekly columns, over 1000 so far, have provided readers with practical guidance and advice on financial and related matters for almost 20 years. Undoubtedly, Julie's toughest task in assembling this book was winnowing her selection of columns into the 92 appearing in this book. She has selected so many that provide practical guidance in useful form for non-professional investors. That is Julie's thing, and she does it so well."

—MANNY BERNARDO (retired), Former Director of
Employee Benefits Tax Services for Deloitte & Touche Tristate,
Benefits Specialist Attorney, and Human Resources Benefits Executive

---

"Julie Jason provides readers with great investment insights for retirement and the rest of their financial lives."

—MARK KANTROWITZ, author of *Twisdoms about Paying for College*

"Julie Jason's book is a 'Must Read' for anyone who wants to learn more about planning for retirement, whether for yourself, or to advise others. Impeccable research, compelling content, all presented in an accessible, informative style that is the hallmark of Julie's books and newspaper columns over the years. I learned so much and enjoyed every page!"

—JUANITA T. JAMES, President & CEO of Fairfield County's Community Foundation

---

"Great investment advice is timeless. These columns from Julie Jason show the way on saving, investing and paving the way to a worry-free retirement."

—JANE BRYANT QUINN,
Author of *How to Make Your Money Last: The Indispensable Retirement Guide*

"Once again, when it comes to sound retirement advice, Julie Jason offers one-stop shopping for a financial feast."

—JOHN WASIK, Author of *Lightning Strikes: Timeless Lessons in Creativity
from the Life and Work of Nikola Tesla*

RETIRE
SECURELY

Insights on
Money Management
from an Award-Winning
Financial Columnist

JULIE JASON

STERLING
New York

To a "Secure Retiree," a physician, who I respect, admire,
and adore: my Mother, GJP. To this day she makes
my life a challenge and a joy.

STERLING
New York

An Imprint of Sterling Publishing Co., Inc.
1166 Avenue of the Americas
New York, NY 10036

Interior text © 2018 Julie Jason
Cover © 2018 Sterling Publishing Co., Inc.

ISBN 978-1-4549-2885-0

Distributed in Canada by Sterling Publishing Co., Inc.
$^c/o$ Canadian Manda Group, 664 Annette Street
Toronto, Ontario M6S 2C8, Canada
Distributed in the United Kingdom by GMC Distribution Services
Castle Place, 166 High Street, Lewes, East Sussex BN7 1XU, England
Distributed in Australia by NewSouth Books
45 Beach Street, Coogee NSW 2034, Australia

For information about custom editions, special sales,and premium and corporate purchases,
please contactSterling Special Sales at 800-805-5489
or specialsales@sterlingpublishing.com.

Manufactured in Canada

2 4 6 8 10 9 7 5 3 1

sterlingpublishing.com

Interior design by Christine Heun
Cover design by David Ter-Avanesyan

Contents

Acknowledgments

A SPECIAL THANK YOU

First and most importantly, you need to know that it is a joy to "talk" with my readers.

You not only made the column more meaningful to me personally, but also helped earn the column some distinctions and awards. I am grateful to you for your continued engagement and support.

I also recognize that the columns would be limited but for the experts who make their knowledge accessible to my readers. I am indebted to these sources who freely tackle thorny issues raised by my readers and offer insights and resources far beyond one person's knowledge.

Then, there are all the people behind the scenes at Hearst and King Features Syndicate who make the column possible, and last but certainly not least, are my Jackson, Grant Investment Advisers, Inc. colleagues who are always prepared to provide perspectives and insights.

I look forward to continuing our dialogue—write to me at readers@ juliejason.com with questions and comments for the column and, if you are interested in learning about Jackson, Grant, please visit our website at jacksongrant.us.

Who Should Read This Book?

This book is about retirement security, a topic that should be meaningful to all, as financial issues from investing to gifting impact so many people, young and not-so-young. If you are looking for context for today's markets, you will enjoy moving through history with me as I advise investors to be patient and occasionally opportunistic in the face of market extremes.

Most adults have an IRA or a 401(k) or both; many of the columns included in this book address investment and technical issues surrounding these tax advantaged savings vehicles, including beneficiary planning and gifting, and even how a child who earns money can set up a Roth IRA, which is the best way to take advantage of time and compounding.

For those seeking advice on their specific financial planning issues, not only do some of the columns speak to common issues, but they also provide advice on how to find good advisers. In this age of identify fraud and other scams, there is a section of columns that will inform readers of a number of practices of which they should be wary. While emails from Nigerian princes may be obvious scams, a phone call from the IRS may seem less questionable.

Improving financial literacy is something that most can work on, and a number of the included columns will be good for parents and their children to review at various stages of their financial planning lifecycles. Estate planning is particularly important for those likely to have to pay estate taxes, so individuals with taxable estates would benefit from both the estate planning and gifting sections of the book.

Foreword

In May 2013, King Features began syndicating Julie Jason's "Retirement Planning and Investment" column. She had written the column for newspapers in Connecticut for a number of years.

When I was initially assigned the task of editing Julie's column, my reaction was . . . well . . . "excited" would not have been the word. You see, her new editor, the child of bankers, had taken one economics course in college (what seemed like 100 years ago) and got an A, but it was a low A, much, much closer to the B level than to the 100 percent mark. Years later, I read Burton Malkiel's *A Random Walk Down Wall Street* and understood almost half of it. That was it on the financial education front.

So there I was, expecting a (don't tell Julie) "boring" column chock-full of concepts that would be difficult to understand. Instead, I found, believe it or not, "passion." You read that right: *passion* in a financial column.

Julie Jason is passionate about financial literacy. She wants to make people as knowledgeable as possible when it comes to saving money and making wise investments for retirement.

She comes to the table with a lot of experience, from being a lawyer on Wall Street to forging a successful career in money management and investment counseling. She has a strong understanding of market trends, studies financial analyses and keeps up with legislative changes. She has a wealth of information to share, and the collection of columns in this book shows the depth of her knowledge.

Julie also understands that it's not easy for the average person to take action on complex financial decisions. And speaking of the average person, it would be easy to assume that since Julie handles clients with substantial wealth, she wouldn't have time for people with simple questions (if such exist) about investing. That's not true. She cherishes her interactions with the readers of her column, and makes it a point each week to ask for their feedback (readers@juliejason.com— just in case you need it).

In a world where Social Security has an ill-defined future, pensions are mostly a thing of the past, and young people often have to be coerced into investing in a 401(k), Julie Jason is on a quest to get people prepared for retirement. People simply are not saving enough, and Julie is standing in that gap with signal flags, pointing them in the right direction.

It's been my honor to serve as Julie's syndication editor for the past five years, and to play a very small role in her quest to help others. I leave you with one final thought: Join the quest! Read this book and learn more about retirement planning. Remember, it's for our own good that Julie is doing this.

CHRIS RICHCREEK
SENIOR FEATURES EDITOR
KING FEATURES

Introduction

Last November (2017) my column celebrated a milestone: 1,000 columns in continuous weekly publication in the *Greenwich Time* (CT) and the *Stamford Advocate* (CT). During that 20-year period, I've interacted with hundreds of people who wrote to or visited with me to discuss their challenges, concerns and questions.

You might ask, what drove me to write weekly columns while running a portfolio management practice (Jackson, Grant Investment Advisers, Inc.) and writing a few books along the way.

This is how all of this writing started: I had a client, a lawyer, who did not participate in his 401(k) at work. Since I knew that any investment he could make on his own outside of the 401(k) was not company-matched and tax-advantaged, I encouraged him to rethink his decision.

To give him a hand, I paid a visit to my local bookstore with the intention of buying a book for him—and found none that told the true story behind the 401(k)'s compounding potential. So, very simply, I decided to write that book for him and everyone else who needed to think of a 401(k) as an investment alternative as opposed to a passive employee benefit plan.

The book *You and Your 401(k)* was published in 1996. The column came in 1998 after another book I wrote on 401(k)s, this time for sponsors (*The 401(k) Plan Handbook*).

Because I began my Wall Street career as a lawyer, I was used to writing (prospectuses and proxy statements) and spending late nights proofreading at the financial printer. As I moved into money management at a major Wall Street firm, I acquired an understanding of investments from a number of different perspectives. I saw investment products created and sold through the firm's retail sales force. Before 9/11, I observed Benjamin Graham's "Mr. Market" first hand during my time on the floor of an exchange that was housed in the World Trade Center. And, at my firm, Jackson, Grant, I experienced direct client relationships leading to an appreciation of the complexity of financial decision-making and the importance of family dynamics.

That's the backstory. The drive behind continuing my writing and speaking is this: How to make good investment decisions is not something humans pick up easily on their own.

Through my dialogue with readers, I want to share a message of both promise and watchfulness.

- "Promise": In today's fast-moving financial world, a family's attainment of financial security is always a work in progress, and there is always room for improvement.
- "Watchfulness": It's far better to develop healthy skepticism than wishful thinking.

I've interacted with hundreds of people who were faced with the need to make important financial decisions without the necessary foundation to do so. Financial literacy is simply not a life skill that we all possess.

But what's even more important is recognizing that for anyone who wants to Retire Securely, more is needed beyond literacy—the "more" being "Financial Fluency," a term I credit to Chris Bruhl, the CEO of the Business Council of Fairfield County, Connecticut, my home state. The occasion was a recent breakfast at Starbucks and a discussion of a series of four public financial literacy presentations I was planning with Hearst, the publisher of the two papers that launched my column in 1998, the *Greenwich Time* and the *Stamford Advocate*. Under the umbrella of retirement security came cash flow management in good markets and bad, charitable gifting, alternative investments, and the integration of estate and financial planning.

Indeed. When we're talking about retirement security, Financial Fluency more accurately describes what is needed.

With that as a backdrop, let me tell you about the purpose of this book. It is to share my dialogue with readers who raised concerns and asked questions over the years, with a special focus on retirement security—and in so doing, to share some tools and insights that might be useful to you.

In this book you will find:

- Market data, insights, and resources from my expert sources, such as Standard and Poor's, Morningstar, and Value Line as well as associations such as the Investment Company Institute and the American Association of Individual Investors.

- Developments from regulators, such as FINRA (the Financial Industry Regulatory Authority), the U.S.

Securities and Exchange Commission (SEC), the U.S. Department of Labor (DOL) and the Internal Revenue Service (IRS). Understanding changing laws and proposed legislation can make your life easier or alert you to potential traps to avoid.

■ References to additional resources. For example: the College Scorecard from the U.S. Department of Education gives parents and high school students vital financial information that can help influence the choice of an appropriate and affordable college.

This book is intended as a resource for historical context and insights on subjects that readers of my column brought to me over the years, updated for today. Before taking any action based on what you read, be sure to check with your tax and investment advisers.

Sections Overview

SECTION 1

History

ARE YOU CURIOUS:

- Should you be concerned about market declines and crises?

- How can understanding history help you stick to your investment plan?

- Should you be an optimist or a skeptic when it comes to investing?

SECTION PREVIEW:

History has a way of putting things in perspective. Looking back over time, the stock market has been a very good investment. As we compile this book, in fact the Dow Jones Industrial Average has been hitting new highs on a regular basis—70 times in 2017 with more records breaking in January 2018. But during the journey, down periods can challenge the steadfastness of even the most knowledgeable and resolute investors. For example, if you had invested in the stock market some 20 years ago, when I started writing this weekly column (September 1998), you would have lived through two bear markets. If you had hung on for the ride through 2017, your investment in an S&P 500 Index fund would be worth far more (7.2 percent average annual return) than a no-thrills bank account (1.6 percent average annual return). If you factored inflation into the picture, your bank account would have left you with a negative return.

In this first section of the book, I'll take you on a historical journey through different market periods, from the 1973–1974 market decline, that erased more than $200 billion in market value from the New York Stock Exchange, to the Internet bubble that had investors convinced that there was a new paradigm (stocks only go up), and finally to the years of the financial crisis through today (December 2017), which has seen a bull market that has risen about 300 percent.

INSIDER'S PERSPECTIVE:

One of the few statements that can be made with certainty when it comes to investing in the stock market is: Bull Markets are followed by Bear Markets—and Bear Markets are followed by Bull Markets. That may seem trite, but the point is that no market is bound heavenward at all times. Historical perspective will give you a foundation upon which to build your investment decisions, especially if you have a long investment horizon. For that reason, you'll see market history in all sections of the book—we can always expect the future to be some variation of the past.

* * *

The first column in this section addresses a question that is always on investors' minds when markets are in bear territory—is this a bottom? To answer the question, I look to an even earlier market crash, the market of 1973–1974 and another from 2000–2002. This column was originally published in July of 2002. While we did not know it at the time, we were a few months away from the bottom caused by the bursting of the Internet Bubble in 2000.

LESSONS LEARNED FROM
1973–1974 MARKET CRASH

Originally published July 28, 2002

On September 1, 1974, the front page of the *New York Times* announced that investor confidence was lost. The Dow Jones Industrial Average dropped 36 percent from a record 1,051.7 on January 11, 1973, erasing more than $200 billion in market value of New York Stock Exchange (NYSE) stocks alone. The "typical" stock dropped more than 70 percent in value. More than 7,000 brokers left Wall Street.

On a day-to-day basis, volume was high and market declines, economic woes, and lack of investor confidence dominated the news. Inflation of 12 percent and double-digit returns on government bonds heightened market problems. The situation was grim. Comparisons to the great crash of 1929 were made by many.

If you had been a diversified investor in 1973, your $100,000 in an S&P 500 tracker would have dropped to $57,000 by the end of 1974.

If you had invested $100,000 in an S&P 500 fund at the top of the market (March 2000), you would have suffered a decline of 43 percent from peak to trough. Just as in 1974, your $100,000 investment would be down to $57,000.

Although there are many differences between the 1973–1974 market and today's (July 2002) market, there are some lessons to be learned.

Trends

First, if you were a trend investor in the up market, you might have had visions of becoming a millionaire. If you are projecting your potential losses now, at this rate, you might think the market will go to zero in no time.

Don't worry. It won't. Up trends don't go to the moon, and down trends don't go to zero. They go far enough to flush out market excesses, and then buyers start to come back into the market.

As Warren Buffett says, when Mr. Market wants to buy, sell to him. When he wants to sell, buy from him. Mr. Market is getting ready to sell, and so the time for you to buy is getting close.

Recover

When did the 1974 market start to recover? Were there clear signals?

A two-day rally of 7 percent at the beginning of October 1974 left Wall Street jubilant but bewildered. Commentators gave little credit to President Gerald Ford's announcement of an economic program to reduce inflation. The promise of lower interest rates was seen as having more of an impact on stock prices, but no one knew for sure.

What is certain, however, is that fearful investors lost ground.

Cashing Out

You may be thinking that you need to cash out now and wait on the sidelines.

What if you had sold out in 1974 with the idea of waiting for signs of a recovery before getting back in? If you had waited six months, you would have recovered your initial $100,000 in 1980 and gone on to bigger gains afterward. But if you had just held on, you would have recovered much more quickly: in two years.

Is this (July 2002) a bottom? We won't know until after the market starts to recover. But there are signs that we could be close.

Focus on the Long Term

Readers who are young and are investing through a 401(k) plan at work are in the best position to take advantage of market periods such as these. Investing systematically through payroll deductions takes away an investor's inclination to try to time the market. Investing small amounts over long periods is always beneficial, even during market declines such as the ones we have been seeing.

Investors who are older and are approaching retirement are at greater risk because, by definition, their horizons are shorter.

It is always best to forgo opportunistic maneuvers in favor of broader diversification. It is also useful to think in terms of life cycles.

Life-cycle investing forces you to think in terms of risk when you consider how far you are from retirement. The closer you are to needing your money, the less risk you should take with your investments.

Weeding Out Losers

No matter how the market is doing and irrespective of your age, risk profile, investment objectives, or experience, remember to weed out your losers. If you are still holding on to an Internet stock that has lost 90 percent of its value, take a close look at your reasoning. Mr. Market is starting to offer some reasonably priced stocks with sound fundamentals. It may be time to start to replace some of the losers with stocks that have better potential for reasonable long-term gains.

It's actually harder to invest in bull markets like the 1998 and 1999 markets that led up to the bursting of the Internet Bubble. [In Section 2, read "Do the Math and Stay the Course on Your 401(k)," October 19, 2008.] Today's (July 2002) market is actually a much better place to be. Speculators will not be happy for a while. Long-term investors will reign. ■

*   *   *

The next column was written earlier (in January 2000) at the height of the Internet bubble, when the average investor thought we were in a new type of stock market, one that never would go down. It was a "new era" in which normal caution was replaced with a feeling of not wanting to be left out. When you see that type of market in the future, reread this column: at those times, caution needs to replace enthusiasm.

TECH STOCKS TOO GOOD TO BE TRUE?

Originally published January 9, 2000; updated 2017

A 70-year-old reader with a balanced portfolio wants to know: Is it time to sell everything and buy Internet stocks?

Returns for some of this year's highest-flying stocks can dazzle just about anyone, and what mutual fund investor would not be gleeful with a one-year return of 100 percent or even 500 percent?

But what about risk?

"This market is different," implies my reader. "Technology and Internet stocks will continue to go up even if they are costly to buy. Things have changed."

Ah, yes. The new economy, the new paradigm.

"Every period has slightly different conditions," explained John R. Hummel, president of AIS Capital Management, LLC, of Wilton, Connecticut. "But the cold hard facts are that there is nothing new about this market that we haven't seen before. The speculation will eventually come to an end."

History has its lessons.

There were major technological advances that fueled speculative fervor in the 1920s, said Hummel. The automobile and the radio were the technological wonders of that time, and both still play a major role in our lives. It took 35 years before the Radio Corporation of America (RCA) recovered its 1929 price peak.

The same was true of the late 1960s bull market. Dominated by the Nifty Fifty [2017 update: Some might say that the Nifty Fifty are comparable to today's FAANG stocks: Facebook, Apple, Amazon, Netflix, Google (now Alphabet)], the S&P 500 Index was driven by consumer goods and technology stocks. However, as Hummel pointed out, higher inflation, monetary tightening, and cheaper and technologically inferior imports from Japan led to stagflation and two bear markets: 1969–1970 and 1973–1974. During the latter period, averages dropped about

50 percent. Many of the Nifty Fifty stocks dropped by as much 80 to 90 percent, some reaching their ultimate lows in 1977–1978.

But what about record-setting business expansion? Doesn't that differentiate the present from prior periods? No, said Hummel. In spite of record productivity, past business expansion cycles were greater.

So what caused major declines in the past? An important factor was the Fed's shift to a more restrictive monetary policy, said Hummel.

What about now? The Federal Reserve is giving us mixed signals, Hummel said. By increasing interest rates three times in 1999, it is restricting. By increasing money supply, the Fed is expanding. The rapid growth of the money supply is fuel for the stock market, Hummel explained. If the Fed starts to tighten the money supply, the stock market will be hit hard, especially if the U.S. dollar falls as foreign economies begin to experience faster growth rates.

So should you abandon your balanced portfolio for a seat on the magic carpet of the new paradigm? No. This is a time to take a deep breath and step back from the fray. "Bull markets such as these create a sloppy, careless attitude on the part of investors," said Hummel. Thinking that this market is different can lure you into complacency. Remind yourself that your goals should be realistic unless you are willing to lose everything. If you still want to speculate with a small part of your portfolio, dear reader, have a strategy to minimize risk. ■

*   *   *

No one knows the importance of minimizing risk as well as Enron investors. Enron's share price fell from about $90 a share in 2000 to pennies to zero in 2001. Enron, at one time the "world's largest energy trading company," closed its doors. As you'll see in the next column I wrote in December 2001, fraud was alleged and bankruptcy anticipated. Both came to be realities. Meanwhile, Enron employees who held Enron stock through company plans and on their own suffered severe losses. The event underscored the importance of diversification for 401(k) participants—and since then (2001), led to the decrease of employer stock in company plans from close to 30 percent in 2001 to less than 10 percent in 2015, as discussed in the column.

LEARN FROM ENRON: DON'T PUT YOUR EGGS IN ONE BASKET

Originally published December 16, 2001; updated 2017

Hidden behind the headlines of Enron's fall from grace are thousands of Enron employees who had millions of dollars in that company's 401(k) plans. Those unfortunate employees had both their employment and their retirement tied to the same risk.

Enron is—or was—a leading energy company with revenues of over $100 billion and assets of over $47 billion. With 21,000 employees active in 40 countries worldwide, 30,000 miles of pipeline, and 15,000 miles of fiber, Enron was hardly a stock that people thought risky.

Yet this large capitalization stock fell from almost $100 a share to pocket change in less than a year. Now in voluntary bankruptcy, the company may not survive. [2017 update: It did not survive.]

Enron is a disaster for its stockholders and its employees. What really happened behind the scenes will not be known for a while.

Stockholder lawsuits have been filed. Investigations by regulators and legislators are under way. Fraud is alleged, and the U.S. Department of Labor is investigating Enron's handling of its retirement plans.

Enron's 401(k)

Enron's 401(k) plans gave employees the option of investing in company stock. In addition, it appears that the company contributed that stock to employee accounts as a match.

If an employee had invested a sizable amount of his voluntary contributions in Enron stock, his 401(k) would have been decimated by the disastrous fall in Enron's stock price.

Indeed, many Enron employees are claiming losses of 70 to 90 percent, according to the Department of Labor's Pension and Welfare Benefits Administration. We won't know the extent of the damage until the Department of Labor completes its investigation.

Blackout

An exacerbating factor was Enron's freeze on employee accounts during a crucial period. The reason for the freeze was a change in 401(k) plan administrators.

In what is called a "blackout period," 401(k) accounts are frozen for a period during which the resigning administrator and the new administrator reconcile records. During the blackout period, employees are unable to act on their accounts.

Individuals who might have wanted to move out of their Enron stock were unable to do so for the length of the blackout, which some believe was a period of three weeks. A three-week blackout is not unusual. Some blackouts can last for months. Some can be as short as a few days.

Sponsors have every interest in speeding up the process. However, many times their hands are tied. Records need to be reconciled before employees can transact on the accounts.

Plans with Stock

According to the most recent comprehensive study of 401(k) plan government filings done by the U.S. General Accounting Office, ownership of company stock by 401(k) plans is rare. Fewer than 2 percent of the 160,000 plans studied at the time held employer stock.

However, since most of the companies that do offer employer stock are large, an estimated 25 percent of all 401(k) participants have company stock in their plans.

At large companies with assets of $1 billion or more, a larger number of plans are affected. According to a survey by Stamford-based Plansponsor.com, over 70 percent of large companies offer company stock in their 401(k) plans. [2017 update: The National Bureau of Economic Research reported that 72 percent of companies offered their stock as an investment option.]

In these plans, 29 percent of participants' balances are invested in company stock. [2017 update: More recent data (2015) shows a dramatic decrease in participants' company stock balances to only 7 percent, according to the Investment Company Institute (ici.org).]

Bankruptcy

Although Enron's situation is extreme, it is not unique. Companies, even sizable ones, do go out of business.

Normally, a bankruptcy does not affect a 401(k) plan. That is, the account balances of the participants do not belong to the company and cannot be attached by the company's creditors. Usually, the only exposure is during the time when money actually is being moved from the company's account into a 401(k) account.

Company Stock

Company stock held in 401(k) plans is likely to rise and fall more rapidly than any other investment offered in the plan. With very few exceptions, the stock of a single company is subject to "event risk" and is much more volatile than a diversified stock fund.

There is no question that plans offering company stock pose additional potential risks to 401(k) participants. Not only is there a job risk, there also is an investment risk.

Your Plan

If your plan offers company stock, take this opportunity to review your investment selections. It is always risky to concentrate in a sector, much less an individual stock. A good rule of thumb is to have no more than 10 percent of your overall portfolio in a single stock even if it is your company's stock.

Keep in mind that your 401(k) should not be used as an aggressive trading account. Think of it as an account you need to protect; invested correctly, it will help pay your bills after you retire. ▪

*   *   *

With hindsight, we know that the bull market that preceded the financial crisis peaked in October 2007. We did not know that when I wrote the next column (August 2007), during a pullback of 8 percent. The sub-prime mortgage crisis was brewing at the time. The column reiterates the need for caution, even when markets are soaring.

WHAT'S AN INDIVIDUAL INVESTOR TO DO? REVIEW YOUR HOLDINGS

Originally published August 19, 2007; updated 2017

What's an individual investor to do?

The full market recovery that officially arrived at the end of May 2007 was short-lived.

The stock market, as measured by the S&P 500 Index, had closed at all-time highs, surpassing the peak it had reached on March 24, 2000, at the height of the Internet Bubble.

Since then, the S&P 500 Index has given up about 8 percent of its value, bringing us back to where we were at the end of 2006.

In between we hit a few more new highs, with the market peaking on July 19, 2007, and then dropping 9.4 percent from there in just a few weeks. During that period, a full 95 percent (477 out of 500) of the stocks in the index were down in price; only 23 stocks had gains.

Four sectors are currently (August 2007) correcting, dropping more than 10 percent, according to Howard Silverblatt, senior index analyst with Standard & Poor's. The worst sectors were materials (−15.5 percent), consumer discretionary (−12.3 percent), energy (−11.8 percent), and financials (−11.4 percent).

How does this turmoil affect individual investors? Big daily drops make everyone worry. The volatility itself is not unusual, however, except that large drops of at least 2 percent on a specific day usually are spaced out more. Some of that worry, however, is misplaced.

On average, there are eight days of declines of at least 2 percent per year, according to Silverblatt. This is based on market data going back to 1926.

But we've only had only five such days over the past four years, Silverblatt explained. The S&P 500 Index had a 2 percent down day in March 2003. We didn't see another until this year (2007), on February 27.

Then we saw four more: March 13, July 26, August 3, and August 9. Thus, although these declines are not abnormal, they are coming fast and furious, giving the impression of greater volatility, Silverblatt explained.

Moreover, you have the uncertainties of credit markets touched off by subprime loan woes, making for a reactive and jittery market. The market abhors unknowns.

But, of course you can't ignore where we've come from since the low of October 9, 2002: Since then, the S&P 500 Index is up 81 percent (through August 2007). The best performers are energy (+196 percent), utilities (+148 percent) and information technology (+117 percent). The worst performers are consumer staples (+31.6 percent) and health care (+30.8 percent).

Where does that leave the individual investor?

If you are a retiree, hopefully you did not jump from a safely diversified portfolio to pursue hot market action late last year. I personally know a few people who did.

If you are one of them, don't wait for things to turn around without doing a careful review of your holdings. There is still much too much uncertainty in this market emanating from the subprime loan fiasco— and the market does not like unknowns.

You'll probably want to do the same thing even if you are at the other extreme. Even an aggressive investor shouldn't throw caution to the wind. ▩

*   *   *

Let's fast-forward to January 2008. Volatility had been increasing. Speculative traders could either lose or win big by making bets on short-term market movements, both positive and negative. I discussed using leveraged and inverse ETFs in this column, cautioning that the technique should only be used by those who could afford to lose money placing bets on the direction of the market.

WHAT'S YOUR GUESS: UP OR DOWN?

Originally published January 27, 2008; updated 2017

The stock market is taking us all on a wild ride, leaving us upended and breathless. It is no different from the fierce Kingda Ka, the tallest roller coaster on Earth.

Kingda Ka reaches speeds of 128 miles per hour, rises 45 stories, and plunges 418 feet. At one point, riders defy gravity and enter weightlessness as they swoop down a valley and up a 129-foot camel hump.

That's what the market felt like last Wednesday when it gapped down at the open only to rebound by the end of the day in a breathless rebound reminiscent of Internet bubble days.

The Dow fell almost 300 points on Wednesday (January 23, 2008), then turned around, recovered the points it had just lost, and added an additional 300 points to close at 12,270—up 2.5 percent from the previous day.

Some might believe that Wednesday's action signaled a "capitulation," a major reversal in the downward trend that we've been experiencing in the stock market. That may indeed be the case, but we won't know for a while. [2017 update: There were several other "false" capitulation days in October 2008 in what had become a unique financial crisis, with the market nadir in March 2009.]

Here are some guidelines.

Investors

If you cannot afford to lose money, don't make bets on market direction. No news, tips, software programs, newsletters, or programs you learn about through an advertisement or infomercial will consistently give you the signals you need to be safely on the right side of the market with your trades. Be especially wary of the programs advertised on TV that promise that even a 12-year-old can apply their system to make huge profits in the market.

Placing bets is not investing. It's speculating—something the average person cannot afford to do.

Speculators

What about people who can afford to place bets on market direction?

If you believe the market is going up, you can buy an ETF (exchange-traded fund) that mimics an index such as the S&P 500 or is leveraged to amplify the move. For example, a double-leveraged ETF can give you a 20 percent return if the market goes up 10 percent.

If you believe the market is due for a drop, you can buy an inverse ETF that makes money when the market goes down. There are a number of bear market mutual funds that accomplish the same result. That is, you win if the market goes down.

Before the advent of bear mutual funds and inverse ETFs, you had to short stocks, sell calls, or buy puts to achieve a profit in a declining market. ▪

*   *   *

We continue to move through 2008. That Fall, the S&P 500 Index experienced massive daily losses and gains. First the losses: September 29, 2008 (−8.79 percent); October 9, 2008 (−7.62 percent); October 15, 2008 (−9.04 percent); December 1, 2008 (−8.93 percent). And the gains: October 13, 2008 (11.58 percent); October 28, 2008 (10.79 percent).

When I wrote the next column (October 2008), six months before the market bottomed, investors were thinking of jumping ship. That timeframe raised these important questions: How do you know when a market is at a top or a bottom? Should you stay the course, or liquidate everything?

With hindsight or without it, the one thing an investor should never do is panic. An investor who cashed out of stocks at the end of October 2008 and stayed there through 2017 would have underperformed the stock market by vast amounts. How much? By about 235 percent. (The S&P 500 Index returned about 235 percent (cumulative) compared to less than 1 percent (cumulative) for a bank account.)

NOW IS NO TIME TO ABANDON
THE INVESTMENT SHIP

Originally published October 12, 2008

What should you do?

These are troubled times in the financial markets, to say the least. The markets are in turmoil, and there is no place to hide.

If you are tempted to abandon ship, don't. There is no need to.

Today is not tomorrow. These bad market periods will come to an end. In earlier times like these, many a steady investor made a fortune when others were panicking.

Since we don't know when the market will find a bottom, the question is what you should do when nothing seems certain.

Open those brokerage statements you received in the mail a few days ago. Don't worry about the dollar amount: The general direction of the market is down, and your account value should reflect that decline. Unless you have been hedging, going short, or keeping it all in cash, your account will be lower than it was last month, last quarter, and last year, and it will be lower still if you check your current values.

Focus instead on the asset allocation. How much do you have committed to stocks, bonds, and cash?

Do the same thing with your 401(k) statements.

If there are any general rules that apply across the board, this is one of them: People investing for income need to have higher allocations in bonds and dividend-paying stocks than do people investing for growth.

If you depend on income from your portfolio, now is the time to review your sources of bond interest and stock and mutual fund dividends.

Address any changes that have occurred recently that will affect your cash flow. For example, Bank of America announced a few days ago (October 2008) that it would cut its dividend because of "recessionary conditions." Have any of your dividends been cut?

Sit down with your spouse to review your cash flow: How much money comes into the household every month, and what is the source of that income? How much goes out, and where does it go? Whether you are working or retired, this will help you be ready for emergencies should any arise. It's always good to be prepared.

Now consider your timeline.

The younger you are, the higher your stock allocations can be on the theory that you will find yourself in better market periods sooner or later. Young 401(k) participants, for example, can put most or all of their 401(k) regular payroll deductions to work in the stock market even today—prices are substantially lower now—and if those prices continue to decline, so much the better for these investors. If the 401(k) has a match, that's even more desirable.

If you have a solid financial adviser on your side, that's reassuring; this is a most difficult time to be going it alone. However, if your adviser is not reaching out to help you, put it on your to-do list to look for another one.

One day in the near future, we will have a trading day that has tremendous volume with a downward move followed by a large upswing; this generally is called a capitulation day. Expect the character of the market to change after that. ▪

* * *

Let's jump to the end of March 2009, when I recounted a presentation I gave to an audience of retirees. What were they thinking at the time? Some were seeing a market bottom and indeed, that was a correct call. However, we were still seeing dividend cuts underway in companies that were conserving cash. In the next column, I also addressed the higher quality dividend payers that were represented in Standard & Poor's Dividend Aristocrats Index, which is still a valuable resource for retirees who are interested in generating dividend income for their retirement portfolios.

WHEN IS IT RIGHT TO REENTER THE MARKET?

Originally published March 29, 2009; updated 2017

Last Tuesday (March 24, 2009), I spoke with a group of 50 or so retirees at the learning and retirement program at Sacred Heart University's Stamford, Connecticut, campus.

What was on everyone's mind?

"When do we get back into the market?"

What a difference a few weeks makes.

This is a decidedly different posture from what I've encountered over the last few months as I've been addressing groups of retirees about how to protect themselves in this turbulent market.

Of course, keep in mind that we had just experienced Monday's (March 23, 2009) 7 percent surge in the S&P 500 after Treasury Secretary Timothy Geithner announced details of the administration's plan to deal with banks' toxic assets.

Monday's upswing was the biggest one-day jump since last October (2008). Some of the major bank stocks ended up almost 20 percent higher that day.

In fact, so far, the month of March (2009) has been the first positive month we've seen since December 2008. After so many dramatically declining months, it's a relief to see what some are calling a bottom.

Year to date through February (2009), the S&P 500 Index had declined over 18 percent, with financials declining 40 percent. Extend that measuring period out three weeks through Monday, March 23 (2009), and the year-to-date numbers look far better, with the S&P 500 Index down only about 8 percent and the financials down only 23 percent.

Looking back to the beginning of 2007, the S&P 500 had fallen by almost 50 percent until returns this month started reversing some of those losses ever so slightly.

When we see positive moves in the market, especially dramatic ones such as the ones we saw on Monday, the tendency is to rush back into stocks for fear of being left out in the cold.

We've seen these kinds of market swings before. Should this one be any different? More important, should the average investor care?

The answer lies in how you define yourself.

If you are an active trader, you've got a perfect market environment to make money on the upside by going long and on the downside by going short. That is something you can do easily (but very cautiously) by using long and short exchange-traded funds (ETFs).

In contrast, if you invest for a goal such as retirement, it's best to ignore the impulse to jump in feet first, especially if you moved all of your money out of stocks and into Federal Deposit Insurance Corporation (FDIC)-insured bank accounts, as many of the retirees I was addressing had done.

Caution, caution, caution is the watchword for today (March 2009). We still don't know what the future will hold considering the need to work out the banking, credit, mortgage, and other recessionary problems, not to mention that substantially increased government spending programs, if not curtailed, will lead to an unhappy future of high inflation.

Dividends, the lifeblood of income investors, no doubt will be cut further as we go into 2009. Standard & Poor's Index Services expects that the dividends on the S&P 500 will decline by more than 13 percent in 2009; that would be the worst annual decline since 1942, when dividends fell almost 17 percent. This is not an unlikely result considering that growth slows in economic recessions and companies can conserve cash by cutting expenditures, with one such outlay being the dividends paid to shareholders.

Of course, some companies actually may be increasing dividends, but according to Howard Silverblatt, senior index analyst at Standard & Poor's, "unless companies believe that their financial future will improve, their need to conserve cash will outweigh their desire to pay dividends."

Given the environment and the unknowns before us all, a conservative investor would do well to put together a good buy of seasoned dividend-paying stocks that could be expected to survive the rough waters ahead.

A good starting point is Standard & Poor's Dividend Aristocrats, a list of solid dividend-paying stocks that you can access for free online at standardandpoors.com [2017 update: a list of 2009 constituents is provided in Appendix A; 2017 constituents in Appendix B]. These are companies that paid dividends for 25 consecutive years, companies you'll recognize, such as McDonald's, PepsiCo, Procter & Gamble, and Walmart.

Caution: Because this list is assembled on the basis of calendar year measures, it also contains stocks that decreased their dividends already this year (March 2009). If those dividends are not increased before the end of the year, those companies will drop off the list. An example is General Electric, whose dividend was reduced last month by almost 70 percent from 31 cents to 10 cents a share (a savings for the company of $9 billion a year). [2017 update: GE was removed from the Dividend Aristocrats List at the end of 2009; GE reduced its dividend in 2017 by 50 percent.]

This is a starting point for further research, of course, not a list of recommended stocks.

Thus, the answer to the question posed is to foreswear emotion. Know yourself. If you have the stomach to trade, now is the time. If you are an investor, don't rush into buying anything because of market moves. Use your time carefully to pick the best stocks to own for the long haul and buy only when you are ready, entering the market slowly over time.

[2017 update: At the end of 2009, S&P 500 dividends actually declined by 21 percent, surpassing the decline in 1942. By the end of 2016, S&P dividends had risen to more than twice the level they were at the end of 2009.]

In the next column, written a few months later (May 24, 2009), Fannie Mae and subprime mortgages are in the news. While the goal was to increase home ownership, the methodology on how to get there was flawed. Regulatory changes followed.

Since being taken into government conservatorship following their 2008 bailout, Fannie Mae has struggled to get back to pre-crisis stability. According to a December 21, 2017 Treasury Department press release, the Treasury Department and Federal Housing Finance Agency (FHFA) have modified terms of the preferred stock purchase agreement with Fannie Mae which will allow Fannie Mae to maintain a $3 billion capital buffer. This is a change to the 2012 agreement that required Fannie Mae to essentially direct all net income to the Treasury, according to the FHFA. Look for more focus on Fannie Mae in 2018 as Treasury Secretary Steve Mnuchin said in December 2017 that "The administration looks forward to working with Congress on comprehensive housing finance reform, a top priority in the year ahead."

HISTORY OFFERS LESSONS ON CRISIS

Originally published May 24, 2009

History tells us that the mortgage mess and the financial crisis that ensued had their start in unsound mortgage lending practices that sprang from a laudable goal: increasing home ownership in America.

As a September 30, 1999, *New York Times* column reported, "Fannie Mae, the nation's biggest underwriter of home mortgages, has been under increasing pressure from the Clinton Administration to expand mortgage loans among low and moderate income people and felt pressure from stockholders to maintain its phenomenal growth in profits."

As reported by Steven Holmes, Franklin D. Raines (then Fannie Mae's chairman and chief executive officer) reduced Fannie Mae's down payment requirements.

"Yet," said Raines, "there remain too many borrowers whose credit is just a notch below what our underwriting has required who have been relegated to paying significantly higher mortgage rates in the so-called subprime market."

Raines subsequently was implicated in unsafe and unsound practices that led to Fannie Mae losses. He entered into a consent order with the Office of Federal Housing Enterprise Oversight in April 2008 under which he agreed to repay $24.7 million to Fannie Mae. The order was based on allegations that Raines "undertook inappropriate earnings management [at Fannie Mae], failed to ensure that adequate internal controls were put in place, released misleading financial reports and permitted the accounting function to operate without adequate resources."

Holmes reported: "In moving, even tentatively, into this new area of lending, Fannie Mae is taking on significantly more risk, which may not pose any difficulties during flush economic times. But the government-subsidized corporation may run into trouble in an economic downturn, prompting a government rescue similar to that of the savings and loan industry in the 1980's."

And, here we are today (May 2009). Fannie Mae was placed under conservatorship on September 6, 2008 and the Treasury promised up to $100 billion of bailout money. Fannie Mae, which was established in 1938 after the Great Depression to support the mortgage market, is only one piece of the puzzle.

We know anecdotally that unscrupulous mortgage brokers convinced unsophisticated borrowers that they could afford a home by getting a mortgage at low teaser rates with little thought about how they could pay a higher mortgage after the rate was adjusted upward.

We know that some encouraged borrowers to inflate house values and income on applications and generally "sold" the benefits of buying the biggest house and getting the biggest mortgage they could acquire with no thought to prudence or criminal consequences. As recently as 2003, more than one in two subprime mortgages were issued by organizations outside the reach of federal bank fraud criminal statutes, according to a White House statement last week (May 2009).

And we know that these "low-doc," "no-doc," and subprime loans fueled securitization on Wall Street, which packaged the mortgages and sold them to investors.

Some of these practices were fraudulent but not illegal until last week.

On Wednesday, May 20, 2009 President Obama signed new legislation to ensure that the "problems that led us into this crisis never happen again."

The President said, "These landmark pieces of legislation [the Helping Families Save Their Homes Act and the Fraud Enforcement and Recovery Act (FERA)] will protect hardworking Americans, crack down on those who seek to take advantage of them, and ensure that the problems that led us into this crisis never happen again."

Although the two acts taken together have a much broader reach, I'd like to focus on the newly expanded antifraud provisions of FERA that will help put a stop to fraudulent mortgage origination practices.

By amending the definition of a "financial institution" in the criminal code (18 U.S.C., Section 20) to include private mortgage brokers and other nonbank lenders, FERA makes those entities subject to antifraud rules.

Among other things, it will be a crime to make a materially false statement or to willfully overvalue a property to influence any action by a mortgage lending business. These are all good changes and certainly a move in the right direction to protect the home buyer.

The act goes further.

By December 15 of 2010, a special committee of Congress (the Financial Crisis Inquiry Commission) must submit to the President a report that summarizes its conclusions on the cause of the financial crisis.

The commission will look at fraud and abuse in the financial (and mortgage) sector; federal and state regulators and the extent to which they enforced or failed to enforce the laws; accounting practices, including mark-to-market rules; tax treatment of financial products; monetary policy; capital requirements and regulation of leverage and liquidity; short selling; derivatives and credit default swaps; financial institutions' reliance on numerical models, including risk models and credit ratings; and the quality of due diligence undertaken by financial institutions, to name a few. For a complete list, link to the legislation at www.congress.gov.

How this commission will fare with such a large task before it remains to be seen. New legislation certainly will follow, possibly leading to a major restructuring of the financial system that we know today. ▦

*   *   *

Market disruptions were not over after the March 2009 stock market bottom. Although the bull market was underway, the market experienced a "Flash Crash" on May 6, 2010, which I write about in the next column. The cause? The rise of high-frequency trading and electronic exchanges.

"FLASH CRASH" REVEALS DOUBT?

Originally published September 12, 2010; updated 2017

The flash crash on May 6, 2010, when the broad market fell 5 percent in five minutes starting at 2:40 p.m., only to recover 90 seconds later, was a product of today's technology.

That's according to Mary Schapiro, [then] chairwoman of the U.S. Securities and Exchange Commission (SEC), who spoke at the Economic Club of New York on Tuesday (September 7, 2010) about the structure of the equity markets, a subject of concern for individual and institutional investors alike, especially on the heels of that day in May.

During the crash, some 324 securities dropped more than 60 percent from their 2:40 p.m. prices, the exchanges canceled more than 20,000 trades, and an estimated $2 billion-plus in stop-loss orders were triggered from 2:30 to 3:00 p.m.

This kind of activity could not have occurred when trades were executed manually. Now trades can be processed in fractions of a second, "in less time than it takes to blink your eye," Schapiro said.

The New York Stock Exchange today executes about 26 percent of the volume of NYSE-listed stocks, down from almost 80 percent five years ago.

Stocks listed on the NYSE, representing 80 percent of the market capitalization of the U.S. equity markets, phased in electronic trading on October 6, 2006, replacing face-to-face auctions on the floor of the exchange.

Now (2010) almost 70 percent of trading is executed elsewhere: other exchanges, internalized broker-dealers, and more than 30 dark pools. Dark pools are alternative trading systems that provide liquidity to the market but do not display price quotes.

"This electronic market structure also has opened the door for entirely new types of professional market participants," Schapiro said.

"The traditional specialist and market-maker roles in manual markets have largely disappeared as the market structure has evolved."

"Today, proprietary trading firms play a dominant role by providing liquidity through the use of highly sophisticated trading systems capable of submitting many thousands of orders in a single second," she continued.

"These high-frequency trading firms can generate more than a million trades in a single day and now represent more than 50 percent of equity market volume," Schapiro said. "And many firms will generate 90 or more orders for each executed trade. Stated another way: A firm that trades 1 million times per day may submit 90 million or more orders that are cancelled."

Regulators are reexamining circuit breakers, which are supposed to calm overly volatile markets, in light of algorithmic trading, high-frequency trading, order cancellations, and the way orders are executed outside exchanges—through dark pools, for example.

Algorithmic trading programs automate buy-and-sell orders for exchange-traded funds and individual stocks.

"Many of these algorithms are programmed to pull back or withdraw from the market entirely in the event of an abnormal price move in one or more broad market index products," Schapiro said. The SEC needs to reconsider the parameters that have to be set for such trading "to provide price discovery and minimize artificial short-term market shocks," she stated.

The volume of orders that are executed in nonpublic dark trading venues such as dark pools and internalizing broker-dealers is increasing, Schapiro pointed out: "They now execute nearly 30 percent of volume, up from approximately 25 percent one year ago. What is the effect of these venues on public price discovery and market stability?"

During the precipitous drop on May 6, 2010 when dark venue volume fell from 30 percent to 10 percent, the public markets were flooded with sell orders.

Schapiro questioned whether the public markets should be expected to "handle nearly all the order flow in tough times, yet be bypassed routinely by a large volume in normal times."

In her words, the important questions left to be answered are "to what extent is our structure meeting or failing to meet its goals of fair, efficient and transparent markets, and how can we modify the structure to preserve the advantages and eliminate the flaws?"

* * *

A few years later, in 2012, the impact of Ponzi schemer Bernie Madoff was still being felt. While the SEC has taken steps to minimize fraud, every investor must be vigilant while examining new investment opportunities.

As the saying goes, "If it sounds too good to be true, it probably is."

MADOFF CHANGED REGULATORY LANDSCAPE

Originally published July 1, 2012; updated 2017

Ponzi schemers are still in the news. We learned last week (June 2012) that Bernie Madoff's brother Peter will soon be serving jail time.

Although fraudsters always will find a way to deceive investors, the regulatory world is a different place since Bernie admitted to his grand scheme in December 2008.

Over the last two years, the Securities and Exchange Commission (SEC) has brought more than 100 enforcement actions against nearly 200 individuals and 250 entities for carrying out Ponzi schemes.

To make Ponzi schemes work, the schemer has to attract investors with promises of riches. After all, the schemer needs new inflows of money to pay out earlier investors, and it helps if the investors are in a nicely defined affinity group.

A 2012 scheme targeted a Jewish community in Los Angeles. Another targeted "socially-conscious investors in church organizations." As to returns, one schemer promised elderly investors annual returns of 9 to 12.5 percent, another guaranteed monthly returns as high as 11 percent from the trading of foreign currencies, and yet another promised returns of 60 to 120 percent per year.

Some schemers also promise security. One promised that "only 1 percent of investors' principal was at risk," and another "falsely guaranteed that their money would be safe and yield lofty returns."

Here are some of the techniques the SEC uses to pursue post-Madoff fraudsters, as reported in an April 2012 SEC Spotlight.

Tips and complaints are gathered in one place: the Enforcement Division's newly created Office of Market Intelligence (OMI). OMI investigates those "presenting the greatest threat of investor harm."

National specialized units launched in May 2010 focus on Structured and New Products, Market Abuse, Municipal Securities and Public Pensions, Asset Management, and the Foreign Corrupt Practices Act.

To build cases against fraudsters quickly, agreements are used to secure the cooperation and testimony of persons who are in the know about fraudulent activity.

To lessen the likelihood of false brokerage statements, advisory firms now are required to submit yearly to an independent public accountant's "surprise exam" to verify custody. In addition, a third party reviews the firm's controls to protect client assets. SEC examiners also routinely verify "the existence and integrity" of client assets by reaching out to custodians and even customers.

Narrative disclosure documents now are required to "improve the quality of disclosure clients receive and allow them to better evaluate the risks associated with a particular investment adviser."

Enhanced risk assessments identify firms that the SEC will examine, such as "advisers whose clients' assets are held with an affiliate, as opposed to an independent entity; funds that seem to have 'smooth' or outlier returns; firms with a disciplinary history; and broker-dealers that sell an affiliate's hedge fund or limited partnership."

Before an examination, the SEC performs "rigorous reviews of firms" to focus "not only on obvious signs of fraud but also more subtle signals that deserve closer inspection, such as a firm using an unknown accountant or no accountant at all."

If an entity has joint or dual registration as a broker-dealer and an investment adviser, the SEC uses joint broker-dealer and investment adviser examination teams.

A quarterly review program helps ensure that "important issues are resolved in a thorough and timely manner and that no examination or investigation falls through the cracks."

On the drawing board is enhanced oversight of broker-dealer back-office personnel who typically perform "critical custody, accounting, account transfer, settlement, and account maintenance functions."

Although ingenious fraudsters will always find a creative way to wriggle through just about any system of regulation, investors can help themselves by adopting an attitude of healthy skepticism and remembering the old adage "If it sounds too good to be true, it probably is."

[2017 update: To see a list of recent Ponzi schemes, go to sec.gov/spotlight/enf-actions-ponzi.shtml. For more information on post-Madoff reforms, see sec.gov/spotlight/secpostmadoffreforms.htm. For testimony on SEC oversight, go to sec.gov and search "testimony on oversight."] ▓

*   *   *

The next column highlights the importance of investing for the long term, especially if you are participating in a 401(k) plan at work.

It's now August 2014 and we are clearly in a bull market, having long recovered the losses of the Financial Crisis.

Since the bottom, the market is up an average annual return of 24.5 percent from March 2009 through August 2014 (and up 19.4 percent from March 2009 through December 2017).

Since the market top of 2007, the market is up an average annual return of 6.3 percent from October 2007 through August 2014 (and up 7.8 percent from October 2007 through December 2017).

Investors who contributed to their 401(k)s throughout the Financial Crisis took advantage of their company match and dollar cost averaging to help ride the market higher through 2017.

401(K) PARTICIPANTS SAW BALANCES
BOUNCE BACK FROM LOWS

Originally published August 24, 2014

If you participated in a 401(k) plan at work during the financial crisis, you may remember seeing a *60 Minutes* segment (April 17, 2009) highlighting the personal tragedies of 401(k) participants who lost their retirement savings.

Now (August 2014), more than five years after the March 2009 market bottom, we have hard data on 401(k) participant returns that recently was released by the Investment Company Institute (ICI).

Employees who continued to participate in their 401(k)s from the end of 2007 through the end of 2012 saw their balances increase about 40 percent.

That's a good result in light of the fact that the average 401(k) account balance dropped by 34.7 percent in 2008. These figures include both employer and employee contributions, investment returns, withdrawals, and loans.

According to the ICI report, from year end 2007 through year end 2012, the average account balance rose from $77,049 to $107,053, for an average annual return of 6.8 percent (cumulatively about 40 percent). The median account balance in this group rose much more—76 percent, from $28,358 in 2007 to $49,814 in 2012, for a compound annual average growth rate of 11.9 percent.

On average, a significant amount (three-fifths) was held in stock funds or company stock, with younger participants holding more equities than did older participants.

The study reviewed about 7.5 million "consistent" participants, defined as the 401(k) participants with accounts at the end of 2007 in the EBRI/ICI 401(k) Database who had accounts at the end of each year from 2007 through 2012.

The ICI report, "What Does Consistent Participation in 401(k) Plans Generate?" can be accessed at ici.org/pdf/per21-04.pdf [2017 update: ici.org/pdf/per23-09.pdf].

According to an ICI report released in January 2014, "Americans' Views on Defined Contribution Plan Saving," a majority of U.S. households have a favorable opinion of 401(k) plans, as they indeed should.

One more point: There is another reason 401(k) participants need to stay the course, especially if the plan offers a match: It's the math behind the 401(k).

As I wrote in my October 19, 2008, column titled "Do the Math and Stay the Course on Your 401(k)" [see Section 2], when you consider the pretax savings you have when you contribute to your 401(k) and add the extra money your company contributes through the match, you have a winning combination even in declining markets.

Here is the math behind a 401(k) with a 50 percent match.

Say your payroll deduction is $100 and your company match is $50, for a total contribution of $150.

Since the $100 doesn't count as taxable income, you have a tax savings that reduces your "cost." Assume your tax savings equals $25 (an effective tax rate of 25 percent). Your cost becomes $75, as opposed to $100.

Each month, $150 shows up in your 401(k), but only $75 of it is your contribution. The rest comes from the match ($50) and your tax savings ($25).

Take a decline as brutal as the Great Depression, with a drop of almost 85 percent from 1929 through 1932.

Over a four-year period, your cost of $75 a month totaled $3,600. Your balance at the end of the four years was roughly $4,340, a profit of $760 achieved during a declining market.

Now take the same period studied by the ICI (starting January 2008) extended through July 31, 2014. Your contributions of $150 monthly totaled $11,850. Your investment in the broad market as measured by the S&P 500 Index fund would have resulted in a balance of $19,600 for an annual return of 15.4 percent.

If you consider your cost of $5,925 ($75 a month), your gain would have been $13,675 ($19,600–$5,925), a phenomenal outcome.

401(k)s are perfect vehicles for long-term investing, especially if they include a match. The lessons from the financial crisis prove that continuing to invest in a 401(k) during good times and bad is a sound long-term investment strategy.

[2017 update: According to a more recent 2015 ICI report, from year end 2007 through year end 2015, the average account balance rose from $77,049 to $143,436, for an average annual return of 8.1 percent (cumulatively about 86 percent). The median account balance in this group rose much more—134 percent, from $28,358 in 2007 to $66,412 in 2015, for a compound annual average growth rate of 11.2 percent.]

* * *

Short-term market timers need to react. Long-term investors need to stay focused on the future. In the next column, written at the end of October 2014, when short-term fluctuations were demanding investors' attention, I discuss long-term holding period returns going back to the 1920s.

Each investor needs to remember that his or her results will be a matter of how well he or she did over a lifetime of investing. Unless you make mistakes, short term periods will not be remembered. What will count, is your progress over the length of your investment horizon, as reflected in long "holding periods."

STOCK MARKET REWARDS LONG-TERM FOCUS

Originally published October 26, 2014

We've been seeing the stock market gyrate over such concerns as the Ebola virus, the economy, ISIS, and possible terrorist actions on U.S. soil. On October 22, 2014, the market as measured by the Standard & Poor's 500 Index closed at 1,927 after rising to a peak of 2,011 on September 18, 2014 and falling to a low of 1,862 on October 15, 2014.

Yet it seems like just yesterday that the *Wall Street Journal's* lead story crowed about the market's rise: "S&P 500 Hits 2000 for First Time." That was August 27, 2014.

Putting aside this short-term volatility, long-term investors need to remember that it's the endgame that matters more than anything else.

For most people, the goal of saving and investment is a comfortable retirement. That's a long-term objective for everyone who is still working as well as for retirees who have 10, 20, or 30 years or even more ahead of them.

Long-term stock market results are a lot different from short-term results even if you factor in the financial crisis. I recently completed a study of market returns going back to the Great Depression. Let me share some of the top-level conclusions with you.

Most important, short-term holding periods are quite volatile, with wide swings between highs and lows. However, long-term holding periods are not.

For example, the difference between the highs and lows range from a single-year gain of about 52 percent to a single-year loss of about 37 percent. That's a very broad range of 89 percentage points.

If you extend the holding period from a single year to, say, 40 years, the length of time in which a 25-year-old would be investing for his or her retirement, the interim ups and downs of the market essentially disappear.

The distance between the highs achieved over each and every 40-year holding period since the Depression is only about 3.5 percentage points.

That is, the highest 40-year holding period had about 12.5 percent average annual returns. The lowest 40-year holding period returned about 9 percent. A 40-year holding period starts with 1926 plus 40 years (ending in 1966), the next 40-year holding period starts in 1927 plus 40 years, and so on.

Longer-period return spreads between highs and lows are modest compared with those in shorter periods.

For example, for all 30-year holding periods in the same time frame, the distance between highs and lows was a high of 13.74 percent and a low of 9.45 percent. That's a high-low spread of 4.29 percentage points.

For all 20-year holding periods, the range was from a high of 17.86 percent to a low of 6.53 percent. The spread was 11.33 percentage points.

For all 10-year holding periods, the range was a high of 20.04 percent to a low of negative 1.38 percent (for the 10 years ending 2008), for a spread of 21.42 percentage points.

People with longer horizons—especially those building wealth for the future—can benefit from understanding the dampening of volatility over time. Volatility affects investors negatively over the short term, especially if they react to the market by selling at the wrong time.

One more point: No one wants to lose money, especially if he or she is retired and needs to protect savings. However, it's usually a mistake to go in and out of the market unless you have a system that you've tested and you trust. The average investor needs to look into the future to have a long-term perspective that accepts interim moves.

All of this presupposes that you are investing appropriately for your goals and situation. If you happened to have purchased the best-performing fund (a leveraged health fund) three years ago, your return would have been over 600 percent. If you bought $1,000 of the worst-performing fund, you would have only $4 of your investment left.

Holding on to the wrong investment is not the answer. Neither is trying to time the market's interim swings. It's best to have a plan that is based on sound long-term objectives and stick to that plan. ▪

*　*　*

Considering the historical periods that we've discussed so far, here is a question for you: If you have a long horizon, can an 8 percent return be attainable? The next column (published February 1, 2015 and updated through 2016), continues the discussion of long-term holding periods, comparing different investments, including T-bills, bonds, and stocks.

At the end of the column, you'll find some additional updates.

CAN AN 8 PERCENT RETURN BE ATTAINED?

Originally published February 1, 2015; updated 2017

In my column, "RMDs for three-year-olds: the benefits of stretching an IRA" (see Section 8, "Estate Planning"), we talked about 8 percent as a potentially attainable return for an investor with a long-term horizon—say, a youth starting his first job, or a young grandchild who inherits an IRA (individual retirement account). Many of you e-mailed me asking to give some examples of such historical returns.

There are a number of studies that focus on historical market returns, most notably "Ibbotson SBBI Classic Yearbook: Market Results for Stocks, Bonds, Bills, and Inflation." [*The 2017 Yearbook* (John Wiley & Sons) provides data from 1926 through 2016.]

Any serious do-it-yourself investor needs to make the Yearbook mandatory reading each and every year. It contains a wealth of information on the markets as well as special studies, for example, on the unpredictability of small stock returns.

Although you have to be careful about viewing historical returns as predictive, they provide useful insights into different types of markets and show how different financial instruments have acted in different economic and historical periods. They also show how they may act in the future in the same or a similar set of circumstances.

For long-term investors, returns in long-term holding periods become relevant, and inflation becomes an important part of the mix, especially since most investors who have a long-term view want to secure a retirement lifestyle of their choosing. That means preserving purchasing power.

If you look at the Ibbotson database from 1926 through 2016, you'll notice that after you factor in the ravages of inflation, there is a clear choice that pulls ahead of all the others.

During the 1926–2016 time frame, Treasury bills returned 3.4 percent compounded annually before inflation but only 0.5 percent after inflation.

Long-term government bonds returned 5.5 percent compounded annually before inflation and 2.6 percent after inflation.

Long-term corporate bonds returned 6.0 percent compounded annually in nominal terms. In inflation-adjusted terms, that was 3.0 percent.

By comparison, large-company stocks returned 10.0 percent compounded annually before inflation is taken into account and provided a 6.9 percent compound annual return after inflation. Small-company stocks returned 12.1 percent before inflation and 8.9 percent after inflation.

Back to our question: Can an individual investor achieve an 8 percent return? The answer is yes if history repeats itself. To replicate large-company stock returns, one invests in a well-run S&P 500 Index fund with low expenses. One has to accept interim price moves, which can be dramatic. Think 2008, when the S&P 500 Index fell 37 percent, or Black Monday (October 19, 1987), when the S&P 500 fell 20 percent in one day. Over long periods, one views those drops as minor blips.

What about mutual funds, which may offer less volatility than the large-company stocks represented by the S&P 500 Index?

Using a database called Steele Mutual Fund Expert, I made a very simple search: balanced mutual funds that had very long track records. Among the seven funds that were started before 1950, all but one had lifetime annualized returns through 2016 [and through December 2017] above 8 percent.

They had different start dates, ranging from the late 1920s through the 1940s, and so the returns are not directly comparable, but they tell a story.

What is interesting is that the most aggressive of these funds had one of the lowest returns (8.6 percent) of the seven. The remaining six less aggressive allocation funds returned (from low to high) 7.7 percent, 8.7 percent, 9.2 percent, 9.6 percent, 9.9 percent, and 10.2 percent.

These funds are survivors of radically different markets over time and have every chance of continuing to survive as time goes on.

I did another Steele search for U.S. equity funds with inception dates before 1950 but, with more aggressive investment approaches than the balanced funds. The lifetime returns of the 28 funds through December 2017 ranged from a low of 3.6 percent annualized since inception to a high of 12.7 percent. ▪

*   *   *

Fast forward to December 2016 (and December 2017). We are still firmly in a bull market that began in March 2009. Do you wonder how long it will last? When will it turn into a bear?

During late 2016, we were wondering whether the Dow Jones Industrial Average (DOW) would break through a psychological barrier of 20,000. It did a month later (January 2017) and is now (January 2018) at another all-time high of over 24,650.

The S&P 500 Index, a broader measure of the stock market, was also at all-time highs as it is now (December 2017). The market has been in bull market territory for 105 months (up about 300 percent) far surpassing the average length of a bull market (52 months), according to S&P Capital IQ. Only one bull market since 1921 was longer and stronger: the 113 months starting October 11, 1990 through March 24, 2000 that returned a gain of 417 percent. The bear that followed lasted from March 24, 2000 through October 9, 2002, dropping a total of 49.1 percent giving up 61 percent of the prior bull market's gains.

WHERE'S THE MARKET HEADED?

Originally published December 25, 2016; updated 2017

I don't think anyone can ignore the surge in the stock market since the (2016) election. We're seeing some dampening, but hardly enough to dislodge long-term trends.

The Dow Jones Industrial Average has been flirting with a new psychological barrier of 20,000 for a few weeks now. We've been close, but we're not quite there as of this writing (December 22, 2016). The question is, will there be a pullback or even a turn in the trend?

The Dow, however, is less significant to investors than the Standard & Poor's 500 Index on a relative basis. This is the case because more people invest in S&P 500 Index mutual funds than in Dow funds.

The S&P 500 Index also is still on a tear. Think back to the bottom of the Financial Crisis. On March 9, 2009, the S&P 500 closed at 676, according to Howard Silverblatt of S&P Dow Jones Indices. On December 21, 2016, 93.4 months later, the S&P 500 closed at 2265.18, for a massive bull run of 234.8 percent. A bull market is defined by a 20 percent rise from a previous low.

Only one bull market since the 1920s has lasted longer: the October 11, 1990, to March 24, 2000 bull run, which ended with the Internet Bubble. It lasted 113.4 months, with a 417 percent return. The average bull market has lasted about 51 months, with a return of about 161 percent.

The bear market (a 20 percent decline in the S&P 500 from its previous peak) that followed (March 24, 2000, to October 9, 2002) lasted 30.5 months; the S&P 500 declined 49.1 percent from peak to trough.

The financial crisis bear market that preceded the current bull market lost 56.8 percent and lasted 17 months, from October 9, 2007, to March 9, 2009. The average bear has lasted 17 months, declining about 38 percent.

It's easy to be swayed by trends and news. "Like a banking airplane, today's stock prices and valuations are at highs, while [interest] rates and inflation remain near historic lows," said S&P Global. Will stock prices decline in 2017? [2017 update: No they did not. The S&P 500 Index ended with a gain of about 21 percent].

Some say that "bull markets don't die of old age, they die of fright." As S&P Global pointed out recently, the fear of a recession would be the turning point. Is a recession on the horizon?

In the fourth quarter of 2016, S&P's one-year forecast was as follows:

1. Inflation of 2.3 percent, up from 2.2 percent (estimated 2016)

2. Gross Domestic Product (GDP) growth of 2.4 percent, up from 1.6 percent (estimated 2016)

3. Fed funds at 1.13 percent

4. Oil prices averaging in the low $50s/barrel

5. Ten-year note yield of 2.45 percent

6. Earnings growth of about 12 percent versus a flat 2016 estimate

That's a forecast for modest GDP growth as well as modest stock gains.

You may hear this market calling out to you to act, but it's more important to focus on your own situation.

Two issues need to be addressed: (1) where you are in your investment horizon and (2) how you make investment decisions.

If you have a long investment horizon and your goal is to accumulate wealth, moving out of the market in anticipation of a decline is not a good strategy. Why? Only hindsight can tell you whether you are making a good decision. If you had done this in January of this year, you would have missed a huge rally and probably never would have gotten back in.

A better strategy is to take advantage of market declines when they come around, as they will by definition: Every bull is followed by a bear, and every bear is followed by a bull.

If you are a retiree whose livelihood depends on your investments, the same thing goes for you, with one major exception: You need to protect your principal unless you have the option of going back to work. There are a number of ways to do that.

For those who have modest savings, there are a number of retirement income products that can augment Social Security with pension-like streams of income.

For those with large assets and large needs, there are more options. There are hundreds of firms that specialize in the needs of the wealthy and can be retained to protect principal in declining markets while producing income to cover yearly expenses and growing assets for legacy purposes.

At the end of the book are three appendices:

- Appendix A: "S&P 500 Dividend Aristocrats Class of 2009"
- Appendix B: "S&P 500 Dividend Aristocrats Class of 2017"
- Appendix C: "Bulls and Bears"

Appendices A and B will be relevant to you as you read sections 1 (*"When is it Right to Reenter the Market?"*) and 9 (*"Stocks for Babies"*), which reference Dividend Aristocrats.

And you will want to refer to Appendix C for bull and bear market data starting in 1921.

401(k)s and IRAs: The Working Years

ARE YOU CURIOUS:

- When is the best time to start investing?

- What should you do if the stock market moves into bear market territory?

- How can you maximize your 401(k) benefits and reduce taxable income?

SECTION PREVIEW:

If you are feeling busy or broke, or both, you may have no time to learn about your 401(k) at work. If you just started working, you may feel that you have no extra money to put away for retirement when you have many competing financial interests like a car, housing, student loans, and family. And, you may mistakenly believe that you have plenty of time between now and retirement, so why not wait before starting to invest?

First, I'll introduce the 401(k) life cycle, which lays out a model to follow after you start participating in your 401(k); then we'll see how a man in his 20's can start to think about and plan his future.

Then, we'll go through some numbers and concepts that will help you take advantage of the power behind the 401(k). You'll find out how to pay for your 401(k) without lowering your take-home pay and the true meaning of a pre-tax contribution that actually lowers your taxable income. If your plan has a company match, don't skip "Make Your Match Matter," where you'll compare the "cost" of participating versus the "benefit."

We'll also talk about how to make investment decisions in down markets, and how to open an IRA if you don't have a 401(k) at work.

INSIDER'S PERSPECTIVE:

The number one financial regret of retirees is that they wish they had started investing earlier, according to a 2016 Bankrate survey. There is no reason to delay saving and investing for retirement and there is every reason to start early (very early) to take advantage of compounding, which can be accelerated through a 401(k) with a match. Once you start saving, the strategies identified in this section will help you get the most from each phase of the 401(k) life cycle.

*   *   *

The markets are often volatile, sometimes running into euphoria, other times falling into despair (as was the case when I wrote this column in April 2001). Are there techniques you should be employing that will improve your 401(k) results? The answer, as this column explains, is that it depends. This column will introduce the ideas of the accumulation, rebalancing, and withdrawal phases of the 401(k) life cycle as well as strategies and timing that are involved in each.

KEY TO PLANNING IS UNDERSTANDING 401(K) LIFE CYCLE

Originally published April 22, 2001

When the stock market disappoints, should you worry about your 401(k) account? Not if you have been basing your 401(k) decisions on your 401(k) life cycle.

There are three phases to the 401(k) life cycle, and each phase has its own set of investment rules. Following those rules will help you avoid sleepless nights when stock prices drop from time to time, which, by the way, is a natural occurrence that should be understood and not feared.

The Accumulation Phase

If you are just starting out, you are in the first phase of your 401(k) life cycle: the accumulation phase. Your job is to grow your 401(k) account to a size that's large enough for you to live on in retirement. In this phase, you will be investing primarily in growth investments such as stocks and riding out the ups and downs of the market. When the market goes down, each of your payroll deductions will buy you more shares. Down markets are actually beneficial as you accumulate stock investments.

Before we look at the second phase of the 401(k) life cycle, let's jump to the third and last phase, which begins after you retire.

The Withdrawal Phase

At some point in the future, you will want your 401(k) to pay you a stream of checks throughout your retirement, which may last for 30 years or more. For most people, this is the real reason for participating in a 401(k) plan: using the income it produces to support oneself in retirement.

In this phase of the 401(k) life cycle, your job is to create income from your 401(k), and this usually is done primarily through income-producing investments such as bonds. You want income from those investments to cover your retirement needs as much as possible, because you want to avoid selling off principal, especially in a correction or a bear market.

If you are in retirement and are taking money out of interest or dividends created by your 401(k), a correction or bear market will have little effect on you.

You will be in trouble, however, if you did not rebalance your portfolio before reaching retirement. That brings us to rebalancing, which is the second phase of the 401(k) life cycle.

The Rebalancing Phase

Rebalancing is sandwiched between accumulation and withdrawal. This is the transitional time before retirement when you are slowly adding income-producing holdings and converting some of your growth holdings to income-producing holdings.

Of the three phases of the 401(k) life cycle, this one is the hardest, since it takes planning and discipline. You will want to start rebalancing your investments when you are 5 to 15 years from retirement. You will be directing that your payroll deductions be invested for income. If you are five years away from retirement, you might direct all of your payroll deductions into bond funds, less if you are seven years away from retirement, and so on.

A stock market correction or a bear market will have little relevance to you when you are acquiring bond funds through payroll deductions. However, if you are exchanging your stock funds for bond funds, you will want to wait until a correction or bear market stabilizes so that you don't sell those funds at a loss. This is one of the reasons for having a longer rebalancing horizon.

Reacting to the market. The biggest temptation that many unprepared 401(k) participants have is to sell in reaction to disappointing stock market performance. Remember, it is not your job to time the market. Your job is to accumulate assets for retirement. You may have 10, 20, 30, or more years until retirement, followed by another 30 years of retirement. You will have many up market and down market cycles to contend with. If you keep your goals in mind for each phase of the 401(k) life cycle, you will avoid panic selling into a correction or a bear market. With a little planning, your 401(k) will serve you well into the future, through good markets and bad.

*   *   *

The next column written in August 2016 is about a young man who wanted to take care of his family and his future. Saving enough for retirement is much easier when you get an early start.

IT'S NEVER TOO EARLY FOR RETIREMENT PLANNING

Originally published August 14, 2016

Meet Tim, a man in his twenties who is thinking about his future. He happens to be one of the very lucky few who are making it big in his sport—enough so that he can take care of his mom and his siblings, something he takes pride in doing.

Tim knows that his career as a professional athlete will end much earlier than his friends' careers. He is very much aware that his big earning years will last for a limited time. In my opinion, that's what gives him an edge over others his age.

He wants to experience the benefits of a high-paying career, but not at the cost of a comfortable future.

With retirement having the longest investment time horizon, that goal has the best chance of benefiting from the math of compounding.

Taking care of retirement is Tim's first priority. Over the next few years, he will contribute the maximum permitted under the law into an appropriate retirement plan. He will deploy the remaining resources for shorter-term goals.

Retirement is on people's minds, even young people like Tim.

A new survey released last week (August 2016) by Schwab Retirement Plan Services, Inc., highlights how saving enough money for a comfortable retirement is in fact the most common "financial stress inducer" for people of all ages, even Millennials. Almost 4 of 10 Millennials (38 percent) named saving for retirement as a source of financial stress above all others, far surpassing student loans (24 percent), monthly expenses (29 percent), and credit card debt (26 percent).

But almost one of two surveyed by Schwab feel it is impossible to save enough in a 401(k) for a comfortable retirement.

In fact, more people know their credit scores than know how much money they may need for a comfortable retirement.

"With so many competing obligations and priorities, it's natural for people to worry about whether they're saving enough for retirement," said Steve Anderson, president of Schwab Retirement Plan Services. "Roughly nine out of ten respondents told us they are relying mostly on themselves to finance retirement. It's encouraging to see people of all ages taking responsibility for their own future and making this a top priority."

But that's not all. Those who are investing for retirement through their company 401(k) plans aren't sure they are making good decisions. Only half (51 percent) of the respondents feel totally on top of their 401(k). More than one-third (35 percent) are stressed about choosing the right 401(k) investments.

Tim is luckier than most since he has perspective and has surrounded himself with mentors who can guide him.

If you have a future retiree in your family, no matter what the age, help him with his "numbers":

- How much money do you need to save to secure your retirement?
- At what age can you afford to retire?
- How much will you need for living expenses?

According to the survey, about 40 percent of the respondents wanted help getting answers to these questions.

Then ask about desires, goals, and concerns. Beyond retirement, what would they like to achieve? How can both long- and short-term goals be achieved at the same time? Talk about lifestyle goals, the future, and leveraging time. Out of that discussion comes a plan for the present that is based on goals for the future and a strategy for how to get there.

*   *   *

Knowing how to manage your tax withholding is a key skill when partici-pating in a 401(k) plan. In the next column published in October 2014 and updated in 2017, I share examples of how withholding allowances can impact your paycheck and your contributions to your 401(k) plan.

UNDERSTANDING THE RELATIONSHIP BETWEEN YOUR W-2 AND YOUR 401(K)

Originally published October 12, 2014; updated 2017

If you work for a company that offers a 401(k) plan, let's talk about how a 401(k) affects your W-2.

You (and the Internal Revenue Service) receive a W-2 from your employer after the close of the tax year showing your taxable earnings in Box 1 (wages, tips, and other compensation). When you do your taxes, you use Box 1 to fill in line 7 (wages) of your tax return (IRS Form 1040 or Form 1040A). Your tax bill is figured from that number.

When you make a pretax 401(k) contribution, that amount does not show up in Box 1. Your employer's contribution, whether it is a match or another type of contribution, such as a "safe harbor," also is not included in Box 1.

Let me give you three examples: an employee who does not participate in his or her company's 401(k) and two who do. In each case, the employee earns $1,000 a week, or $52,000 a year, and is single.

Employee A is not participating in a 401(k). His W-2's Box 1 shows $52,000 of taxable wages. As a single filer, his federal income tax bill will be approximately $6,145 (2017).

Employee B is contributing 5 percent of her salary to the pretax 401(k) ($2,600 for the year). Her Box 1 shows taxable wages of $49,400 even though she earned $52,000. Employee B's federal income tax bill will be roughly $5,495 (2017) or $650 less than Employee A's.

From the IRS's point of view, Employee B earned $2,600 less than she really did. That's one tax advantage of your pretax 401(k). The other is tax deferral that lasts until you start to withdraw money from the 401(k).

Employee C is contributing the same amount as Employee B, but his plan provides for a dollar-for-dollar match. His Box 1 will show taxable income of $49,400 as does Employee B's, but he earned an additional

$2,600 because of the match. Keeping in mind that his match has to vest in accordance with his 401(k) plan's provisions, Employee C's "income" is $54,600, but he is taxed on only $49,400.

If he were to pay taxes on the full $54,600, his federal tax bill would be about $6,795 (2017). Instead, his tax bill is only $5,495 (2017), which you can think of as "savings" of $1,300.

Again, that's identical to Employee B's tax bill even though Employee C earned $2,600 more because of the match. An important thing to remember about matching is this: If Employee C leaves the company before vesting, he won't be able to take the match with him.

Let's look at these three examples from a cost/benefit point of view.

Employee A, who does not participate in his plan, has no tax benefit and no savings.

Employee B saved $2,600 of her own money through payroll contributions. In addition, she got a break from Uncle Sam, saving $650 that she would have had to pay in taxes but now doesn't.

Employee B is ahead of Employee A by $650, plus Employee B has $2,600 saved for retirement, whereas Employee A has zero savings.

Employee C saved $5,200, which was $2,600 of his own money through payroll contributions plus the employer match. In addition, he saved $650 in taxes, just as Employee B did.

Employee C is ahead of Employee A by $650 in tax savings, plus he has $5,200 saved for retirement.

You can look at these examples another way. You can ask yourself what it actually "cost" each employee to save money for retirement after accounting for tax savings.

Employee B's cost was $2,600 minus $650 in tax savings, or $1,950. You can think of this as buying a $2,600 investment for only $1,950, a discount of 25 percent.

Employee C's cost was the same as Employee B's ($1,950), but his 401(k) balance was twice as high ($5,200 versus $2,600). Employee C paid only $1,950 for his $5,200 investment, a deep discount of 62.5 percent.

Although you'll have to pay taxes on withdrawals from your pre-tax 401(k) after you retire, there is no way to beat the power of the 401(k) as a savings vehicle, especially if your employer contributes to the plan.

*   *   *

If you believe you can't afford to participate in your 401(k) but get a tax refund at the end of the year, read the next column published in April 2014. It will tell you what you can do to keep all or most of your take-home pay and participate in a 401(k) at the same time.

MAKING YOUR 401(K) AFFORDABLE

Originally published April 27, 2014; updated 2017

If your employer offers a 401(k) plan that you think you cannot afford to contribute to, consider this: It may be possible for you to contribute without lowering your take-home pay dramatically.

Let me give you some background first, and then I'll share the technique.

The nice thing about 401(k) plans is that they offer tax advantages, one of which is the ability to contribute on a pretax basis. What that means is that your contribution is not taxed at tax time.

This is how it works:

First, say you don't participate in your 401(k) at work. Your compensation is $26,000 a year. Your W-2 reports $26,000 of taxable income on line 1. The tax you owe will be calculated on the basis of your income of $26,000.

Let's suppose you do participate in the 401(k) with a contribution of 6 percent of compensation (6 percent of $26,000, or $1,560).

Even though your compensation is $26,000, the IRS considers it only $24,440. That's the amount your employer reports as taxable income on line 1 of your W-2. Why not $26,000? Because the 401(k) contribution of $1,560 is deducted from your gross pay.

Let's take the next step to understand the significance of the difference in the W-2s.

You owe federal tax of $1,878 (2017) in the first case with a W-2 of $26,000 and no 401(k) contribution. However, you owe only $1,638 (2017) with a W-2 of $24,400. Because you contributed $1,560 to your 401(k), you saved $240 in taxes.

That may not seem like a big deal, but it is.

You can apply that $240 to your 401(k) contribution. Here's how:

Everything we've been talking about so far assumes you are single and are claiming one withholding allowance for federal income tax purposes. When you start working, you tell your employer how many withholding allowances you want to claim on IRS Form W-4, the Employee's Withholding Allowance Certificate.

By changing your Form W-4 with your employer, you can increase or decrease the amount that is withheld from your paycheck for income tax purposes. Since you will owe less in taxes by contributing to your 401(k), you can increase your withholding allowances.

Let's explore withholding allowances by using a calculator called "Payroll Deductions Calculator" that can be found at bankrate.com.

There you can enter your income of $26,000 (as $1,000 biweekly) and one withholding allowance under your "current paycheck." Your net paycheck shows as $821 (2017).

Then below, under "new paycheck," fill out the gross pay line as $1,000 and change the withholding allowances to two and add 6 percent to "401(k)/403(b) plan withholding." You can leave all the other lines blank for now. Click "view report."

Compare your "current paycheck" with your "new paycheck." In the example we are discussing, you can see that the new paycheck is $25.48 less than your current paycheck.

However, in exchange for losing $25.48 each paycheck, you will have $1,560 in retirement savings at the end of the year. Let's say your 401(k) has a 3 percent company match, as many do. That would add $780 from your employer, increasing your 401(k) balance to $2,340.

In this example, your two withholding allowances will cover your taxes in full.

What have you accomplished? You've lowered your paycheck by $662 ($25.48 × 26 pay periods). You've lowered your tax obligation and covered it through withholding. And you've socked away $2,340 in your 401(k) for your retirement.

Ask yourself: Was it worth it?

Your $662 paycheck reduction brought in $2,340. If you look at this commitment to a lower paycheck as an investment, your $662 investment gave you a profit of $1,678 ($2,340 –$662). That's your "gain" before any earnings that you will make on the 401(k)—a "profit" of 250 percent, not a bad investment.

*   *   *

If you want "free" money from your employer and the IRS, the next column published in November 1998 (updated through 2017) will show you how to get it. It's a matter of maximizing your company match.

MAKE YOUR MATCH MATTER

Originally published November 29, 1998; updated 2017

Your boss walks into your office and hands you an envelope. He says, "Here's $3,000 to help you save for your future." With a firm handshake, he wishes you the best of luck and says good-bye.

You open the envelope in search of a check. Instead you find a letter and a copy of your company's 401(k) plan's summary plan description.

The letter says that the money's already set aside for you, but there's one small catch: You have to read about the 401(k) first to find out how to get it.

Wait, you think to yourself. Are you missing something? Doesn't your boss know you're already participating in the company's 401(k) plan?

You review your participation. You are making $60,000 a year. You are contributing 1 percent, or $600, and you receive a match of $600 from the company.

SWORD

Your 401(k) plan is a double-edged sword. It gives you great financial power over your retirement. But as with every fine weapon, you have to hone your skills to do it justice.

Now let's find that $3,000 your boss wants you to have.

THE SPD

The summary plan description (SPD) describes the features of your plan. A more detailed description is also available, but more often than not, you can find all you need in the SPD. If you don't have your SPD, you might want to get it from the human resources or benefits department.

Usually the SPD covers the basics: how and when you can enroll, employee contributions, company contributions, the investment options offered under the plan, loans, plan distributions, leaving the company, in-service withdrawals, designating beneficiaries, pretax and after-tax accounts, and more. Another subject that is covered is vesting, which applies to company matches.

COMPANY MATCH

The financial services company you work for is in Stamford, Connecticut. The company calls your SPD the "Company Savings Plan Highlights." The index has a section called "Company Match." That's what we want. Looking there, we can see that the company will automatically match 100 percent of an employee's contribution to the plan up to 6 percent of compensation.

All right, you think. I am getting the maximum 100 percent match. I contribute 1 percent myself and get 1 percent from the company. That's pretty good, isn't it?

No, it isn't. You are not fully utilizing the match the company has set aside for you.

MAXIMIZING YOUR MATCH

You might assume that you are taking full advantage of your match if you contribute even 1 percent, since you do qualify for the full dollar-for-dollar match, but you are not. You are actually leaving money on the table, and the money you are leaving behind is additional compensation that the company wants to give you. And its money the IRS won't tax until you take it out in retirement.

Let's look at some other percentage contribution levels. At 2 percent, the company match is $1,200. At 3 percent, the match is $1,800. At 4 percent, the match is $2,400. At 5 percent, the match is $3,000. Here's what your boss is talking about: At 6 percent your company contributes $3,600 to your 401(k) account on your behalf. That means that if you are contributing only 1 percent, you are leaving behind $3,000.

In each of these cases, this is money that is due you without your working an extra minute. It's an extra company bonus for saving for your own retirement. And it is tax-free to you until you start withdrawing your money in retirement.

Very nice, you say, but I just have a feeling this is going to cost me.

Well, let's think about that. You do have to do something to trigger that extra money coming from your company. But as I'll explain below, it certainly does *not* cost you.

To qualify for the extra $3,000 from the company, you have to put up an extra $3,000 too. Through payroll deductions, you have to contribute 6 percent of your compensation to the plan into an investment account in your name that you control. Thus, you're not spending it or giving it away; you are investing it for your future.

WHAT YOU GET

If you do that, at the end of the year you will have your contribution of 6 percent and the company's contribution of 6 percent for a total of $7,200. Half of that is an extra company bonus to reward you for taking care of yourself, plus you get whatever returns your investments of those monies provided you.

WHAT IT ACTUALLY COSTS

Let's see what you had to pay. Your 6 percent payroll deductions are $3,600. But because this 401(k) contribution of yours reduces your W-2 earnings, your taxable earnings drop by that amount (from $60,000 to $56,400).

Because of that, you spend less on federal and state taxes. [2017 update: If you are single, for example, the federal tax due on $60,000 gross income is $8,145 compared to $7,245 on gross income of $56,400, for a difference of $900.]

Now you have to subtract the tax savings from your contribution to see how much you are really paying ($3,600 − $900 = $2,700). When you do that, you see your out-of-pocket cost drop by $900 to $2,700. That means that you are paying $2,700 to get $7,200 of 401(k) benefit. That puts you ahead by almost $4,500 ($7,200 − $2,700) just for participating in your 401(k).

So does it cost you? No, it costs the company and the IRS.

If you hear people complaining that they can't afford to maximize their company matches or, worse, can't afford to participate in their plans, do them a favor. Talk to them about the extra $3,000 you found in your SPD. And tell them your boss made a mistake. Tell them you actually improved your situation by about $4,500.

*   *   *

Just how does one decide on 401(k) options? The next column written in October 2000 talks about choosing 401(k) investments. The approach applies to all types of markets.

STOCKS VERSUS BONDS IS THE AGE-OLD QUESTION

Originally published October 29, 2000

A reader of this column is 55, single, and works for a large company. Having just received a disappointing 401(k) quarterly performance report, Janice wants to know if she should change her investments. She plans to work another 10 years until she reaches age 65.

Among the eight options offered by her company's 401(k) plan, five are stock holdings, two are bond options, and one is a money market fund.

Janice has chosen to invest most of her 401(k) account in the stock market. She has one stock, that of her employer, a publicly held financial services company, and five stock mutual funds, one of which is a balanced fund that holds both stocks and bonds.

The first issue to tackle is how much should be invested in stocks as opposed to bonds or money markets. That depends on six interdependent factors: the size of your 401(k), what is held outside of your 401(k), whether you have a pension, whether the pension is indexed to counteract inflation, the amount of money you need to live on after retirement, and how much time is left before retirement. None of these factors alone should lead you to a decision. Weigh them all before making a move.

If your 401(k) is your largest asset and you are inexperienced as an investor, you may need to include a bond or money market position. Generally—but not always—the volatility of your portfolio will decrease after the addition of bonds and money market funds. If your 401(k) is not your largest asset but you are concerned about its current performance, your jitters may move you to less volatile investments. That is not always the right choice. A lot will depend on the following factors:

- *Outside assets:* If your 401(k) is your only asset, you need to be conscious of protecting it. That is a reason to add some bond or money market positions. However, if you are young and have no pension and understand that markets fluctuate, you may want to be 100 percent in stock investments while you build the portfolio over time.

- *Pension:* If your retirement expenses are covered by your pension and that pension is indexed to increase with inflation, your situation is ideal. You can invest your 401(k) any way you wish.

  However, if you have a 401(k) in lieu of a pension, you must invest it in a way that will create your own personal pension that will supplement your Social Security payments. You will need to invest for growth while you are working and for income when you need to pay yourself a pension check in retirement. This is not an easy task. You have to learn how to do this as soon as possible.

- *Indexing for cost of living increases:* Not many pensions increase over time. If you have a pension, check to see whether your payments will increase as you get older. If they don't, you will need to plan on saving enough to offset inflation.

- *Living expenses:* You need to know how much you spend. Assume that you will need 70 percent as much as you spend now after you retire. If you have no pension, you need to invest your 401(k) so that it will pay you enough money to live on throughout your retirement.

- *Time horizon:* In Janice's case, she has a time horizon of 10 years until retirement plus another 10 years until she has to start withdrawing money from her 401(k). A long horizon such as this gives Janice a chance to ride through just about any underperforming period in the stock market, and this supports her desire to be 100 percent invested in stocks.

  Someone with a shorter horizon may wish to have a portion of the 401(k) invested in the bond and money market options.

To sum it up, there are a number of personal factors to consider before one decides on stock and bond allocations. Most people can follow this general rule of thumb: Invest in stocks for growth when you need to grow your 401(k) account but be ready to ride out the fluctuations of the market. Invest in bonds for income when you need money to live on or for diversification. Invest in money markets to stabilize a portfolio at any age.

Having a prescreened investment menu is one of the advantages of participating in a 401(k) plan. That is, the participants do not have to take the time to screen the tens of thousands of investment options they could buy for retirement. Acting as your fiduciary, your company does that for you and comes up with a list of options that it deems suitable for you and other employees.

That makes your job much easier. Your role is to make your stock versus bond allocations and then study your investment options to determine how they differ.

If you are unsure about how your company chooses and monitors its 401(k) investment options, it's fair to ask. Typically, sponsors have investment committees composed of human resources and finance personnel whose job it is to monitor investment options for the plan. The company should have written guidelines or an investment policy statement to follow. If there is nothing in writing, that does not mean there is no policy. Any time an investment is chosen for a plan, de facto, someone is acting on a policy. In the best case, it is well reasoned and prudent. In the worst case, it is ad hoc. In any case, you need to have some comfort that your 401(k) investment options are being followed and reviewed regularly.

In the next column, I review how to become the master of your 401(k), with a focus on responsibilities—yours and management's. There is a process to go through, starting with disclosure documents, and working through investment options. The goal is to tie your investment selections to where you are in your 401(k) life cycle.

BE THE MASTER OF YOUR 401(K)

Originally published November 15, 1998

Are you in control of your 401(k) investments?

A question from a reader raised some concerns that I would like to share with you. This participant had not considered his investment options since he enrolled in his 401(k) account three years ago. He wasn't certain how his 401(k) account was invested. In fact, he said he couldn't remember the last time he looked at his 401(k) statement.

One of the benefits of having a 401(k) plan is being able to invest for your retirement painlessly through payroll deductions. Money is deducted from your earnings and transferred to your 401(k) account on your behalf. In most plans, the way these monies are invested is up to you.

As an investment adviser, I cannot overemphasize the importance of managing your 401(k) investments. If you, like this reader, don't know the options available to you or how your 401(k) is invested, you are not managing your 401(k). It is managing you.

This is bad enough if you have a pension plan that can support you in retirement. But if you are relying solely on your 401(k) to supplement your retirement income, drop everything and do your 401(k) homework. Your 401(k) can provide you with a wonderful retirement if it is managed well. Conversely, it can be a lost opportunity if it is ignored.

HOMEWORK

Here are the minimal steps I would take in assessing and managing my 401(k) account. I encourage you to take all of them no matter how much or how little investing experience you have. The time commitment is not great. The payoff is.

MANAGEMENT'S RESPONSIBILITIES

First, understand who is responsible for what. The investments made available to you by your plan are screened carefully by your company's management. In the process, they are acting as fiduciaries under the Employee Retirement Income Security Act (ERISA), the federal law governing 401(k) plans. In that role, they are responsible for engaging in a due diligence process in choosing and monitoring the investments that are made available to you.

REASONABLE EXPECTATIONS

You should be able to rely on management having executed its fiduciary responsibilities. As a result, you need not second-guess the selections themselves unless of course you have cause to believe that there are problems, such as an offering that is not performing as expected.

YOUR RESPONSIBILITIES

Your job is to compare the investments with one another and determine what each one can do for you.

TOOLS

There are a number of tools available to help you, but before you begin, make sure your data is current. One might perhaps expect smaller companies to be less likely to keep up with current data, but one would be surprised. Even at the largest employers, it is usually up to you to make sure you have the most current information. Do not rely on what you have in your 401(k) file at home; many times these are the materials you received years ago, when you first enrolled in the plan.

WHAT YOU NEED

Make sure you have the current summary plan description (SPD), which describes your plan. Also get a current listing of the investment menu and a description of all current offerings, including prospectuses and financial reports, current performance data, and, of course, your personal 401(k) account statement. All of this is obtainable through the human resources department.

Your goal is to use these tools to assess the investments you should be choosing now and in the future as you move through the different stages of your 401(k) plan.

For example, when you are just starting out, your primary concern is growing your 401(k) account. You will need to determine which investments offer growth potential.

Much later, after you retire, you will need to have your 401(k) produce income for you to live on. You will need to know which investment options offer income potential.

Sometime before you retire, you will have to start thinking about moving from growth investments to income-producing investments. You will be looking for investment options or techniques you can use to accomplish that result.

In each of the three stages of retirement investing—accumulation, rebalancing, and withdrawal—you also may wish to hold investments that lower your risk. Determine which options are appropriate for lowering the risk of your 401(k) portfolio.

HOW TO JUDGE WHAT YOU SEE

How do you make these judgments if you are not a seasoned investor? To simplify things, let's say you have three investment options: a stock fund, a bond fund, and a money market fund.

Of the three, let's see which fund is designed for the accumulation phase of your 401(k) life cycle. Remember that when you are accumulating assets, you have years of saving and investing ahead of you. Your goal is to grow your account as much as possible.

Let's take the options one at a time. What you are looking for is clues to what each option is intended to do for you.

MONEY MARKET FUND

If you look at the money market prospectus, you'll see that its objective is stability of principal. Is that fund designed to grow your assets? No.

It is designed to protect your principal. You won't want to use it to grow your 401(k).

But what can a money market fund do for you? It may offer you some peace of mind if you are worried about volatility. If you have your 401(k) invested in a money market fund during the accumulation phase, you may be protecting your principal, but is that your goal? And will a money market fund help you beat inflation?

BOND FUND

If you look at the bond fund prospectus, it tells you that the fund's objective is the production of income. Is the bond fund designed to grow your assets? No. It is designed to pay dividends that you can use for income. This fund might be more appropriate after retirement to produce income when you need it.

As described in the prospectus, bond funds fluctuate in price. In contrast to money market funds, they do not provide stability of principal. However, you may use a bond fund during the accumulation phase to diversify your portfolio.

STOCK FUND

When you look at the stock fund prospectus, you see that this fund's objective is growth of capital. Among the three alternatives offered, this may be the fund that management intended you to use for growing your capital during the accumulation phase.

Unlike the money market fund, the stock fund will not offer you stability of principal. Volatility is the price you pay for the prospect of growth. The risk of loss is also described in the prospectus.

NEXT STEPS

This analysis is just your starting point. You also have to determine how much you wish to direct into each fund on a regular basis. Do you want to direct 100 percent of your contributions into the stock fund? Do you want to dampen your volatility by directing 20 percent into the money market fund? That will depend on how comfortable you are with interim price fluctuation versus how important the long-term goal of building retirement assets is to you.

HOW IMPORTANT IS PERFORMANCE?

Performance is a matter for management to consider when it monitors the investment selections. For example, management would compare the stock fund with other similarly managed stock funds. Its goal is not to find the highest-performing fund of the moment. Rather, it is looking for signals that would cause the fund to be no longer suitable to offer in your plan. Is performance in line with expectations? Has the investment manager changed its investment objectives or investment policy? Has the fund shown problem signs such as assets trending downward or expenses trending upward? And so on.

ACTING ON PERFORMANCE NUMBERS

An inexperienced 401(k) investor may misuse performance data. I have seen 401(k) participants switch their holdings each quarter. When they receive their quarterly reports, they move their holdings to the highest performer of the moment. That is a good way to dig yourself into a hole and never get out.

You need to base your investment decisions on your investment goal.

Invest for growth when you are growing your 401(k) account. Invest for income when you are taking money out of your 401(k) account in retirement. Rebalance your portfolio in the in-between stage so that you are not forced to sell equity holdings into a down market if you happen to find yourself in one at retirement. At all times, consider whether you need to diversify your holdings with money market funds or stable assets if volatility makes you nervous.

TIME AND EFFORT

Take the time to follow your 401(k) account. This is not the type of benefit plan that you can ignore. You don't want to be in the position of looking back at retirement and asking yourself, Why didn't I pay more attention to my 401(k) plan? By then, the wonderful opportunities your 401(k) can offer will be lost. ▪

*　　*　　*

Do you work somewhere that does not offer a 401(k) plan? Have you changed jobs? Have you inherited retirement assets from a deceased spouse? Have you retired from a company at which you accumulated 401(k) savings? If you answered yes to any of these questions, you may find that you have the need to open an Individual Retirement Arrangement (IRA) account. In the next column, I explain how to open, fund, and designate beneficiaries on an IRA account.

WHAT YOU NEED TO KNOW TO OPEN AN IRA

Originally published March 9, 2014; updated 2018

You've decided to open an IRA. What's next?

"Herbert" has been investing for retirement through his 401(k) plan at work for 20 years and "Susanna," a recent college graduate, has never invested on her own. Both want to know how to open an IRA account.

IRA is an acronym for individual retirement arrangement, which is the official Internal Revenue Service term. But most people call IRAs individual retirement accounts, and indeed, an IRA is a type of account as opposed to an investment.

Why would Herbert and Susanna want an IRA? Simply to help them save and invest for retirement in a tax-advantaged way. Let's dive into the mechanics.

If you want to open an IRA, start with your local bank, brokerage firm, or mutual fund company. You will be provided with IRA account paperwork to complete or will be encouraged, as Susanna was, to go online to fill out the paperwork on your own. You also can search for a financial institution that offers IRAs online.

The paperwork is relatively straightforward. Some items are obvious, such as your name (by the way, you are the "owner" of the IRA), address, and Social Security number. But other items can raise questions for a new investor.

When Susanna looked at her paperwork, she was caught off guard by these items:

1. *Type of IRA.* The form asks you to choose among a traditional IRA, rollover IRA, inherited IRA, Roth IRA, Roth inherited IRA, and Roth rollover IRA. As a new investor, Susanna will choose either a traditional IRA or a Roth IRA. The other types deal with inheriting an IRA from someone or having an IRA funded with money coming from a company retirement plan. At age 22,

Susanna would choose a Roth over a traditional IRA for its superior long-term tax advantages even though Roth contributions are not tax-deductible. Briefly, a Roth offers tax-free investment opportunities as opposed to the traditional IRA's tax deferral benefits. However, a traditional IRA can be tax-deductible in many cases, whereas funding a Roth never results in a tax deduction.

2. *Funding your account.* Next, you are asked to state how much you want to contribute to the IRA. There are limits. Susanna earned about $10,000 (during the current year), and is due to earn about $40,000 (the following year). The most she can contribute is $5,500 (2018 limit; check current limits at irs.gov), which is the top limit for someone under age 50. Herbert earned more than $200,000. Because he is over 50, the maximum he can contribute is $6,500 (2018 limit; see irs.gov for current limits).

3. *IRA contribution tax year.* You can choose to make your contribution effective for the current tax year (2017) or even for the prior tax year (2016) if you haven't filed your 2016 tax return and you fund the IRA before the deadline (the due date of your tax return, plus extensions). If you meet those requirements, what's best for a new investor? Choosing 2016 as the tax contribution year. Why? So that you also can make a contribution for the 2017 tax year.

4. *Designated beneficiary.* Your beneficiary receives the IRA in the event of your death. You'll see a primary beneficiary and a contingent beneficiary on the form. You'll want to name both. To maximize the beneficiary's tax deferral possibilities, it's not a good idea to have "my estate" or "my will" as the beneficiary. A beneficiary does not have to be a family member, and it is possible to designate a charity as one.

5. *Options account.* If the form asks you to sign up to trade options, you'll want to decline. Options trading should be left to experts.

How many people have IRAs? Almost 44 million U.S. households (more than 35 percent of all households) owned IRAs (in 2017) according to the Investment Company Institute's (ICI) "Frequently Asked Questions About Individual Retirement Accounts."

Most owned traditional IRAs (35.1 million); 24.9 million owned Roth IRAs. Some owned both. According to the ICI, 13.9 percent of households that own traditional IRAs also own Roth IRAs. Another 6 percent own employer-sponsored IRAs.

For more information on the differences between a traditional IRA and a Roth IRA, listen to a podcast offered by the Financial Industry Regulatory Authority (FINRA) by going to finra.org and searching "Should You Open an IRA?"

* * *

Every 401(k) participant will experience down market periods. The next column, which was written in 2016, discusses how to make good decisions during market corrections. What actions should you take regarding your 401(k) contributions and balances in a market correction? The answers may surprise you, as often the best thing to do is nothing at all, assuming you have made appropriate investment selections.

MANAGING YOUR 401(K) DURING
A MARKET CORRECTION

Originally published January 23, 2016

If you are a 401(k) participant, you may be wondering if you should bail on equities, as the stock market is in a correction, having lost more than 10 percent from its last peak. From my perspective as a professional money manager, I can tell you that the answer is no.

First, let's get some perspective.

Your 401(k) is nothing like an investment you can make on your own.

First, taxes. When you buy an S&P 500 Index fund in your taxable brokerage account, during the entire holding period you will be paying taxes on dividend income, capital gains distributions, and capital gains taxes on profits.

Those taxes are a huge barrier to optimal long-term performance, and you need to think long term when you think 401(k)s. What's long term? Your entire working career, which spans 40-plus years, plus retirement, which can add another 30 years or more.

If your investments are subject to tax drag over a 40-year period, your growth is impeded. Not so with your 401(k) (or IRA), which is taxed only when you begin making withdrawals, typically after you retire.

Another tax benefit is this: You reduce your taxable income dollar for dollar when you contribute to a 401(k). If you earn $50,000 and contribute $5,000 to your 401(k), your W-2 reports taxable income of $45,000, not $50,000 (and not $55,000 if your employer contributes another $5,000).

Next, your 401(k) plan may offer a contribution from your employer. Many do. More than 90 percent of the plans that Vanguard administers offer employer matches or other contributions. An employer contribution is not something you can do for yourself.

Why is that important? If your employer gives you money for your 401(k), that's above and beyond the money you put at risk in the market.

Although your entire balance is at risk, it helps to view your employer's contribution itself as profit.

Combine these factors (avoiding taxes for the long term plus employers giving you money to save for retirement) and you have an investment that surpasses anything you can do on your own.

The next question is, When the markets are dire, should you sell your stock market holdings or stop contributing to your 401(k) altogether?

Once again, let's get some perspective. Your freedom to change your investments is usually quite liberal. Normally, you are not constrained in making investment selection changes.

There are two types of investments that must be considered: (1) your payroll contributions and (2) your balance.

You may be contributing $100 a month every payroll period. Your balance may be $10,000. You direct the way your contributions are invested; you also direct the way the investments making up your "balance" are invested. Thus, there are two types of investment decisions that you need to make, and they are not based on the same investment principles.

Your payroll contributions are periodic, with the period depending on how often you are paid. If you want to take advantage of volatility, put those contributions to work with more volatile investment options. For example, say you have an S&P 500 Index fund option. When the market is declining, you'll be buying more shares of the fund at lower prices. You build wealth by acquiring more shares, and if you can do that at cheaper prices, you are ahead of the game.

As to your balance, different rules apply. You'll want to assess how long you have until you retire. If you have only a few years, you'll want that balance invested cautiously. Less volatile investments, such as balanced funds, will be better options than an S&P 500 Index fund. Why? You'll lose less during market declines.

If you are decades away from retirement, you can take on more risk. If you have a pension that will cover your living expenses in retirement, you can be more aggressive with your investments.

When should you worry? If your 401(k) is your largest asset and you are going to retire soon. But should you react by selling or stopping contributions? Not if your personal plan has been crafted to achieve these goals: (1) making sure your income covers your expenses throughout retirement even as cash outlay increases over time as a result of inflation and taxes and (2) possibly creating a legacy for your family or for charity.

If you are thinking of stopping your 401(k) contributions because of the market, don't. You'll miss out on returns. According to the Employee Benefit Research Institute (EBRI), "consistent participants" had 401(k)s worth four times more than those of other participants. This data is from EBRI's study of account balances from 2007 to 2013.

Don't react with fear. Work market declines into your personal plan and engage a skeptic to work with you. ▪

*   *   *

While the previous column provided more general advice, the following was written in October 2008, the worst month of the Financial Crisis. In it, I provide the numbers to demonstrate the rationale that continuing your 401(k) contributions through down markets will leave you in a much better situation in the long run.

DO THE MATH AND STAY THE COURSE ON YOUR 401(K)

Originally published October 19, 2008

When severe market declines strike home as they are doing now (October 2008), people tend to run for cover and ask questions later. That's not always the best course of action.

Some people are thinking about stopping their 401(k) contributions. That's not a good idea, especially if the plan offers a match, irrespective of how the market is doing.

But to give you the worst-case scenario, I'd like to walk you through the math behind your 401(k) so that you can see the value of holding on.

Let me give you an example using a plan with a middle-of-the-road 50 percent match in the worst market in history: the Great Depression, when the market dropped about 85 percent over four years (1929–1932).

Say you started contributing $100 a month to your 401(k) in the beginning of 1929 and continued until the end of 1932. Because 401(k) contributions are made in pretax dollars, let's factor in a tax rate of 25 percent to make the math easy.

Although you are actually contributing $100, it's costing you only $75 ($100 – $25 in tax savings at a 25 percent tax rate).

Your contribution is $100 and another $50 is coming from the match, for a total contribution of $150.

Here is the important point to remember: Your personal investment in a 401(k) is a lot less than goes into the 401(k) because of the pretax nature of the contribution and the match.

When you take that into account—which you must if you consider your 401(k) an investment—you see that you are using $75 of your own money to "buy" a $150 contribution to the 401(k). Each month, $150 shows up in your 401(k), but only $75 is your money. The rest comes from the match ($50) and your tax savings ($25).

Let's see what happens over the four-year period during which the market declined almost 85 percent. Over that four-year period, your cost for making these $100 monthly contributions was only $75 a month over 48 months, or a total of $3,600. At the end of the four years, you have a profit of $760 for a total ending value of $4,340. That's a return on your investment of about 21 percent over the four-year period.

Why should you look at your 401(k) this way?

If your plan has a match, you need to stay the course regardless of your age. What if your plan does not have a match? You'll lose less because of your monthly investing and the pretax advantage.

As before, the cost of your contribution was $75 a month over 48 months for a total of $3,600. At the end, you have a balance of $2,893 for a loss of $707, or about 20 percent, instead of a loss of about 85 percent if you had invested one chunk of money at the beginning of 1929 outside your 401(k).

Even though we're not in Depression-like times, the financial markets could not be more uncertain. We saw a huge surge on Monday, October 14, 2008, when the market was up over 11 percent on the day.

However, the worst single-day decline of the current market followed on Wednesday, when the Dow fell over 7 percent on the day.

Although it's too early for the average investor to jump in to buy stocks outside a 401(k), it is worth looking at investing your monthly payroll deductions in your 401(k), particularly if you have a match. If you have a large balance in your 401(k), different rules apply, however. A large balance needs to be invested appropriately for your age and financial circumstances.

* * *

What is the most important asset you are going to have at retirement? With the rapid decline in company pension offerings, the answer is likely to be a 401(k). In the next column from 1999, I tell a story of how important it is to be aware of what is happening in your 401(k) and retirement accounts. I also detail some steps that you can take to engage your company and co-workers in meaningful dialogue regarding your retirement accounts.

GET INVOLVED IN RETIREMENT PLANNING

Originally published May 2, 1999

Someday in the future . . .

You and your neighbor "Sam" are retiring soon. You are both in good health and expect to live long and happy lives. In fact, you are looking forward to 30 years of retirement or more. You meet over coffee to discuss your 401(k) investments.

Now that you are retiring, you will be using your 401(k) account as a source of monthly income. There is a little Social Security money coming in, but most of what you need is going to come from your 401(k).

Who would have thought that you would be paying yourself your own pension?

You think back.

"It was a lucky day when we got interested in our 401(k)s," you say.

Sam laughs in agreement. "Yes. If it weren't for our 401(k)s, we'd still be working . . . or moving in with our kids."

Getting interested means two things: educating yourself about your plan and asking your company for help when you need it.

Let's say you do your homework about your own plan. You compare its features with others and find that it falls short of your expectations. It could be a simple matter of not being provided with current investment information about the plan. Or it could be worse. Perhaps your plan provides investment options that you cannot understand.

Here is what you need to do.

First, bring your questions and concerns to your company. Management needs employee feedback on the benefit plans the company is offering. Your interest in the plan should be appreciated and encouraged. Employee interest is a sign of a healthy plan.

Second, suggest a mechanism for feedback if there is none. This could be as simple as a suggestion box. Or you could ask that the 401(k) plan be put on the agenda at monthly management meetings.

Third, consider organizing a 401(k) lunch club. Your company should be helpful in posting notices and providing a room. If you meet once a month, you can have volunteers report on different aspects of the plan at each meeting. For example, two people could volunteer to educate themselves about the plan's matching provisions and report on their findings.

It's better in the long run if employees find the answers for themselves instead of relying on the benefits department. Why? You may be living with the plan long after you retire. You need to know how to find the answers.

Fourth, let your company know you are paying attention to the plan. Your 401(k) is a valuable retirement tool, perhaps the only tool you have. You need to build your retirement assets to pay for your retirement, which may last a long time.

If your company doesn't feel the plan is important to you, will management make the plan a priority? If you want your company to improve your plan, you need to make it aware of your interest and concern.

If you do this, when you retire, you'll be able look back and say, "I'm really glad I started paying attention to my 401(k) when I did."

401(k)s and IRAs in Retirement

ARE YOU CURIOUS:

- Have you saved enough to retire securely?

- What is a "safe" withdrawal rate?

- How do the retirement account tax rules work?

SECTION PREVIEW:

This section contains columns you'll want to read both when you are retired or near retirement. We'll discuss safe withdrawal rates, when you need a portfolio review, and how to avoid making retirement mistakes. This section is helpful for retirees looking to move from saving to investing and stresses the importance of effective tax strategies. It also addresses consequences of improper planning.

INSIDER'S PERSPECTIVE:

If you are like most people, you are concerned about outliving your money (seven out of ten U.S. adults over the age of 18 surveyed were concerned that they would outlive their retirement savings, according to a 2016 study from Northwestern Mutual). That is a real concern that needs to be addressed through a careful review of your spending and your income sources. It is not enough to rely on an adviser's cheery outlook. You don't want to hear: "Don't worry, you'll never run out of money," unless and until a full cash flow analysis is done for you.

Here's why: Anecdotally, I can tell you about a corporate executive with $10 million of investable assets. His adviser told him he could retire at the age of 55—without running out of money. Who knows why the adviser believed that, since he never asked the executive about his living expenses—$2 million a year.

If you have a financial adviser who is telling you "Don't worry, you'll never run out of money" you may need to find a new adviser (skip to section 5 of this book). In my experience every situation is unique, and your personal circumstances are the most important determinant of your preparedness for retirement.

* * *

In the next column, written in February 2018, I discuss five ways retirees successfully prepare for retirement.

FIVE SECRETS TO RETIRE SECURELY

Originally published February 4, 2018

A while ago, I met with someone whose 70 year old father had been living beyond his means.

The father, a retired businessman, confided to his 40-something son that he had $100,000 of credit card debt that he could not repay. "How could that be?" asked the son. The father answered that he didn't realize anything was wrong in the beginning and life was proceeding along as usual. Eventually, he became aware that he was dipping in to credit, but he felt he had to "keep up appearances" as a leader in his community.

In another situation, a teacher on a limited income received a letter from her retired father asking her to send him money so that he could stay in his home. He had been paying his bills through home equity lines of credit that finally dried up. Could she and her two siblings each send him $1,000 a month so he could stay in his house?

In my role as financial columnist, author and money manager, I'm hearing more and more stories like these.

Over the years, I have seen retirees successfully navigate the retirement minefield. Let me share some of their secrets with you.

1. *Do a situation audit.* The transition to retirement calls for a situation audit that goes something like this. "Alright, my spouse and I will no longer be working. Just how will we support ourselves for the rest of our lives? Do we have to do things differently? Can we continue to use credit cards? Should we change our lifestyle? How can we be sure that our resources will last a lifetime, in sickness and in health?"

2. *Do a cash flow analysis.* Cash flow management is the very simple process of making sure that outflow (your monthly expenses) never exceeds inflow (monthly income from pension,

Social Security, and dividends and interest). Retirees who know how to do this have successful retirements, by which I mean, their finances are healthy throughout their lives. Anyone of any means can arrive at this result.

3. *Obey coverage rules.* The ideal situation is to cover essential expenses with "guaranteed" sources of income, such as Social Security retirement benefits, pension, and pension substitutes.

   Then, pay for discretionary expenses only when there is extra cash generated from your investments. If you can't do that, you'll need to consider lowering your lifestyle desires to fit the reality of your pocketbook.

4. *Address social changes that will occur after you retire.* Consider what the future may bring. What happens if you predecease your spouse or you become ill or incapacitated? What do you want to see put in place to help your spouse manage? What happens if your spouse predeceases you, or becomes ill? How will you manage? What role do you want your children to play? What about your financial, legal, and tax advisers?

5. *Engage your spouse as a partner.* Before retirement, one spouse usually drives financial decisions and the other jumps in the back seat. That has to change in retirement for one very good reason: what happens if the leader predeceases the follower, or becomes ill and incapacitated? Successful retirees realize that retirement is a joint venture between spouses, calling on both to share decision-making, planning, and importantly, managing the financial team, comprised of the family's adviser, accountant and lawyer.

Every life transition—retirement, divorce, loss of a spouse, loss of a job, sale of a house or sale of a business—calls for a re-examination of your personal economic, lifestyle, and social drivers. The sooner you get started, the better off you and your family will be. If you don't want to think of your own well-being, think of the burden your children may need to shoulder if someday you had to write a letter saying, "I've got bad news. I've outlived my money and I need your help." ▨

* * *

The arrival of your retirement will give rise to solicitations to roll over your 401(k) assets into an IRA. While there are advantages to rollovers, such as having more control over your investment options, there may be disadvantages that may make a particular scenario a bad idea for you. The next column will take you through the things you should know before you consider any rollover proposals. The column has been updated to consider proposed Department of Labor (DOL) fiduciary rules. The DOL rules are still under review at the time of writing. It is yet to be seen which fiduciary standards will ultimately be enforced, but it is clearly a priority for the regulators.

DON'T LET YOURSELF BE RUSHED INTO A ROLLOVER DECISION

Originally published May 13, 2001; updated 2017

A reader is retiring at age 58. "Sam" started thinking about retirement about a year ago, when he attended some company-sponsored retirement planning seminars. It occurred to him that he could expect to spend more hours retired than he spent working.

"Say we work 8 hours a day for 40 years. That's 80,000 hours of work during a lifetime," said Sam. "If I'm retired, I'm not working 24 hours a day, 365 days a year. That's 87,600 hours in 10 years. In just 10 years of retirement, I will have chalked up more retirement time than I spent working over an entire lifetime."

Sam started thinking about retirement in a different light. This was going to be an important phase of life that he hoped would be long and satisfying. Sam was ready to address his finances, the most important part of which was his 401(k) plan.

When a stockbroker approached him with the idea of rolling over his 401(k) plan into an IRA, Sam was ready.

Any time a commissioned salesperson recommends taking money out of your 401(k) account, your job is to take a step back and consider the whole picture. [2017 update: Under proposed Department of Labor (DOL) fiduciary rules, more client interactions, such as advice about rollovers to IRAs, will require retirement advice providers to operate under a DOL fiduciary standard.]

Let's look at some of the basics you have to cover before deciding if a rollover is right for you.

A rollover involves moving money. Typically, you would set up an individual retirement account (IRA) at a financial institution such as a brokerage firm, bank, or mutual fund company to receive the money moved out of your 401(k). Sam is eligible to do a rollover because he is retiring. You are also eligible if you change jobs; in that case, you have the additional option of transferring your old 401(k) to your new company if the new plan is set up to accept transfers.

Pretax Account

Sam has both pretax and after-tax money in his 401(k). The pretax account can be rolled over into an IRA. The after-tax money cannot. Most plans will not allow Sam to roll over just his pretax account. That means that if Sam wants to roll over his pretax account, his after-tax account will be distributed as well. [2017 update: New IRS guidelines were released in 2015 regarding after-tax 401(k) contributions. The pretax portion of the 401(k) would roll over to a traditional IRA; the after-tax portion can roll to a Roth IRA to preserve tax advantages.]

Company Stock

Sam also has a substantial amount of company stock in his 401(k) account, which he acquired over the years at a very low cost basis.

If you hold highly appreciated company stock in your 401(k), you cannot roll that over to your IRA without losing possible tax advantages. The gain or Net Unrealized Appreciation (NUA) of company stock held in a 401(k) account is given special treatment under the law. The minute it is rolled out of the 401(k) into an IRA, that special treatment is lost.

Gains on company stock held in a 401(k) plan have favorable tax treatment if and only if certain procedures are followed.

To take advantage of this special tax treatment of company stock, the stock must be transferred in kind to a taxable account. (The administrator of the plan can help you figure out the tax consequences.) Because of the distribution, the stock is now outside the tax-deferred environment and can be sold just as any other stock would be. Future gains will be taxed at capital gains tax rates. The stock cannot be placed in an IRA.

If instead of taking a distribution of the company stock you roll over that stock into an IRA, you will lose the option of selling the stock at a future date at the lower capital gains tax rate. In a sense, once the stock is rolled, you cannot "unroll" it.

Whether this benefit is a significant one for Sam needs to be addressed by doing a few what-if calculations. Sam will have to run some numbers assuming he takes an in-kind distribution and compare them with a rollover. He will have to think about different scenarios, such as holding on to all or part of the stock for his own portfolio or to leave to his children.

In Sam's case, his largest 401(k) holding happens to be the stock. After he retires, he may want to diversify. That alone does not indicate that he should do a rollover. Depending on his particular situation, it may make sense to take the stock in kind first, pay taxes on the distribution, and diversify outside of an IRA, particularly if Sam intends to buy individual stocks that he wants to hold for the long term.

Estate

Although you generally want to build tax-deferred assets, there are cases in which you don't. Dying with a large sum of money in tax-deferred accounts has its drawbacks if the overall estate is substantial.

The difference in tax treatment can be great. In a taxable situation, when a security is inherited, the basis is stepped up. That is not the case with an IRA.

Say you inherited stock from your father. He bought the stock at $10, and when he died, it was worth $100. Your cost basis is $100, not $10. That translates into a tax advantage for you. When you sell the stock, your gain will be figured from the $100 value, not the $10 value, and that means a tremendous tax savings in this example.

There is no comparable concept when it comes to IRAs. The cost basis of a stock held in an IRA is irrelevant to the taxation of the IRA you inherit. Distributions will be taxed at ordinary income tax rates.

Before deciding whether to roll over your 401(k) into an IRA, it pays to look over your plan, consider your options, and do some what-ifs. Don't forget to consult your accountant and tax adviser. If you have company stock in your 401(k), get a tax explanation from your 401(k) plan administrator so that you can assess tax consequences. Above all, don't rush into a rollover decision. ▪

*   *   *

When you retire, one of the major questions to address is whether your nest egg can support you through to the end of your life. It will be tempting to micromanage the investments, particularly when markets are going through emotional gyrations between fear and greed. In this 2010 column, I discuss how to not let emotion drive your decisions. I review how to take a needs-based approach framed by your own circumstances that will satisfy your requirements for cash flow and security.

RETIREES' GOALS ARE INCOME, GROWTH

Originally published November 21, 2010

What should retirees do with their savings?

A local retired couple, ages 65 and 63, are do-it-yourself investors with $2.5 million in savings. They e-mailed me with a series of questions.

Question: The first question asked by financial advisers is, "What is your risk tolerance?" In days past, that referred to whether you could tolerate a 10 to 15 percent decline in the market, but in today's environment does it mean can you tolerate a 30 to 40 percent decline in the market?

Answer: Most people don't like the idea of losing any money in any amount, most certainly not 30 to 40 percent in any investment at any time or even for an entire portfolio.

However, history tells us that such declines can and do occur. In fact, stock losses can be higher, even to the point of losing 100 percent of one's investment.

Retirees with a 30-year horizon should brace themselves for both market declines and bubbles during their lifetimes. Why? Because during such a span of years, there will be recessions, depressions, inflation, deflation, political instability, wars, disease, innovation, exploration, progression and regression, catastrophes, and triumphs.

The fact is that times change, and as they do, prosperity ebbs and flows.

In booming markets, the complaint is about loss of opportunity: "The stock market just made a major move; I want to do the same." "So-and-so is making a killing in gold; I feel left out."

In depressed markets, the question is "Where can I get guaranteed returns?"

Question: How can you keep your savings safe in uncertain economic times?

Answer: The safest place to put money is not always the best place; money under the mattress may burn up in a fire.

Fear should never motivate an investment decision; neither should the feeling of being left out spur someone to speculate in a rising market.

Leaving behind those emotions permits a rational approach to retirement investing, which is required in both good markets and bad if one is to survive the different types of markets that will come the way of most long-term investors.

Question: What is the appropriate asset-allocation plan for stocks, bonds, and cash for retirees? Does it really vary from one circumstance to another?

Answer: The appropriate asset allocation is indeed a matter of personal circumstances.

Allocations flow from the needs of the client; they are calculated on the basis of personal cash flow (the money coming into the household minus the money going out). Incoming cash flow is figured from lifelong income streams, such as pension and annuity income plus Social Security retirement benefits. Outgoing cash flow is simply living expenses.

Inflow needs to cover outflow. If it does not, the assets are not structured in such a way that they cover the net cash flow needs. That's the first priority of a retirement portfolio: to cover the retiree's expenses now and as they rise over time because of inflation.

That part of the portfolio is fixed by using a demand-based formula that starts with income needs. The remainder is invested for (1) growth and (2) preservation of capital.

Let's go through an example.

Assume you need additional cash flow of $50,000 a year. Assume you have $2.5 million in savings. Assume you can find high-quality bonds that yield 5 percent. Your bond allocation will be $1 million. Your growth allocation (stocks) will be $1.25 million (this part of the portfolio has a long-term objective: to grow for future needs and for a legacy). The rest will be allocated to cash.

Someone else may need more income, which would mean a higher bond allocation. Yet another person might need less, hence a lower bond allocation.

Every component of the portfolio has a job to do. You manage the portfolio to meet those goals with the understanding that the markets will not cooperate from time to time. No matter what direction the markets are heading, the first priority is to produce the income the retiree needs to live on. Safety is achieved by carefully planning the portfolio, carefully monitoring how each position is doing, and pruning and weeding as necessary.

Question: With interest rates as low as they are today, can one invest in bonds or is it inevitable that the principal will be in danger because the only way rates can go is up?

Answer: Interest rates are historically low, which means that they will rise eventually, and when that happens, your bonds will decline in price. However, if you hold your bonds to maturity, you will not lose money even though your statement will show declines in value.

The likely decline in the value of bond holdings should be factored into expectations.

Where can you find other income-producing investments today? If you can accept the risks of investing in stocks, look to solid dividend-paying stocks and hybrid (stock and bond) mutual funds. The dividend yields are attractive. Various "guaranteed" income products that are pure insurance products, such as immediate annuities, are possibilities, as are variable annuities with income guarantees. However, they should be approached with caution since these products are easily misunderstood.

Question: What should retirees do with their savings?

Answer: Manage your portfolio to meet three distinct objectives: income, growth, and capital preservation. Do not invest on margin, do not concentrate in a particular sector or security, do not make bets on the direction of the market, do not speculate, and most of all, do not let emotions make your decisions for you.

* * *

While it is tempting to look for a yardstick against other retirees to assure yourself that you are in a good position when it comes to your retirement savings, the most important metric is how your assets will meet your own personal needs. In the next column, originally published in 1999, I suggest seven steps to take that will give you a good idea as to how prepared you are for retirement. The results of these assessments will suggest areas you can work on and areas where it might be prudent to seek professional advice.

ASSESS YOUR FINANCES

Originally published January 10, 1999

If you are 25 or 65 or anywhere in between, consider taking these seven steps now to feel more prepared for retirement.

Step 1. State your investment goals. What are your objectives? Goals determine how much you need to add to your investments each year, how much you should invest on a tax-deferred or tax-free basis, and how you need to allocate between stocks and bonds.

Let's look at how to set goals for two individuals, age 65 and age 25.

Say you are age 65 and retired. You need to create an income stream from your portfolio to cover the gap between your living expenses and what you will be getting from your company pension and Social Security.

After you figure your pension and Social Security income, you estimate your expenses and calculate the dollar amount of the gap. Say the gap is $10,000 a year.

Knowing your gap, you can state your goals: Cover the gap by creating $10,000 of after-tax income from the portfolio. Invest the rest for growth.

With a specific investment goal statement such as this, all your investment planning falls into place. Now you know that you need to divide your portfolio into two portions, each with a different investment objective. The first and most important is the income portion of the portfolio, which will be invested in income-producing assets that pay interest or dividends. The second portion will be invested in stocks for long-term growth opportunities.

Say you are 25. You believe you will be paying for your retirement in full, since you don't work for a company that offers a pension and you don't want to rely on Social Security.

Your long investment horizon allows you to take on more risk. You can invest in growth investments such as stocks and stock funds, including growth funds and aggressive growth funds.

Take advantage of savings opportunities at work by contributing the maximum possible to your 401(k) and other contributory plans. Invest your accounts with a focus on long-term growth. In addition, every year, invest the maximum permitted in a Roth IRA for long-term growth. (Go to irs.gov and search for "Roth" to look up current limitations and maximums permitted.)

Step 2. Check your tactics. Make sure you are not trying to reach your goals through a current market fad. For example, you may be tempted to log on to a trading service to buy and sell stocks on margin. Or you may be attracted to some of the Internet stocks that have had tremendous price gains. But are these tactics right for you? Remember that an investment portfolio is like a bar of soap: The more you handle it, the smaller it gets. Most investors will do much better by going slowly and sticking to the basics.

Step 3. Reassess your investment strengths and weaknesses. If trading high-flying stocks is enticing but not an area of expertise, think twice about practicing with your retirement money. If you know nothing about stocks or stock mutual funds and you need to grow your assets for retirement, recognize that as a definite weakness and make it a point to learn.

Ask your company to provide investment education if it doesn't already do so. Lecturers can be arranged for lunchtime investment education series at low or no cost through local investment firms. Or you can sign up for continuing education programs at local high schools or colleges. Make sure that your instructor sees you as a student, not a prospect.

Step 4. Reassess your tax planning. Are you making the best use of all tax-advantaged investment opportunities? Your 401(k)? Your IRAs? If you are earning outside income, are you setting aside funds in a Simplified Employee Pension?

If you do not have enough tax-deferred assets working for you because you started late, are you exploring other tax-deferred opportunities? If you have not looked at tax-deferred variable annuities recently, you may wish to do so. There have been great improvements in these products, making them quite attractive for investors who do not have enough tax-deferred money saved for retirement.

Step 5. Look at your estate plan. Check your will and don't forget your beneficiary designations for your company retirement plans and IRAs. Beneficiary designations should be reviewed each year, and copies should be kept with your important papers.

Step 6. Measure how you performed last year. Reviewing performance helps you see if you are on track. Measure yourself against your goals, not someone else's winning trades. Ask yourself if you invested in a way that moved you toward your goals. Did you invest for growth if you were seeking to accumulate assets? Did you take yourself off course when the market corrected between July and September? How would you have fared if you had stayed the course?

Step 7. Finally, determine whether you will need to make major financial decisions this year. The start of a new year is a good time to review your overall financial picture and set your plan in motion. It's also an important time to plan for major events such as selling a house or business, changing your marital status, and retiring. If a major event is in the cards, start exploring the tax and investment consequences early. ▪

*   *   *

The next column highlights the importance of effective tax planning and the disastrous consequences of improper planning.

AUTOPILOT WORKS FOR AIRPLANES, NOT RETIREMENT ACCOUNTS

Originally published February 24, 2002; updated 2017

Tax Deferral

A tax-deferred account is one of the best ways to grow your assets for retirement. Indeed, encouraging retirement savings was the intention of Congress in permitting tax deferral for IRAs and company savings plans such as 401(k)s and 403(b)s.

To help taxpayers maximize their savings, lawmakers were willing to give up tax revenue for otherwise taxable transactions. Tax revenues on distributions such as dividends, interest, and capital gains distributions were deferred. A capital gains tax on profits from the sale of a security was also deferred.

Until the relatively recent adoption of the Roth IRA, there was simply no better way to avoid current taxation and thus enhance long-term growth.

Congress's rationale for allowing an individual to defer taxes was the idea that tax revenues would be recaptured eventually. Indeed, the law provides that taxpayers are required to start taking money out of their IRAs, 401(k)s, 403(b)s, and other tax-deferred accounts after age 70½.

When money is withdrawn, a tax is triggered on the withdrawal. Sometimes 100 percent of the withdrawal is taxable, sometimes less, generally depending on whether the initial contributions were made in after-tax dollars.

Here is the problem and a warning to people approaching retirement.

When your largest asset is your tax-deferred account, you need to put tax planning at the top of your priority list. Here's why.

Inappropriate Use

There is a correct and an incorrect way to use a tax-deferred account such as an IRA. A tax-deferred account is best used to grow your assets in preparation for retirement and to create a flow of income after retirement. The idea is to maximize growth as long as possible and minimize withdrawals and thus taxes.

Optimal Usage

In the ideal situation, required minimum withdrawals after age 70½ are taken in kind and tax is paid out of another account.

Let me illustrate. Say you have 500 shares of XYZ mutual fund worth $100,000 in your IRA. If you need to make a required minimum distribution of $1,000, you can transfer $1,000 worth of the fund into a taxable account. (The transfer triggers $1,000 of taxable income.)

Instead of paying taxes from your IRA account, it's best to pay taxes out of another pocket. This strategy protects your tax deferral benefits as long as possible.

Worst Usage

In one reader's situation, Bill found himself in a tailspin because he used his IRA incorrectly, albeit while following the advice of his broker.

Bill was paying an annual $40,000 life insurance premium with his IRA money and making two $10,000 gifts per year to his sons. The account also was coded for tax withholding. This caused a structural failure.

The drain on the $2 million IRA went from about $82,000 a year to account for the minimum required to be withdrawn to $282,000 to pay for insurance and gifting. These excessive withdrawals put too much pressure on the IRA in this market. The IRA could not withstand the stress and fell from $2 million to $800,000 in two years.

If you want to withdraw money from your IRA above the minimum withdrawals required by law, compute the tax impact first. Let's look at the scenario that creates the highest risk: You have only one account, and it is an IRA.

As in Bill's situation, assume your effective tax rate is 40 percent [2017 update: you can use the formula below to run examples at different effective tax rates]. Say you need to withdraw $1,000 from your IRA. Assume your taxes cannot be paid from another account.

To net $1,000, you actually need to withdraw $1,667: $1,000 plus $667 for taxes. In this situation, for every dollar you need to take out of your IRA, you need to take out an additional 67 cents to pay for taxes.

To estimate how much you need to withdraw in the same circumstances, apply this formula. Take the amount you wish to withdraw ($1,000) and divide it by 1 minus your tax rate (1 − 0.40). In this example, that's $1,000 divided by 0.6 = $1,667.

Planning

Doing the math will help you determine whether you should be paying for life insurance and gifts with your IRA. In Bill's situation, neither his accountant nor his broker called attention to the fact that he was in danger of going to zero if he kept up those withdrawals. Neither was Bill even faintly aware of his out-of-pocket cost for the insurance and gifts, both of which were discretionary expenditures.

Lessons Learned

First, before using your IRA as a checking account, run the numbers. Don't make discretionary purchases with precious IRA dollars.

Second, plan ahead. If your tax-deferred account is your biggest asset, do you have pension income that will pay for retirement expenses? If not, think about building up taxable accounts.

Third, if the value of your IRA account starts to fall dramatically, stop the withdrawals immediately. Figure out the problem. You may be invested incorrectly. Or you may be stressing your IRA with withdrawals that are too large for it to support.

Finally, don't forget that you need to put some effort into your investments. Watch your account. Read. Learn. Ask questions. Identify problems quickly to avoid disasters. Keep in mind that autopilot works for airplanes, not IRAs. ▪

*   *   *

In the next column, I provide a quiz published by Ed Slott. It will help you identify how to take advantage of all of the tax benefits available to retirement account holders.

TEST YOUR TOLERANCE FOR
TAX RISK ON YOUR IRA

Originally published February 16, 2003

Ed Slott, the author of *The Retirement Savings Time Bomb*, has spent a good deal of time and energy flushing out the biggest mistakes people make with their retirement plans. Considered to be the nation's foremost IRA expert, Slott is a CPA who publishes a popular newsletter called *Ed Slott's IRA Advisor*.

Take Slott's test to see if you are at risk of blowing up your IRA, 401(k), or other retirement savings account. Then count your "yes" and "no" answers. I'll tell you how to score yourself below.

1. Do you have most of your retirement savings in a company 401(k), 403(k), or 457 retirement plan? Yes ☐ No ☐

2. Do you have company stock in your 401(k)? Yes ☐ No ☐

3. Is your retirement plan one of the largest assets you own? Yes ☐ No ☐

4. Have you recently left your company or retired, or will you be retiring soon? Yes ☐ No ☐

5. After you retire, will you be leaving your retirement account with your former employer? Yes ☐ No ☐

6. Will you be taking a lump-sum distribution from your company plan at any time? Yes ☐ No ☐

7. Will your retirement savings account pass to your beneficiaries according to the terms of your will? Yes ☐ No ☐

8. Have you named a trust to be the beneficiary of your retirement plan? Yes ☐ No ☐

9. Is your estate the beneficiary of your retirement plan? Yes ☐ No ☐

10. Will you be leaving your retirement assets to your spouse?
Yes ☐ No ☐

11. Have you put off instructing your beneficiaries what to do and what not to do with your retirement plan when they inherit? Yes ☐ No ☐

12. Do you want to be able to control the payouts on your retirement accounts(s) after your death to prevent your beneficiaries from squandering the money? Yes ☐ No ☐

13. Will you be inheriting a retirement account from anyone? Yes ☐ No ☐

14. Are you confident that your bank, broker, or mutual fund company will have all the documentation on your retirement account that your beneficiaries will need? Yes ☐ No ☐

15. Are you unsure of the exact amount the IRS requires you to withdraw from your retirement account and when? Yes ☐ No ☐

16. Do you own a life insurance policy? Yes ☐ No ☐

17. Will you be rolling cash, stock, or other property over from one retirement account to another? Yes ☐ No ☐

18. Has it been more than a year since you last updated the beneficiary forms for every retirement account you own? Yes ☐ No ☐

19. Will you need to tap into your retirement savings before you reach age 59½? Yes ☐ No ☐

20. Have you heard of the Roth IRA but taken no steps to find out more or set one up yet? Yes ☐ No ☐

The total number of "yes" points represents the approximate percentage of your retirement savings that probably will go to pay taxes, says Slott. The total "no" points represent the percentage you or your family can expect to keep after taxes.

If you are at risk, you need to get in gear, says Slott. Regardless of the type of tax-deferred retirement savings plan you have, whether it's an IRA, 401(k), 403(b), 457, Keogh, SEP IRA, or Simple IRA, the tax man will show up at distribution time and everyone will be in jeopardy of losing money unless you all do some advance planning.

Although income and estate taxes on retirement plans are extremely complicated, as with everything else, there are some ways to simplify the distribution-planning process. Slott helps organize your options by offering five planning steps. Step 1: Time your distributions "smartly." Step 2: Insure it. Step 3: Stretch it. Step 4: Roth it. Step 5: Avoid the death tax trap.

Retirement distribution planning is fast becoming a new technical discipline. As baby boomers continue to age, millions will need to become more knowledgeable about taking money out of their retirement plans wisely and preparing their families for postdeath distribution options.

Slott's book is a good start for anyone who wants to get a grip on the issues, and his newsletter, though technical, is second to none. Of course, be sure to involve your tax adviser before making any decisions that will affect income taxes and review any changes you might want to make to beneficiary designations with your estate planner. For more information about retirement distribution planning, go to Slott's website at irahelp. com. As Slott says, "Your retirement savings is your money. It's your job to protect it from taxes."

*   *   *

There are so many factors that go into how much a retiree should withdraw from his or her retirement accounts per year, many of which are impossible to know for sure; market gains and losses and remaining lifespan are the most difficult to predict. Because of the unknowns, there is no correct answer that will serve all readers. While I provide some current thinking on the subject in the next column, a thorough and realistic assessment of your personal circumstances should always guide your ultimate decision.

HISTORY AND "SAFE" WITHDRAWAL RATE

Originally published November 6, 2016

I received an e-mail from a reader about how to start retirement without the fear of running out of money.

He asked: "What do you consider to be a safe withdrawal rate today to ensure that a portfolio is not depleted over 30 years? I've learned that traditionally there was the '4 percent rule,' but now that people are living longer, and given such meager safe returns, low interest rates, and market uncertainty, I've read that some suggest no more than a 2.5 to 3 percent withdrawal rate."

The 4 percent rule that the reader refers to comes from an October 1994 *Journal of Financial Planning* column by William Bengen titled "Determining Withdrawal Rates Using Historical Data." The methodology is based on a 1952 paper by Andrew Roy, "Safety First and the Holding of Assets," in *Econometrica: Journal of the Econometric Society*.

In a May 11, 2004 press release, Merrill Lynch recommended a 4 to 6 percent annual withdrawal rate. A more recent 2013 study published by Morningstar, "Low Bond Yields and Safe Portfolio Withdrawal Rates," lays out a 2.8 percent rule. The study is an excellent review of the underlying concepts and theories of withdrawal rates.

As a professional "investment counsel" whose expertise is in structuring and managing retirement portfolios of $5 million-plus, I can tell you that there is no magical percentage withdrawal rate that applies across the board to all retirees.

I also can tell you that investors are not likely to know what's best for them. When individuals were asked in 2004 (Merrill Lynch's "Retirement Preparedness Survey") how much they could safely withdraw each year, the answer was over 20 percent, and the "average expected rate of return from assets" during retirement was 22 percent— yes, 22 percent per year. Remember that 2004 was just a few years after the Internet Bubble burst.

Investors need help on how to make an appropriate assessment of the options before them. (A lot will depend on their investment experience and expertise.)

To get some guidance, a retiree needs to face the dilemma of having to project 20 or 30 or more years ahead. How does someone assess the future with all of its unknowns, including inflation, taxes, health, longevity, and, of course, the uncertainty of the financial markets themselves?

The starting point is always the same: How much are you spending now? How much nonportfolio income are you taking in? How much will you need to withdraw from your portfolio to maintain your lifestyle over a lifetime that could last 30 or more years after retirement? And are you an expert as an investor?

In the real world, investment counsel, as at my firm, starts with a cash flow analysis that looks at how the portfolio will be affected by different withdrawal and return scenarios. We do that with a sensitivity analysis that is driven by different assumptions for longevity, inflation, taxes, returns, and so on.

An alternative approach is a Monte Carlo simulation, which gives you a probability of success (or ruin) of a total-return portfolio. You can search for Monte Carlo simulations online and give them a try. If you go that route, be careful in reviewing the underlying assumptions for inflation, spending, returns, and so on. Be especially alert to whether the program accounts for withdrawals from your portfolio to cover your spending. ▪

* * *

For more on "safe" withdrawal rates, the next column published in March, 2017 provides some additional insight. Importantly, "savers" may make decisions differently from "investors."

NO MAGIC NUMBER FOR RETIREMENT SAVINGS

Originally published March 12, 2017

The subject of retirement preparedness is always coming up, and for good reason: We're minting new retirees at a fast clip. The baby boom generation is reaching age 65 at a rate of 10,000 Americans per day, according to the Pew Research Center.

Are these newly minted 65-year-olds prepared? That's the question a recently released study wanted to answer. Called the "Retirement IQ Survey," it is Fidelity Investments' "first-ever" study to gauge how well the average American understands how to make money last for a lifetime.

Let's talk about this survey question: "About what percentage of your savings do many financial experts suggest you withdraw annually in retirement?"

The right answer, according to Fidelity, is "limiting portfolio withdrawals to no more than four to five percent of your initial retirement assets, adjusted each year for inflation, over the course of your retirement horizon."

Some of the pre-retirees who were surveyed agreed (42 percent) with 4 to 5 percent, but an almost equal number (38 percent) thought 7 percent or more was the right figure. Fifteen percent thought a safe withdrawal rate was 10 to 12 percent.

If you want my opinion, based on my experience as a professional money manager who specializes in retirees, it is that there is no magic number for this very good reason: Retirees' financial and lifestyle situations are unique, and, more important, when you retire and how you invest control your results and thus the withdrawal rate appropriate for you.

Let's take two extremes: a saver and an investor. Say a 65-year-old invests 100 percent into an S&P 500 Index fund the day after he retires, and that day happens to be a market bottom. He could potentially withdraw 10 percent without running out of money.

Assuming the investor bought an S&P 500 Index fund with $1 million on March 9, 2009, the beginning of the current bull market, he could have withdrawn 10 percent yearly ($100,000) and would have about $2.6 million left, for an average annual return of 20.8 percent.

Contrast the saver who put her money in the bank. If she withdrew 10 percent per year, only $218,000 (average annual return of 0.04 percent) of her original $1 million CD would be left.

If the withdrawal had been 4 percent ($40,000) instead of 10 percent, the saver would have about $690,000 left (average annual return of 0.05 percent), compared with the investor's $3.4 million (average annual return of 19 percent).

But what if these 65-year-olds retired a few years earlier, the day the last bear market started (October 9, 2007)? At the 10 percent withdrawal rate, the saver's $1 million would be worth about $107,000 (average annual return of 0.6 percent), compared with the investor's $113,000 (average annual return of 0.7 percent).

In the end, the saver and the investor would be pretty even. But the investor would have seen his $1 million drop to $500,000 by the end of 2008. In contrast, the saver would have had about $913,000 at that time. Although interest rates were at historic lows during this period, the stock market dropped by almost 60 percent from peak to trough (from October 9, 2007, to March 9, 2009), according to S&P Capital IQ.

Compare the 4 percent withdrawal rate. The saver's $1 million would be worth about $664,000 (average annual return of about 0.4 percent), and the investor's would be worth about $1.1 million (average annual return of about 5 percent).

Thus, there is a lot involved in coming up with a safe withdrawal rate. These are pure returns. Inflation and taxes also would have to be taken into account.

For more information on the survey, read "How Much Do You Know When it Comes to Preparing for Retirement? Fidelity's Retirement IQ Survey Uncovers Significant Knowledge Gaps" released on March 6, 2017 (fidelity.com/about-fidelity/individual-investing/how-much-do-you-know-about-retirement). For some helpful resources, check out Fidelity's website, especially its Retirement Score (https://communications.fidelity.com/pi/2015/retirement/). Performance data for this column was provided by Thomson Reuters. ▩

*   *   *

How confident are you that your retirement portfolio will last a lifetime? While few can answer that question with certainty, I wrote the next column in 2007 to share an example of how to structure a portfolio. The thought process and framework for understanding if your portfolio will last a lifetime are as relevant today as when the column was written a decade ago.

PAYING FOR A VACATION THAT
LASTS A LIFETIME

Originally published July 15, 2007; updated 2017

There is a dividing line between work and retirement. One day you're commuting to the job. The next day you're on vacation.

Your daily routine changes, and your paycheck stops coming in the mail.

Investment goals also change.

Before you retire, you want to increase your wealth. After you retire, your first and foremost objective is to replace your paycheck.

How confident are you that your retirement portfolio can do that?

Confidence is a funny thing. You need enough but not too much. Overconfidence is a common reason for investment mistakes, according to behavioral economists such as Terrance Odean, [then] professor of banking and finance at the Haas School of Business at the University of California, Berkeley.

Odean's point is essentially this: Overconfident people overestimate their ability to make good investment decisions and in the end lose out.

With that backdrop, let me ask you this: Will your retirement portfolio serve as your constant friend and benefactor? If you are not sure (which is probably a good thing), consider getting a second opinion.

Here's an example of what you can find out, based on a reader's situation.

At age 73, "Matt," a widowed father of three and grandfather of six, has a good future ahead of him. He is healthy and fit and has the genetic predisposition to live well into his nineties.

He gifts money to his kids and grandkids yearly. "I like to see them smile while I'm above ground," he explains.

Matt's expenses come to $78,000 a year, and happily, more than one-half is covered by his pension and Social Security, both of which have consumer price index (CPI) inflators; that is, the payments increase to offset the ravages of inflation.

The $1 million Matt invested in municipal bonds earns tax-free interest that more than covers his remaining expenses. Matt bought those bonds at a premium, which means that he paid more than the face value of the bonds at the time he bought them. Some of the bonds mature in 30 years.

Matt has an additional $250,000 invested in high-quality corporate bonds that will mature in four years.

Matt wants to know if his portfolio will last a lifetime. Here are a few considerations for him to think about.

First, when interest rates rise, the price of a bond declines. Some of Matt's bonds mature in 30 years, and that exposes them to greater risk than would be the case with shorter bonds. If Matt needs to liquidate a long bond in an environment of rising interest rates, he will lose principal. In the rising interest rate environment of the late 1970s and early 1980s, high-quality bonds lost more than 50 percent of their value.

Second, if Matt decides to hold the bonds to maturity, he will lose the premium. For example, if Matt paid $1,200 for a bond with a face value of $1,000, he will get only $1,000 at maturity, thus losing the $200 premium. Effectively, because the premium is amortized over the life of the bond, he is spending the premium with each payment he receives.

Third, when Matt's bonds mature, will he be able to replace the income stream? That will depend on interest rates at that future date, which of course is an unknown.

Fourth, should the extra $250,000 invested in bonds be invested for moderate growth instead? Investing for growth through the stock market—buying a basket of well-chosen diversified individual stocks or stock mutual funds—if done properly can grow that portion of the portfolio for future needs.

Finally, although inflation is not a major concern for Matt because both his pension and Social Security increase with inflation, it should not be ignored. That's another argument for adding a moderate growth component to the portfolio.

Although these are quick observations, a portfolio evaluation would get into much more detail, including a review of each holding and its contribution to the overall plan. That way, you can pave the way to a worry-free vacation of a lifetime. ▪

*   *   *

Retirement success, which I define as a stress-free and financially secure retirement, doesn't come automatically. In the next column (written in 2005, updated in 2017), I provide an excellent resource from Ernst & Young that focuses on mistakes that retirees make and how to avoid them. The advice is built around a model that is a "trade-off tool." Very simply, "failure," is running out of money. "Success" is living your desired lifestyle and leaving money for your heirs and charity, if you are charitably inclined.

10 RETIREMENT MISTAKES TO AVOID

Originally published May 8, 2005; updated 2017

When you retire, you can afford to make only so many mistakes with your finances. Recovering from losses is harder to do. Time is not on your side. Going back to work or moving in with your kids may not be good options.

The insurance and actuarial advisory practice of Ernst & Young has built a model for financial services firms to use in helping retirees avoid some common mistakes. The model is a "trade-off tool," said Joseph Weiss, that considers a multitude of random scenarios that allow people to see the potential success or failure of different courses of action.

"Failure," for example, is running out of money. "Success" is living your desired lifestyle and leaving money for your heirs.

Here are 10 retirement mistakes to avoid that are based on this model.

1. Planning to a specific age (or assuming who will live the longest). Most planning tools have a fixed time horizon, assuming death at a certain age. Weiss said, "What if you're wrong in your assumption?" If you die too soon, there will be money left over. If you die too late, there will be no money left.

    The order of death between spouses is another tricky assumption. Many programs assume the older spouse will die first. If the order of death is reversed, the final ramifications of the plan will change. For example, assume "Preston's" pension and Social Security benefits total $30,000 and his wife, Daphne, receives $50,000 for a total of $80,000. If Preston dies first, household income drops by $30,000. If Daphne dies first, household income drops by $50,000.

2. Hoping the law of averages works out (one can't rely on average rate of return on assets). Most planning tools assume a fixed

percentage rate of return, which is not realistic, Weiss said. When you project retirement needs using an investment return of 8 percent, the retiree may reasonably assume that he will get 8 percent year in and year out. The reality is something quite different. Although someone might be able to achieve 8 percent looking back over a long period, the yearly return will vary quite a bit. You need to have a very good idea of the probability of meeting your income needs considering how you are invested.

3. Trade-offs must be personalized: Don't follow the herd. People have a tendency to do what other people do even when they are making retirement decisions. Your needs and means can hardly be the same as someone else's. For example, a 62-year-old retiree might want to trade off the near-term benefits of starting her Social Security benefit at age 62 for a higher payment beginning four years later at age 66.

4. Forgetting Uncle Sam (inefficient liquidation strategy). Most people have two types of retirement assets: qualified and non-qualified, Weiss said. Nonqualified assets are taxable accounts and holdings, such as your house, your bank account, and your brokerage account. Qualified assets are your 401(k), 403(b), 457, individual retirement account, and other tax-deferred assets. Your liquidation strategy will be inefficient unless you treat your tax-deferred assets with care.

5. Avoiding the stock market and panicking during market fluctuations. Buying high and selling low is a costly mistake that is hard to recover from.

6. Failure to anticipate health-care costs. Many plans ignore health issues. Mistakes include spending too little for long-term health care and spending too much. Don't forget to consider the chances of needing nursing home care considering your health and age.

7. Lack of 401(k) asset management. Many retirees don't consider how to maximize their 401(k)s, which can lead to unnecessary taxes and cash flow problems. Your 401(k) may be your largest or second largest asset; get help with managing this asset.

8. Distinguishing dreams from reality. Weiss said that spending decisions should be based on what you can afford versus what you want to have.

9. Going it alone. In the area of retirement planning, you may not be aware of the things you don't know that you need to know. Weiss recommends working with a competent adviser.

10. Failing to understand retirement risks. Many retirees are unaware of the risks they face. They can run out of money. The markets can hurt them. The order of death can affect their planning. There can be a catastrophic event that changes their plan. They also have to deal with the inherent conflict between a wealth transfer goal and an income goal.

Keeping in mind that most people retire only once, these are excellent points to take to heart. ▪

*   *   *

While champagne and a favorite chocolate cake may be your immediate responses to the title question of the next column, if you have an IRA, you need to be aware of the rules governing the required minimum distributions (RMDs) that must start around the time you reach that age. The next column, written in June 2017, walks you through the convoluted rules (though it does not provide an answer to "Why 70½?") that direct how much you are required to withdraw and when.

HOW WILL YOU CELEBRATE YOUR 70½ BIRTHDAY?

Originally published June 18, 2017

There are 3.3 million Americans who need to read this column: those who will be turning 70 this year. The question is, will you be turning 70½? You need to know the answer if you have a retirement account such as a tax-deferred IRA or 401(k).

First, figure out when you will reach age 70½. That's when tax rules force you to start withdrawing from tax-deferred retirement accounts. Failure to do so results in substantial tax penalties.

If your seventieth birthday falls in the first half of the calendar year (January 1 through June 30), you will reach 70½ in the same calendar year that you turn 70. For example, if your birthday is January 31, 1947, you turned 70 and 70½ in 2017.

If your birthday falls in the second half of the calendar year (July 1 through December 31), you will reach 70½ in the calendar year in which you turn 71. For example, if your birthday is August 31, 1947, you will turn 70 in 2017, but you won't turn 70½ until 2018, the year of your seventy-first birthday.

Don't ask where this 70½ rule comes from. It seems to be a mystery.

Second, if your birthday is between January 1, 1947, and June 30, 1947, dig out your IRA and 401(k) statements from December 31, 2016. You don't need to do that if you turn 70 in the second half of the year (July 1, 1947, through December 31, 1947); you will need your December 31, 2017, statements next year when you turn 70½.

Third, write down the year-end balances of each account. You will need your balances to calculate your mandated withdrawals (required minimum distributions, or RMDs). You can add together your IRA balances to take the withdrawals from any one of the IRAs. This is not the case with 401(k)s; each 401(k) must be handled separately.

Fourth, consider your spouse's birthday. If he or she is 10 years younger than you, your RMD will be lower than the RMDs for others. See IRS Publication 590-B (Uniform Life Table II covers spouses who are 10 years younger than the IRA owner).

Fifth, contact the person who does your taxes. You will need his or her help to decide whether to take your RMD in the year you turn 70½ or two RMDs the next year. For example, if you are 70½ in 2017, you can take your 2017 RMD in 2017. Or you can take two RMDs in 2018. One is for 2017, which must be taken before April 1, 2018, your "required beginning date"; the second is for 2018 (based on your December 31, 2017, balance), which can be taken any time before December 31, 2018. Delaying your first RMD is permitted under a special rule that applies one time only.

Your tax adviser will want to run a few what-if tax returns for 2017 and 2018 to help you decide. If you take two RMDs in 2018, your taxable return for 2018 will include both RMDs (2017 and 2018). For clarity, let's say your RMD for 2017 is $10,000 (based on your December 31, 2016, IRA balance) and your estimated RMD for 2018 (based on a hypothetical December 31, 2017 balance) is $12,000.

If you take your 2017 RMD in 2018 (by April 1, 2018), your 2018 tax return will pick up $22,000 ($10,000 plus $12,000) of income for the RMDs. Your 2017 tax return will show no RMD taxable income as a result.

In contrast, if you take your $10,000 RMD for 2017 in 2017 and your 2018 RMD of $12,000 in 2018, your 2017 tax return will show income of $10,000. Your 2018 tax return will report income of $12,000.

Sixth, if you are still working and participating in a 401(k) at work, be aware that you may delay your mandated withdrawals from your 401(k) while you are working (but not if you own 5 percent or more of the stock of the employer). You still will need to make RMDs from your IRAs.

If you would like to do some figuring, there is an excellent online resource sponsored by the U.S. Securities and Exchange Commission at investor.gov. Search for "IRA." Choose "401(k) and IRA Required Minimum Distribution Calculator."

The IRS has an excellent chart comparing RMD rules for IRAs and defined contribution plans at irs.gov. Search "RMD Comparison Chart."

Also check out "Retirement Topics—Required Minimum Distributions (RMDs)."

Investors: Read Before You Buy or Sell

ARE YOU CURIOUS:

- How should you set up rules for buying and selling?

- Where can you access publicly available investment research and analysis tools?

- How can you take advantage of down markets?

SECTION PREVIEW:

In this section, we'll talk about when to hold, add, or sell investments you currently own. I'll show you how to read a prospectus, how to tell if you are getting a good deal in buying different classes of mutual fund shares, and how to research the buys and sells of corporate insiders. We'll also cover where to access research from providers such as Morningstar, the American Association of Individual Investors, Value Line, and *Investor's Business Daily*.

INSIDER'S PERSPECTIVE:

A 2017 Legg Mason study found that 80 percent of investors felt "somewhat" or "very" optimistic about their investments in the coming year. Confidence in the market is a positive indicator of our economic health, but remember that markets change. Without a set of rules, how will you know when it is time to buy or sell? Portfolio construction and monitoring is all about protocol. At my money management firm, we follow a rule set that guides our investment decisions, helping us remove emotion from the process. I wrote the columns in this section to help you develop your own set of rules for research and designing an investing decision process for yourself.

* * *

What does Warren Buffett identify as the single most powerful factor behind his investing success? Compound interest. I selected the next column as the lead for the section because it explores this fundamental concept of investing. This column, originally published in January 2015, goes on to lay the foundation for your buying and selling rule set by examining how stock analysts across the industry begin their fundamental research.

DO YOU WANT TO BE A MILLIONAIRE?

Originally published January 25, 2015

If you want to be a millionaire, Morningstar, the research house known for its mutual fund star ratings and independent research, will teach you how.

Seasoned investors know that the secret is twofold: starting to invest early in life and taking advantage of compound interest. But just how do you do that?

Start with some basic knowledge of compounding.

Here is a quote from Morningstar's Investing Classroom: "When you were a kid, perhaps one of your friends asked you the following trick question: 'Would you rather have $10,000 per day for 30 days or a penny that doubled in value every day for 30 days?' Today, we know to choose the doubling penny, because at the end of 30 days, we'd have about $5 million versus the $300,000 we'd have if we chose $10,000 per day.

"Compound interest is often called the eighth wonder of the world, because it seems to possess magical powers, like turning a penny into $5 million. The great part about compound interest is that it applies to money, and it helps us to achieve our financial goals, such as becoming a millionaire, retiring comfortably, or being financially independent."

Again quoting from Morningstar's Investing Classroom: "A dollar invested at a 10 percent return will be worth $1.10 in a year. Invest that $1.10 and get 10 percent again, and you'll end up with $1.21 two years from your original investment. The first year earned you only $0.10, but the second generated $0.11. This is compounding at its most basic level: gains begetting more gains. Increase the amounts and the time involved, and the benefits of compounding become much more pronounced."

How do you choose investments with the goal of earning more than you would in a bank account? Start with questions that stock analysts ask themselves:

1. What is the goal of the business?

2. How does the business make money?

3. How well is the business actually doing?

4. How well is the business positioned relative to its competitors?

You'll also want to judge the company's competitive advantage through an "economic moat" analysis, a Warren Buffett term. First, evaluate the firm's historical profitability. Second, assuming that the firm has solid returns on its capital and is consistently profitable, try to identify the source of those profits. Third, estimate how long the company will be able to keep competitors at bay. Fourth, think about the industry's competitive structure.

These are just a few samples of what you can learn through the Morningstar Investing Classroom.

There are four course offerings (stocks, funds, portfolio, and bonds). Within stocks, courses are organized in five levels, starting with the basics in the 100 series and advancing in complexity into the 500 series. The 200 series focuses on stocks and stock selection. The 300 series reviews financial statements; the 400 series discusses value, or what a stock is actually worth; and the 500 series is a collection of subjects from portfolio construction to unconventional equities such as master limited partnerships (MLPs) and real estate investment trusts (REITs) and great investors such as Benjamin Graham and Buffett. It ends with 20 stock-investing tips.

There is no charge for using the Investing Classroom. If you register, you'll be able to track your results in the quizzes at the end of each chapter. If you answer the questions correctly, you accumulate credits that you can monetize. If you accrue enough credits, you can earn a free 60-day premium membership to Morningstar.

As Morningstar says in the course: "Your goal as an investor should be to find wonderful businesses, and invest in them at reasonable prices. If you avoid confusing a great company with a great investment, you will already be ahead of many of your investing peers."

From my perspective as a professional money manager, I can tell you that taking the full series of classes—there are more than 100—will make you a better student of the markets and, if you can apply the lessons to your decision making, a better investor.

Morningstar Inc. is a provider of independent investment research (morningstar.com). You'll find the Investing Classroom at morningstar.com/cover/Classroom.html. ▪

*   *   *

The next column, originally published September 2016, looks at the American Association of Individual Investors (AAII) screening software. The software allows you to understand, replicate, and modify screening methodology employed by some of the greatest stock gurus of all-time—or to create your own. This type of research and screening is an essential aspect of developing your personal investing rule book.

SCREENING SOFTWARE CAN HELP YOUR EFFORT TO OUTPERFORM THE STOCK MARKET

Originally published September 22, 2016

How would you like to find the stocks that will outperform the market over the next few years?

The starting point is to study the experts, such as Warren Buffett, Benjamin Graham, and Geraldine Weiss.

You might say, "Good advice, Julie, but who has the time?"

Well, truth be told, computer software has made the process much easier. Let me share one program with you.

There is a nonprofit organization whose mission is to educate investors. Called the American Association of Individual Investors (AAII), the organization creates educational materials written by CFAs (Chartered Financial Analysts), academics, and investment practitioners.

I know the AAII through my work as a writer, and I'm a fan. The AAII was kind enough to supply me with the appendix materials to my latest book, *Managing Retirement Wealth: An Expert Guide to Personal Portfolio Management.*

By far the most interesting tool investors will want to use is the AAII's screening software. Buffett, Graham, Weiss, and dozens of other managers' screens are replicated for you to study.

By using the screens, you can compare one manager's criteria with another's and then make your own judgments on the basis of what you hope to achieve when you are buying stocks.

For example, if you want to beat the market, you could study the 45 screens that beat the Standard & Poor's 500 Index over the last 10 years. The S&P 500 Index returned 5.2 percent annualized in that period.

Here are the top seven screens. (The screens are defined online at AAII.com.)

1. Estimated Revisions Top 30 Up, an earnings estimates screen (20.2 percent annualized)

2. Estimated Revisions Up 5 percent, an earnings estimates screen (19.6 percent annualized)

3. Graham Enterprising, a value screen (19.2 percent annualized)

4. Driehaus, a growth screen (18.9 percent annualized)

5. Piotroski, a value screen (17.3 percent annualized)

6. Price-to-Free-Cash-Flow, a value screen (16.5 percent annualized)

7. Stock Market Winners, a growth screen (14.7 percent annualized)

How many of these placed at the top for five-year returns? A few. Price-to-Free-Cash-Flow ranked first, returning 21.7 percent annualized for the five-year period. Second was Piotroski, with returns of 20.5 percent annualized. Estimated Revisions Top 30 Up returned 17.7 percent annualized, taking sixth place. The S&P 500 Index returned 12.2 percent annualized for the period.

Price-to-Free-Cash-Flow ranked third for the three years ending August 2016 (19.7 percent annualized). In comparison, the S&P 500 Index returned 9.9 percent annualized.

We all know that returns that beat the market come at higher risk. The AAII codes each screen with a "risk index," a standard deviation score comparing the stock with the S&P 500 Index. The risk index for the S&P 500 is 1.

All the top performers were substantially more risky, as you might guess. A 2 is twice as risky (volatile) as the S&P 500.

1. Estimated Revisions Top 30 Up—risk index of 1.8

2. Estimated Revisions Up 5 percent—risk index of 1.8

3. Graham Enterprising—risk index of 1.8

4. Driehaus—risk index of 2.2

5. Piotroski—risk index of 2.1

6. Price-to-Free-Cash-Flow—risk index of 1.8

7. Stock Market Winners—risk index of 1.4

Before I go any further, don't even think of investing by just replicating a screen. There is a lot more involved. You'll want to compare and contrast the screens, study the stocks that pass the screens, and focus on risk.

To see a sample screen, read "Tweedy, Browne: 'What Has Worked in Investing,'" by Wayne Thorp of the AAII (go to aaii.com, click "AAII Journal" and search "Past Journal Issues" for April 2011). Another essential resource is AAII's "Constructing Winning Stock Screens," which you can find online at aaii.com/stock-screens/constructing winningstockscreen.

If you put in the effort, this type of research will make you a better investor whether or not you want to beat the market. It also will help you know when to sell. ▪

* * *

Another great research tool is Value Line. Unlike the AAII software we discussed in the last column, Value Line uses a proprietary ranking system to rate aspects of a stock's profile such as "safety" and "timeliness"—both of which are defined in the following column originally published in December 2013. Like the AAII screening software, Value Line can serve as an essential component of the research toolbox.

USING VALUE LINE TO PICK STOCKS

Originally published December 8, 2013

Let's look at how you can use Value Line as a tool to find stocks you may want to buy when the timing is right.

Say you are an aggressive investor who wants to buy stocks that will outperform the market over a short period.

With thousands of possible choices, narrowing the list becomes imperative. This is where research services and screening tools come into the picture.

By using research tools, you can develop a screen to weed out stocks that don't meet your needs. An aggressive screen would be different from that of a conservative investor who wants to sleep at night.

The Value Line Investment Survey starts with its universe of 1,700 stocks that make up about 90 percent of the market capitalization of all stocks traded in U.S. markets. Value Line ranks those stocks into quintiles based on three proprietary measures called Timeliness, Safety, and Technical.

The quintiles place the stocks into five categories so that you can quickly grasp which equities are at the top, bottom, and middle of the pack.

For Timeliness and Technical rankings, the very top (Rank 1) and very bottom (Rank 5) both have 100 stocks. The middle (Rank 3) contains 900 stocks, and Ranks 2 and 4 contain 300 stocks apiece. The distribution of Safety ranks is not arranged in a set parameter.

An aggressive investor would look for stocks ranked 1 or 2 for Timeliness, based in part on recent earnings momentum and stock-price performance. These are stocks that Value Line believes will lead the pack for relative price performance during the next 6 to 12 months. They tend to be more volatile and have smaller capitalizations than the general market.

Stocks ranked 3 are expected to be "average performers" but still might be quite appropriate for more conservative investors. Stocks ranked 4 and 5 probably would be weeded out by most investors, since those stocks are viewed as being less likely to perform well during the next 6 to 12 months than the vast majority of the 1,700 stocks.

The Safety ranking is more useful for conservative investors, who will want to search for stocks ranked 1 or 2, whereas aggressive investors may be happy with 3, 4, or even 5 as long as they keep a watchful eye on the stock.

Safety is based on the company's Financial Strength grade, a measure of the financial condition of the company, as well as the stock's Price Stability, which is based on the stock's volatility (standard deviation of weekly percentage price during the last five years).

Aggressive investors also will want to focus on the Technical ranking, which predicts short-term (three to six months) price changes, based on a proprietary model evaluating 10 recent price trends.

Before choosing a stock that you find in such a screen, you'll want to study the company's financials. Value Line provides key data sets for different time periods, including projections for the future for sales, cash flows (net income), earnings (profits after expenses and taxes), dividends (payout to shareholders), and book value (net worth).

Value Line also computes a Target Price Range, which is its opinion on where the stock probably will trade in three to five years.

In case you're wondering if you can screen for stocks ranked 1 for all three rankings, that's an unlikely combination. The same is true for the worst-ranked stocks (all 5s).

How successful is Value Line's ranking system? According to Ian Gendler, executive director of research: "Our ranking system for Timeliness has been forecasting the relative price performance since 1965, and over that span, the favorably ranked equities have easily outperformed the major market indexes."

Another way to screen is to start with industries instead of individual stocks. Value Line ranks the 97 industries that make up the market on a scale of 1 to 97, with 1 being the best. To derive the industry rank, Value Line takes the individual rankings for each stock, averages them out, and compares them with each of the other evaluated industries. Value Line suggests picking at least six industries that are the most timely: those ranked 1 through 6.

The six top-ranked industries right now are Home Building, Foreign Electronics, Thrift, Precious Metals, Insurance (Life), and Banks (Midwest).

You can try your own screens online by signing up for a free trial at valueline.com. ▓

*   *   *

In the next column, originally published in May 2006, we will talk about the Investor's Business Daily (IBD) database of market data. Former content editor of the IBD, Ken Shreve, shared with me a few rules which you should consider when formulating your own personal buying and selling criteria. Shreve's advice is as relevant today as over a decade ago when we first spoke.

BY FOLLOWING RULES, INVESTORS CAN BECOME MARKET-SAVVY

Originally published May 21, 2006

As I write this column in May 2006, all the major stock indexes are down in heavy volume, including the Dow, the S&P 500 Index, and the NASDAQ.

The NASDAQ Composite Index, an index of over 5,000 companies and a bellwether for the market, has fallen below its 200-day moving average. The 200-day average is an important psychological indicator that many professional investors follow. If a stock price falls below its 200-day average, it's time to sell.

Technically unhealthy for some time, the NASDAQ has been experiencing heavy selling by institutions. Through Wednesday, May 17, 2006 the NASDAQ marked five heavier-volume sell-offs in the past seven trading sessions.

Moving averages are graphical depictions of price movement (averaging closing prices over a rolling period) that smooth out prices and make it possible to spot trends.

Pensions, mutual funds, insurance companies, and hedge funds are dumping stocks. Sectors that led the market are tumbling.

Should you sell everything and run for cover? Or is it time to hunt for bargains?

I turned to Ken Shreve, senior markets writer for *Investor's Business Daily*, for some insights drawn from *IBD*'s vast body of market research. *IBD*, a weekly financial newspaper, is published by William O'Neil + Co., which collects and maintains the most extensive computer database on the markets in the United States. The data is featured in *IBD*.

Shreve's rule no. 1: Don't hunt for bargains when the odds are against you. "Professional selling in the market and weakness in market leaders make it a risky environment to be buying stocks," says Shreve. "Investors who missed out on the run in gold stocks, steel stocks, oil and gas, and the like may try to buy those sectors on weakness but that's not a good idea amid the institutional selling that we're seeing in these sectors."

The goal for an investor is to swim with the market tide, not against it. When the major market indexes are signaling a clear decline, you can still find some stocks that are outperforming, but it isn't worth taking chances. Three out of four stocks will follow the market trend.

Pundits will continue to opine on where investors should put their money now, but investors should listen to the market, not to personal opinion, says Shreve.

Shreve's rule no. 2: Don't hold on to a losing stock hoping for a turnaround. *IBD* teaches investors to use a 7 percent sell rule. If your stock has fallen 7 percent below your purchase price, sell. Consider it an insurance policy.

Don't try to predict changes in market direction; let the market tell you where it's going. Buy only when you see the general market direction changing in your favor.

By doing extensive market research, *IBD* has identified a few simple tools to use to spot a shift in the direction of the market. To see if we're ready to make a move up, watch for a "follow-through" day after a "rally attempt."

A rally attempt is an up day, and we didn't see anything but down days through Thursday of this week. Watch for an up day and count that as day 1.

Then watch for a follow-through day between the fourth and seventh days after day 1, the rally attempt. A follow-through day is a day on which the market is up a minimum of 1.5 percent on higher volume from the previous day.

If the market closes below day 1, start over again with the next up day.

The last follow-through day we saw in the market occurred on October 19, 2005, which was five days after the rally attempt of October 13, 2005. Volume was 1.98 billion shares on October 19, up from 1.5 billion the day before. If you go to the NASDAQ chart at investors.com, you can see the nice rally that followed.

After the market is back on track, watch for emerging leadership. Which stocks are outperforming others? Which sectors do they represent? These are stocks that could be new leaders.

For serious investors who want to learn more about *IBD*'s data and how to use it to make money in stocks, consider attending one of *IBD*'s workshops (investors.com).

* * *

Now let's talk about selling rules. Whether you are a younger aggressive investor, a retiree with an income portfolio, or a short-term trader using leverage, you need to have clearly defined rules for when to sell. In the next column, originally written in August 2003, I give you a basis for developing your selling rules (using some of the tools we've reviewed in the previous columns) and go over some bad habits that I recommend you avoid.

BEFORE YOU PICK STOCKS, ESTABLISH SOME SELLING RULES

Originally published August 10, 2003; updated 2017

There are many research tools available to help you pick stocks for your portfolio.

Don't put those research tools away after you've made your purchases. The act of buying a stock does not put an end to research but begins a process of careful monitoring to determine whether you should continue to own that stock.

When should you sell a stock? That depends on what you are trying to achieve. An investor's goal is to accumulate money for a specific need, such as retirement. A trader's goal is to make as much money as possible in as little time as possible.

If you are trying to trade for a profit, your selling rules will focus on near-term data such as price and volume.

A successful trader will sell out before losses mount while letting his profits run. He may set a stop loss at 10 percent below his purchase price. If the stock has a run-up, he may sell it after he achieves a certain profit. Or he may hold on to the stock until it starts a retreat from a high.

If you are a trader, you may want to see the selling rules published by *Investor's Business Daily* at investors.com.

Most people are not traders, however, and they should not be. Someone who invests for retirement has a longer horizon than a trader and a different motive for owning stocks. The purpose of the rule set remains the same: to allow you to profit from the stock while protecting you against losses. However, the methodology is different.

Instead of focusing on intraday changes in prices, investors with a longer horizon will sell when the stock fails to meet selection criteria.

Let's say you chose a stock because it was a leader in its industry, with solid earnings growth and low debt. After a few years, you see that the company begins to lose its leadership position to a rival and significantly increases its debt load. Because it no longer meets the criteria you used to buy it, you sell it regardless of whether you've made a profit.

Here's another example. If you are using Value Line for stock selection, you might be buying stocks that are ranked 1 or 2 for Safety. You would sell when the stock falls in rank to a 3 or below.

What about taxes? Taxes should not get in the way of your selling discipline. Many people did not sell at the top of the bubble to avoid capital gains taxes and held on until their profits disappeared. Taxes are a fact of life. [2018 update: Long-term capital gains tax rates under the 2018 tax act range between zero and 20 percent based on taxable income]. If a stock needs to be sold, sell it.

Bad Habits

Studies of investor behavior point to some bad habits that you will want to avoid to improve your results.

First, don't sell in reaction to the news.

Second, don't sell your winning stocks too soon.

Third, don't hold on to your losers with the idea that you'll sell them after they turn a profit.

Fourth, don't overestimate your knowledge or skills. Sell the stocks that were mistakes to make room for better choices.

Fifth, sell stocks that you shouldn't own because they are too risky for your financial situation.

Sixth, recognize that you are not investing to win a contest. Outperformance is not the goal.

Seventh, don't trade too much. Studies of individual investors revealed that those who trade the most earn the lowest returns.

Eighth, don't act impetuously. Fish are caught because they snap at the bait. There will be plenty of opportunities to make a profit, all in due time and after careful consideration.

Finally, develop your own set of selling rules and follow them. If you don't, you'll find yourself using the "cross your fingers" method, hoping that your losers will recover and that you'll catch the next boom before riding it all the way down.

Good investing is a result of planning, careful stock selection, and knowing when to sell. Losing portfolios are made up of random activity in reaction to a sales idea or something you see on the news.

*　*　*

Having developed a basis for your research practices and an outline for your buying and selling rules, it's a good time to think about how the buying and selling rules correspond to each other. In the next column, originally published October 30, 2016, I present a 5-step outline for investors. Once you have defined your buying rules, your selling rules fall into place. It could be as simple as following a leading analyst's buy advice and subsequent sell recommendation (though that isn't necessarily what I'd advise you to do). Each investor will have a unique rule set based on a review of the factors that lead their decision-making process.

KNOW WHEN TO HOLD 'EM.
KNOW WHEN TO FOLD 'EM

Originally published October 30, 2016

If you are an investor, you probably like picking stocks, but then what? Do you have a set of rules you follow that address when to hold, add to, or sell all or part of your stock position?

Before going any further, note that we're talking about individual investors, not professional money managers. Among professionals, there will be differences that depend on whether someone is managing a mutual fund, a closed-end fund, a managed account, a pension, or customized portfolios for individuals, which is the role that I play as my clients' personal portfolio manager.

An individual investor's rule set will be unique to that individual. If you stop to think about it, it has to be.

Why? Hold, add, or sell rules flow from the way you make your buys and your uniquely personal decision-making makeup.

Let's start there. Here is a list of questions that will help you audit yourself to uncover how you make buy decisions:

1. What stock(s) do you own now?

2. How did you find the stock? A tip from a friend, a newspaper column, an independent research publication such as Value Line or Morningstar, a recommendation from your broker, a service such as *Investor's Business Daily's Leaderboard*, an advisory news-letter, something you saw on the news or heard on the radio, an online chat room, or an online blog? Or perhaps you found the stock through a screen, using software such as the American Association of Individual Investors' online tool.

3. What did you want the stock to do for you? Were you looking for growth of capital over a long period or a quick profit on a

short-term trade? Perhaps you wanted to create dividend income or diversify your holdings. Or were you building out a portfolio?

4. What tools, resources, and investment theses did you rely on to make your purchase decisions? For example, were you relying on technical analysis, fundamental analysis, a combination of both, or an advisory service? Were you considering the developing economic picture? Were you buying a certain type of stock with the expectation that it would do well in an environment of rising interest rates? Did you buy the stock because you saw trends in sales and earnings? Because you thought the stock was cheap compared with others in the industry?

5. How did you measure success? Did you compare your stock's return with that of its sector or industry? Did you make a profit within the expected time frame? Did you create the dividend income you were aiming for?

When you examine your answers, selling rules can begin to emerge. You will learn, therefore, that if you bought a stock because of a tip from a friend, only your friend can tell you when to sell.

Although this is way too simplistic for most situations, it is an example of reversing the buying rationale to come up with a selling rule. Say you bought a stock because of a recommendation from a major analyst. If the analyst later issues a sell recommendation, that could be the trigger for unloading the stock.

Say you bought your stock to create a pensionlike dividend stream. Did the stock continue to pay dividends as you expected? A selling rule can emerge that focuses on dividend safety. Remember Kodak? Its dividend was a hefty 6-plus percent for a number of years before declining to just under 2 percent and finally to zero. (Kodak later was restructured after filing for bankruptcy in 2012.) Anyone who buys a stock for its dividend yield (especially if it's a higher yield than that of the general market) needs to watch the stock's fundamentals carefully over time. Consider a selling rule that addresses potential and actual dividend cuts.

The ultimate question is this: What has to happen for you to sell the stock (or buy more)? That approach will help you take the uncertainty—and the emotion—out of the decision. With effective selling rules in place before you buy a stock, you won't be crossing your fingers and hoping your stock will come back someday. ▪

* * *

Understanding your personal risk tolerance is one of the most important aspects underlying the development of your buying and selling rule set. Many of the readers I speak with are risk averse—some to the extent of only holding cash in their portfolios. However, bank account or money market holdings are subject to loss of purchasing power due to inflation and taxes. In the next column, which was originally published in August 2013, I address some of the common concerns of risk-averse investors and present some questions to help these investors determine their personal course of action.

FINANCIAL ADVICE FOR
RISK-AVERSE INVESTORS

Originally published August 23, 2015; updated 2017

A couple pulled out of the stock market at the bottom of the financial crisis in March 2009 to be "safe." Still in money market accounts, Mary and Bob want to know where to invest, but they have a handicap: They are not interested in the financial markets or investing, and they don't want to do any research. They just want someone to tell them where to put their retirement money.

I gave them some insights and advice on what to read. I also offered to discuss a portfolio for the couple to consider in light of their aversion to risk.

Since I cannot follow my normal process of portfolio construction in a column, I will share the factors that I consider when planning a portfolio for a particular family, a subject I've written about in two of my books: *The Retirement Survival Guide: How to Make Smart Financial Decisions in Good Times and Bad* [which was updated in 2017] and *Managing Retirement Wealth: An Expert Guide to Personal Portfolio Management*.

First, some insights: There is no such thing as a risk-free investment. A FDIC-insured bank account is subject to inflation risk and tax risk. A broad stock market investment such as an S&P 500 Index fund is subject to volatility, with daily price increases and declines.

Bonds, even ultrasafe U.S. government bonds, react to interest rate moves. Bonds drop in price when newer bonds that pay higher interest become available to investors. Real estate is illiquid and subject to housing market fluctuations. Annuities issued by insurance companies are subject to the risk of the insurance company going belly up.

What that means is that risk needs to be understood and in fact embraced. But who can embrace losing retirement money? During the financial crisis, the S&P 500 Index fell 57 percent over 17 months from peak (October 9, 2007) to trough (March 9, 2009). And what about volatility? On three days in 2008, the market fell close to 9 percent, according to Howard Silverblatt of S&P Dow Jones Indices. On two days in 2008, the S&P 500 rose more than 10 percent. And what about the following rebound? In the next 77 months, the S&P 500 rose more than 200 percent.

Bear markets can be brutal. Not recovering from losses can be devastating.

Professional money managers have the advantage of research and experience that forms the foundation for conviction during different market periods. For example, I recently completed a study of the worst holding periods since the 1920s, updated through the financial crisis and beyond. This type of in-depth study provides insights that lead to effective strategies for retirement investing. After all, bad markets and volatile markets will always be with us, as will bubbles.

Without this type of knowledge, people can only react to market news. Remember the *60 Minutes* exposé of 401(k) plans that aired a month *after* the bottom? People who bailed after watching the show locked in their losses, and if they are still sitting on the sidelines, they have not recovered.

If you are a risk-averse retiree who has little interest in the financial markets, here are the questions you need to answer before you start choosing investments:

1. Do you need to withdraw funds from your savings to cover living expenses during retirement? If so, how much do you need for basics versus discretionary expenses?

2. Do you have any legacy or charitable interests? If you do, you'll need to think in terms of growing your savings to achieve "positive terminal value"; that means that you have something left over to leave your heirs.

3. Since you want safety, are you willing to invest some time in learning about risk?

If the answer to number 3 is no, your best bet is a bank account.

If your answer to number 2 is no, you only have to focus on yourself and your own needs.

If, in response to number 1, you do not need to withdraw funds to live on, a stock market crash won't leave you homeless. However, if you do need to live on your savings, your personal risk is high. You will need to face the fact that getting a financial education is not an option; it's a necessity.

The "safest" way to learn is by studying three diversified investments: a stock index fund, a balanced fund, and a bond fund. Compare and contrast the three to see how they work. These three investments can form a simple "portfolio" for you, but only if you reach a solid level of understanding of what these investments can and cannot do for you.

To find information, you can start with a research house such as Morningstar.com or visit a mutual fund provider such as Vanguard.com. It's not smart to start with a commissioned salesperson before you know enough to avoid misunderstandings.

* * *

Very rarely in my career have I come across the unique individual who enjoys reading an investment prospectus. The next column, originally published in August 2014, provides you with a methodology for reading (or at least scanning) a prospectus—a very important tool for researching most type of investment offerings and products. I always caution people that a prospectus is more akin to a warning label than any other type of literature. That's reason enough to read one, yes?

REASONS AND METHODS FOR
READING A PROSPECTUS

Originally published August 10, 2014

"Paul" knew that he should have read the prospectus for the "risk-free" stock market investment before he bought it, but the prospect of reading 130 pages of small print stopped him cold. Instead, he threw away the prospectus and relied on verbal explanations from the person who recommended the product to him.

If you are one of the many people who are averse to reading prospectuses, let me explain something: Prospectuses are like kung fu. They teach you self-defense.

Having written prospectuses as a young Wall Street lawyer, I can share a few tricks on how to make it through the legalese.

First, don't confuse a prospectus with literature. Forget about reading one from start to finish as you would an column or a story. Read it as you would a warning label on a bottle of prescription medicine, remembering that the prospectus is there to protect you. Read it for signs of danger, that is, anything that you can misunderstand to your detriment.

What's an example? If you are attracted to the product because of guarantees presented to you orally, you'll want to confirm your understanding with the language in the prospectus. You can ask the person recommending the product to point out the relevant language in the prospectus (or in the contract if the product is insurance).

Other examples: What about penalties for early withdrawal (contingent deferred sales charges)? Or something that can work to your advantage, such as a waiver of sales commissions for IRA accounts?

Second, remember that your job is to be a skeptic. Read the prospectus to find reasons you may *not* want to make the investment. Example: Costs are too high.

Third, scan a few prospectuses. You'll see that they follow a formula. One section will explain the investment; another will discuss risks;

others will set out how to buy, how to sell, charges and fees, taxes, and so on. Some products come with prospectuses in multiple parts. Be sure to get them all if you are investing serious money.

Fourth, when in doubt, compare and contrast. For example, if you are presented with a variable annuity with guarantees that are hard to understand without an interpreter, ask a competing salesperson to present you with a product he or she would recommend. Have each person present the pros and cons of each product, but don't stop there. Compare and contrast each prospectus as well, section by section.

Fifth, don't buy something before getting answers to these key questions:

1. What does the investment promise to deliver?

2. In what conditions will the promise not be delivered on?

3. If there are guarantees, against what, by whom, and in what circumstances? Guarantees of any sort need to be studied closely, since they can be misunderstood. Unconditional guarantees don't exist.

4. What are the risks associated with the investment in normal markets as well as in the worst-case scenario?

5. What is the most you can lose and in what circumstances?

6. How can you get your money back?

7. Are there any penalties of any sort or limitations on liquidating the investment?

8. What are the tax consequences?

9. What are the costs of buying the investment compared with the cost of owning the investment and the cost of liquidating the investment?

10. Assuming you are being shown the product by a person who recommended it to you, what does he or she make if you buy the product?

With the information you find in the prospectus, you can ask more direct questions and ultimately make a more reasoned investment decision.

As a rule, you don't want to buy something until after you have read about and understood the benefits and risks, especially if there is pressure to take advantage of a special feature. I hope you won't come across this one: a bonus payment that is "only available until 3 p.m. today."

The more you go through this process, the easier it gets. You are comparing and contrasting and looking for anything that is not clear. If you are uncomfortable about your understanding of what you are getting, pass up the opportunity. Others will come along.

*　*　*

If you are a mutual fund investor, are you aware of the different share classes that affect pricing? Mutual funds that have more than one share class have different fee structures. For example, The Income Fund of America had 17 different share classes at this writing. The next column, originally published in May 2012, contains some cautionary advice when making a mutual fund purchase and presents a valuable tool offered by the regulators that helps to assess the effect of fees and expenses over time.

UNDERSTANDING HOW TO CHOOSE
BETWEEN MUTUAL FUND SHARE CLASSES

Originally published May 6, 2012

On a visit to a bank, I couldn't help notice a couple speaking about an investment opportunity.

The representative recommended that the couple invest $100,000 in a particular mutual fund and offered them a choice between two share classes.

She explained that one class (Class A) cost about 0.6 percent per year in operating expenses, whereas the other class (Class C) cost twice as much. Then she explained that the commission to purchase the Class A shares was 4.75 percent, compared with zero for the Class C shares. Then she asked the couple to choose between the two share classes.

This scenario takes place in bank lobbies and brokerage firms every day. If you are in this situation, how do you make a reasoned choice?

Before we tackle decision making, let me give you some context.

First, when you buy investments in a bank lobby, that person is regulated as a registered representative of a brokerage firm (not the bank itself). He or she is licensed to sell investment products such as mutual funds, insurance products such as annuities, and hybrids such as variable annuities.

Second, you pay the broker when you make the purchase and possibly for as long as you own the fund. The amount depends on the share class you purchase and the payout rate that the salesperson earns in line with her arrangement with the broker-dealer she works for.

The fund pays the broker two ways: an up-front payment at the time you make the purchase and an ongoing quarterly payment for as long as you own the fund. The payments to her come from the money you invest.

In this case, the broker would get paid more up front if you bought the Class A shares. With a $100,000 purchase, $4,750 comes off the top. The remaining $95,250 is invested in the fund. The broker would receive between $1,900 and $4,275 (or more or less) depending on her payout arrangement with her broker-dealer. In addition, she would receive another $250 a year in ongoing compensation (12b-1 fees).

The A share would be a more lucrative immediate commission for the broker than the C share, which would be a better financial result for the broker if you held on to the fund for a long time.

Let me explain further.

If you bought the C shares, the broker would receive substantially less up front (only $400 to $900) but more on an ongoing basis ($1,000 a year assuming a full payout).

Third, since the broker can have an incentive to suggest one class over another on the basis of her own earnings, it's a very good idea to be clear on the benefits and drawbacks of each share class before you make a purchase.

Fourth, because of the homework involved, it would be a mistake to make a quick purchase. Although this bank broker offered only two share classes, there are usually more to consider.

Where can you get help in understanding how to choose between share classes?

Your decision will depend on two things: your returns and how long you intend to hold the fund.

Luckily, there is an online tool that can help you do projections that will show you which class is a better choice for you.

The tool is the mutual fund analyzer offered by the Financial Industry Regulatory Authority (FINRA), the largest independent securities regulator in the United States (go to apps.finra.org/fundanalyzer/1/fa.aspx). You'll want to see the effect of fees and expenses over time.

You will need to look up the fund in question. Then you will be asked to enter the investment amount, the assumed rate of return, and the holding period.

I assumed a two-year holding period for the $100,000 investment and a 5 percent annual return. The C shares came out ahead (a profit of about $6,000 for C shares versus about $3,800 for A shares). The longer the holding period is, the more profitable the A shares will be. For example, at 10 years, the A shares had a profit of about $39,000 versus $34,500 for the C shares. At 20 years, the A shares were $20,000 ahead of the C shares.

One more point.

Conflicts of interest can arise even if you are not working with a broker; investment advisers may have a dual role that puts them in the same position as this broker. Most large brokerage firms are now dually registered, for example (as broker-dealers and investment advisers).

If you choose to work with a firm that does not get revenue from product sales, be sure to check its conflict disclosure in its ADV Part 2A disclosure document to make sure that the firm does not receive any payments from the funds it purchases for your portfolio. You can find a firm's ADV Part 2A online at sec.gov/investor/brokers.htm.

In any event, exploring share classes (and potential conflicts of interest) is something you'll want to do, especially if you are investing important (to you) sums of money.

* * *

Did you ever wonder about how corporate insiders view their company's stock? That is, are the executives buying or selling? In the next column, originally published in March 2013, I detail the forms that officers and directors of publicly traded companies must file with the SEC when transacting in their company's stock—and where you can find these filings. While an insider purchase or sale does not always indicate good or bad news, it does represent valuable information that should be part of your research methodology.

INSIDER TRANSACTIONS—
WHERE TO FIND THEM

Originally published March 10, 2013

Before you invest in a stock, would you like to know whether company insiders are buying or selling that stock? You can think of insiders as people in the know, such as officers and directors of the company.

After all, as some have said, there are many reasons insiders sell a stock but only one reason they buy it: They believe the price is going up.

Where do you find information on insider buys and sales?

Look to Securities and Exchange Commission (SEC) Forms 3, 4, and 5, which are publicly available on the SEC's EDGAR database at sec.gov/edgar/searchedgar/. Search for the company name or ticker. Click "include ownership Forms 3, 4, and 5."

To help you read these forms, you'll find this SEC investor bulletin helpful. Go to sec.gov/investor/alerts and search "Insider Transactions and Forms 3, 4, and 5."

Let me go through the forms one by one. Form 3 has to be filed within 10 days after a person becomes an insider to disclose ownership of the company's securities.

Form 4 has to be filed when an insider buys or sells securities, including the amount purchased or sold and the price per share. "Securities" includes common stock as well as derivative securities such as options, warrants, and convertible securities. Form 4 must be filed within two business days after the transaction date.

Form 5 is filed when at least one transaction, because of an exemption or failure to report earlier, was not reported during the year.

The bulletin states: "For example, some transactions, such as certain purchases by an insider of less than $10,000 in a six-month period, don't have to be reported on Form 4 when they occur but do have to be reported on Form 5. The Form 5 filing doesn't have to disclose transactions that have been previously reported. When reporting transactions on Form 5, insiders use the same transaction codes as when reporting on Form 4."

Keep in mind that sales don't always indicate bad news. Insiders could be selling for personal reasons, such as needing cash or to diversify their holdings.

You might want to look at some blank forms first to get your bearings. You can find them and their instructions at sec.gov/forms. You also can find third-party websites offering insider ownership and transaction information. Search for "insider transactions."

I'm sure you'll agree with the SEC that it helps to understand insiders' economic stake in the success of the company.

If you are interested in other SEC educational materials, you can call (800) 732-0330 for more information or go online to Investor.gov or to the website for the Office of Investor Education and Advocacy at sec.gov/investor.shtml.

*   *   *

The next column I selected to conclude in this section does not necessarily represent a specific tool, but more of an opportunity that is periodically presented to all investors—A Down Market. This column, written in September 2002 during the dot.com bubble bursting, presents the calculus behind investing in a sideways and down market.

WAYS TO MAKE MONEY IN A DOWN MARKET

Originally published September 22, 2002

Some people believe we may be entering into a flat market reminiscent of the period 1972–1982.

Those of you who remember that time have "Dow 1000" etched into their memories.

The Dow Jones Industrial Average reached 1000 on November 14, 1972. By March 1974, the Dow was down to 577. It took until October 12, 1982, for the Dow to come back to 1000.

Imagine going into another protracted sideways market lasting from 2002 through 2012.

Can anyone make money in that type of market?

Let's look at the period 1972–1982 for some answers.

Suppose you invested in a well-respected growth and income mutual fund at the beginning of the 10-year period. On November 14, 1972, you bought $10,000 worth of shares. Now it's October 12, 1982.

You may think your investment would be worth just what you paid for it 10 years earlier: $10,000.

Not so. Your original investment of $10,000 is now worth $27,422 after all fees and expenses.

How can that be explained?

The day you made your $10,000 investment, you bought 1,464 shares at $7.91 a share, which included a sales load. Before the sales charge, the share price was $6.45 a share.

Even though you didn't make any additional investments, during the 10 years you held the fund, you acquired an additional 1,808 shares. Those shares were purchased for you with the dividends and capital gains distributions paid by the fund to shareholders who owned the fund. Your dividends were reinvested during the bear market of 1974, when prices dropped to a low of $4 a share.

You sold the fund when the Dow came back to 1000 and the fund was selling at $8.38 a share. Your $10,000 investment was worth $27,422, for an average annual return of 10.72 percent in a market that lost about 40 percent in 1973–1974 before recovering slowly over the next eight years.

Did I single out a fund that outperformed everyone else? No. But I did choose a growth and income fund that is run by a sound, well-respected team of advisers.

During the same period, the average growth and income fund returned 7.7 percent according to Lipper, a provider of mutual fund and market data, for an ending value of $20,900. That is not a shabby return for a sideways period that included a bear market that looks very much like the one we are experiencing today.

401(k) participants are the big winners in a sideways market.

The 401(k) Advantage

What happens if you are investing in a 401(k) in a 1972–1982 type of market?

Most people who invest for retirement through their 401(k) plans do so by means of payroll deductions. That means that you are purchasing new investments each pay period, which is usually monthly or biweekly.

It is not uncommon for a company to provide employees with a 50 percent match up to 6 percent of compensation.

Let's see what happens in a 1972–1982 sideways market to "Marylou," a young woman who is contributing $100 each month to her 401(k) plan at work to purchase the same growth and income fund. Let's assume that she receives 3 percent salary increases during the period and that her company pays her a 50 percent match, which starts out at $50 a month.

In 10 years, Marylou invested $100 of her own money each month for a total of about $14,000.

Her employer contributed an additional $7,000 on her behalf, which represents the company match.

The same growth and income fund would be worth $44,000 in 1982, for an average annual return of 25 percent on her $14,000 investment. A similar investment in the average growth and income fund as measured by Lipper resulted in $36,000, for an average annual return of 21 percent.

If Marylou had invested in the average balanced fund, she would have an ending value of $35,000, for a 20 percent average annual return. The average growth fund would have resulted in a final value of $35,494, for a 21 percent average annual return. A well-managed growth fund offered by a major mutual fund family would have returned $59,000, for a 30 percent average annual return.

Keep in mind that this period included the 1973–1974 market decline of close to 40 percent.

Sideways and downward markets are not "bad" markets for savvy investors. They are probably the best markets for 401(k) participants, especially if the company provides a matching contribution.

If we find ourselves in a long protracted sideways market reminiscent of the period 1972–1982, patient investors with sound investment practices will be rewarded handsomely.

Financial Advisers

Part 1: How to Judge

Are You Curious:

- Is your adviser acting in a fiduciary capacity?

- How is your adviser compensated and does that compensation create conflicts of interest?

- Is it time to change advisers?

SECTION PREVIEW:

If you have significant assets, it is highly likely that you have one or more brokerage accounts with major Wall Street firms, along with retirement plans at work, one or two online accounts, and perhaps a professional money management firm ("registered investment adviser"). That puts you in the position of having to manage those accounts and service providers, some of whom operate under different sets of rules.

In this section we'll distinguish between types of advisers, as differentiated by regulation. Keep in mind that "financial adviser" (or just "adviser") is a term I use as a catchall for any type of person you might engage. We will also address when it's time to review your current adviser and how to do that, how your adviser gets paid and how to assess potential conflicts of interest.

INSIDER'S PERSPECTIVE:

An executive was shopping for an advisory service to set up and manage his retirement portfolio. He asked his colleagues what they liked (and disliked) about their advisers. The executive told me that his colleagues shared what they didn't like, but none could share what they liked.

As an industry insider, I would conduct the search by looking for a combination of three things: skill (is the professional skilled in the particular role I am retaining him for?); integrity (is the professional trustworthy, which is most important in avoiding misunderstandings, and a "fiduciary," with a duty under the law to put my interests ahead of his own should a conflict arise?); and can the professional achieve the results I'm looking for, based on my specific objectives?

I also want to see transparency, with full disclosure of all elements of the relationship. That means disclosure of all fees and financial and other benefits that the adviser receives directly or indirectly as a result of the client relationship.

The columns selected for this chapter represent a base of knowledge that investors should be armed with when reviewing their current advisory relationship(s) or considering a new engagement.

*   *   *

This first column was written in October 2004 and updated for this book. I discuss the regulatory framework that sets the standards of care for financial advisers.

ARE FINANCIAL ADVISERS ALL THE SAME?

Originally published October 17, 2004; updated 2017

Not being aware of the differences between stockbrokers (registered representatives) and investment advisers can lead to misunderstandings, losses, and even lawsuits. Our regulators would like to make it easier for consumers to understand the differences or, better yet, some would like to raise everyone to the higher "fiduciary" standard that applies to registered investment advisors.

Regulation is the key to understanding the distinctions. Very simply, no matter what they call themselves, financial advisers are regulated as "registered representatives" or "investment advisers" or both. This is important to consumers because the law determines the standard of care that applies to the relationship between the client and the financial adviser.

Registered Representatives

Regulation of registered representatives revolves around transactions.

A customer buys a security: That's the transaction. Regulation focuses on the point of sale. Most transgressions involve unsuitable recommendations or unauthorized transactions.

To be "suitable," the broker's recommendation must be appropriate for the customer's age, financial situation, investment objective, and investment experience. A recommendation of speculative stocks, for example, would not be appropriate for an elderly widower who could not afford losses.

"Unauthorized transactions" are just what they sound like. A broker may not buy a security for your account without getting your authorization.

Other actionable activities include switching a customer from one mutual fund to another for no legitimate purpose; using deceptive or fraudulent devices to induce the purchase or sale of a security; charging the customer excessive markups, markdowns, or commissions on the purchase of securities; guaranteeing customers against losses; and failing to use reasonable diligence to see that a customer's order is executed at the best possible price in prevailing market conditions, among others.

If you grant your broker discretionary power over your account, the broker is held to the higher standard of a fiduciary. In some states, a broker has a fiduciary duty but only with respect to a transaction.

Otherwise, there is no legal duty of loyalty to the customer, and because of that, there is no legal responsibility under federal securities laws to provide you with information that could point to potential conflicts of interest, such as indirect or hidden fees or incentives to sell a certain product or service. Likewise, a registered representative has no legal duty to volunteer information about his background or training, customer complaints, disciplinary actions by regulators, or customer arbitrations or lawsuits.

Registered representatives can be licensed to sell insurance, and some also may be registered as investment advisers.

[2017 update: To complicate matters, now even the biggest transactional firms (broker-dealers) are "dually" registered as investment advisers and broker-dealers. That puts the burden on a customer of such a firm to initiate a dialogue about the capacity under which the adviser is acting (fiduciary or suitability). Since 2011, the idea of "harmonizing" the two sets of standards has been discussed by regulators, but the issue remains unresolved.]

Investment Advisers

Regulation of investment advisers flows from the relationship with the client, not the transaction, and is founded on a duty of loyalty owed by the adviser to the client that extends to all dealings with the client. As a result, the adviser is a fiduciary at all times and must put the client's interests ahead of her own in all dealings with the client.

As a fiduciary, the adviser must disclose potential conflicts of interest in writing. The adviser also must provide information about his background, training, years in the business, education, the basis for his investment recommendations, complaint history, and other matters that can help you assess his competence and self-interest.

Differences Blurred

These distinctions may be important in your hiring decision, yet they are easily missed, especially in an industry that chooses titles for their marketing panache, such as the now ubiquitous "wealth manager." Don't conclude anything from a title.

People who need help to invest important sums of money, such as 401(k) rollovers, pension distributions, or inheritances, need to be particularly aware of who they are retaining.

Potential confusion is increased when registered representatives also act as advisers when they offer advisory services such as managed accounts.

* * *

Whether you have a long-established relationship with your financial adviser or are interviewing a replacement, you'll want to read the next column to confirm the scope of your engagement. Originally published in October 2013, the column will prepare you for a conversation to make sure your expectations are met.

REVIEW THE SCOPE OF YOUR ENGAGEMENT

Originally published October 27, 2013

Even if you have a happy long-term relationship with your financial adviser, you owe it to yourself—and to him or her—to review your understanding of the scope of the services being provided.

This should be a regular practice, and it may be of particular interest to you now, since regulators are focusing on investor confusion about services and considering changing legal standards of care.

Start the inquiry by asking for a meeting to review progress and talk about the future. Your adviser should be happy to oblige, since it helps ensure smooth sailing for both of you.

Ask your adviser to bring documents or reports that are relevant to your relationship. The documentation will differ with the type of firm the adviser works for.

If your adviser works for a broker-dealer, you'll be reviewing a new-account form that you signed when you opened the account as well as monthly brokerage statements and confirmations. The new-account form is important, since it records your adviser's understanding of your experience as an investor, your risk tolerance, and your objectives.

Some broker-dealers provide additional reports, such as quarterly or annual performance reviews and financial plans.

If the firm is also registered as an investment adviser, be sure to review the firm's Form ADV Part 2A (also called a "brochure") as well as the adviser's Form ADV Part 2B.

These documents cannot be ignored, as they disclose conflicts of interest such as compensation arrangements and referral fees. They also disclose disciplinary information about the firm (Part 2A) and the financial adviser (Part 2B).

If your financial adviser works for a major brokerage firm, it is not unlikely that you are invested in managed accounts. Each of the managers of those accounts has Form ADV Part 2A disclosure documents that you will want to review. Another important document is your contract for advisory services.

In many cases, these documents will have been sent to you in a large packet at the time you opened your account. Form ADV Parts 2A and B will have been sent to you at the beginning of your relationship and updated later when or if material changes occurred.

If your adviser suggests that ADV Parts 2A and B are not important to review, consider whether you agree: Do you need to understand how your adviser is paid? Does she receive sales incentives to recommend one product over another? Do conflicts of interest exist in the relationship? Are there disciplinary disclosures? Can your adviser sell other financial products to you under a different compensation arrangement?

At the meeting, confirm that there are no misunderstandings about investment experience, objectives, and risk tolerance. You'll find those on your new-account form or investment policy statement. Are they consistent with your understanding? Do they need to be updated?

Next, confirm your understanding of the services your adviser is providing and how you are compensating her for those services.

Is she providing transaction-based services; that is, is she recommending that you buy a certain investment from time to time? If so, is she paid a commission (or markup or markdown) for each trade? Is she also receiving any payments from product sponsors, such as mutual fund 12b-1 fees, that will not be visible on a confirmation? Does she receive more compensation for selling you certain products over others?

Is your adviser providing access to a professional money manager through a managed account? If so, is he paid a fee that is based on the assets you invest in the managed account? How much are the total fees you are paying to all the involved parties? Are there any other costs you are bearing?

You may have an adviser who has multiple bosses. For example, some registered investment advisory firms also have arrangements with independent contractor broker-dealers. In this case, it can be tricky to understand when he is being paid for the sale of a product and when he isn't.

Perhaps the easiest relationship to comprehend involves someone providing a single fully disclosed money management service paid for exclusively by the client with no other source of income muddying the waters.

No matter what service you believe you have, it's a good practice to confirm your understanding in writing after the meeting.

Finally, make sure you are receiving all the reports you need to assess how you are doing.

It pays to be in sync with your financial adviser. This dialogue will help you understand what to expect of each other. ■

*   *   *

Are you curious about how to best interview a financial adviser? There are many different advisers, wearing different hats, working under different regulatory structures, selling different products, and providing lots of information to sort through. In the next column, originally published in August 2014, I provide a list of questions published by the Investment Adviser Association. The list will be helpful to you when you interview your current adviser (something I recommend everyone do) or potential advisers if you are shopping for a new adviser.

In addition, I highly recommend that you read a publication called "Cutting through the Confusion," published by the Investments Adviser Association (investmentadviser.org).

QUESTIONS TO ASK A FINANCIAL ADVISER

Originally published August 31, 2014; updated 2017

Here is a list of questions to ask financial advisers that is provided by the Investment Adviser Association, a nonprofit of which my firm is a member. Founded in 1937, the IAA played a major role in the enactment of the 1940 law regulating "investment advisers." Investment advisers are required by law to put your interests ahead of their own under what is called a "fiduciary" standard. This is a good list to use for any financial adviser you might retain. It will help you understand the services provided.

Under "Questions to Ask," the IAA says this:

"After identifying your investment goals, you should interview investment advisers to decide which one would best be suited to help you achieve your goals. Asking detailed questions will help you determine your comfort level with the prospective adviser on both a personal and professional level. Some questions you might ask include:

1. "Are you a fiduciary, i.e., are you required by law to place my interests ahead of your own at all times? Are you willing to acknowledge your fiduciary duty in writing?

2. "How are you paid? Do you make more money if I buy a particular stock, bond, or mutual fund over another investment? If so, would you still recommend this investment and why? Does your firm hold prize contests for sales?

3. "What products and services does your firm offer? Are recommendations of products and services limited? If so, why?

4. "What are the potential conflicts of interest surrounding the investment advice that you will give me? What policies have you instituted to avoid or at least mitigate any such conflicts?

5. "What is your investment philosophy? How does your investment philosophy differ from other investment adviser firms?

6. "How often will we meet? How often will I receive written reports about my portfolio?

7. "What happens when you place an order for my account? Could I get a better price (cost and/or commission) if you sent my orders to a different market or broker to be executed?

8. "Describe your typical client. May I contact your long-term clients as references?

9. "How long has your firm been in business? What are the qualifications of the investment and professional personnel in the firm?

10. "With respect to the person who will manage my account, what experience do you have, especially with people in my circumstances? Where did you go to school? What training do you have in the investment management field? What is your recent employment history? What other firms have you been registered with? What is the status of those firms today? What licenses do you hold?

11. "Where does your firm invest its own money? Is it invested similarly to that of your clients?

12. "Have you ever been disciplined by any government regulator for unethical or improper conduct or been sued by a client who was not happy with the work you did? How many lawsuits or arbitration cases have been filed against you and against your firm? What were the outcomes?

13. "Can you provide me with a copy of the registration documents that you filed with the SEC? For Registered Investment Advisors, ask for a copy of Parts 1 and 2 of their Form ADV.

(Note: Also ask for the firm's "Brochure" [also called Form ADV Parts 2A and 2B].) For investment adviser representatives of the adviser, ask for a copy of their Form U-4."

If you would like to access IAA information, go to investment adviser.org.

*   *   *

Are you wondering about how financial advisers get paid? The next column written in June 2015 discusses why it's important to know the answer. The column discusses the various forms of compensation and fees that a financial adviser receives. Since you are the person paying those fees, you have every right to fully understand the fees you are paying and the services you are receiving in return.

FINANCIAL ADVISERS SHOULD BE CLEAR ABOUT COMPENSATION

Originally published June 14, 2015

How much is your financial adviser earning?

This is a simple question in a complex setting, since financial advisers come in all stripes and compensation comes in many forms, some of which can be hidden from view.

In my mind, the best practice for an adviser to follow is to be completely open about compensation, whether it is direct or indirect, visible on a trade confirmation or not.

There can be some hesitancy on the part of some advisers who are not obligated to make full disclosure, but I believe that an honorable adviser will welcome the inquiry. After all, transparency helps build long-lasting relationships.

Here are the questions to ask: "How are you compensated for my doing business with you? What can you give me in writing on that?"

You'll want to hear and read about the general practices of the firm the adviser works for, and you'll also want some specifics relating to your own account.

For example, a major brokerage firm publishes a booklet on mutual fund fees that is nine pages long, single-spaced. There you will see the firm's policy: Adviser compensation "differs by share class and whether mutual fund shares are purchased through an asset-based fee program, traditional brokerage account or a self-directed investing account."

Further: "Some fund classes carry higher front-end sales charges or asset-based fees than others (e.g., Class A shares may have higher front-end sales charges and therefore pay higher up-front compensation than Class B shares). As a result, [an adviser] may receive more or less compensation depending on the fund or class you purchase."

That disclosure won't help you very much in understanding what's happening in your account, so you have to go further. Go through your brokerage statement and your confirmations with your adviser and have him point out examples.

Take a mutual fund that you own. Ask how much the adviser received in payment when you bought the fund and how much she receives on an ongoing basis. This information is not reported on trade confirmations or brokerage statements.

The question to ask when making an investment is: "What will you be paid as a result of my purchasing this investment?"

Notice, I did not ask "How much will I pay to buy the investment?" The latter question might not uncover payments that don't show up on confirmations or brokerage statements.

After you get answers, you'll be better able to judge whether there are conflicts of interest embedded in the relationship. If there are, you'll need to ascertain whether a recommendation is being made for your benefit or for the adviser's. One product may be as suitable for you as another but may generate a bigger payment to the adviser. That's something I would want to know as a client.

Other types of fees may come into the picture that might not wind up in the adviser's pocket. For information, you'll want to read the North American Securities Administrators Association (NASAA) report "Are You an Informed Investor? Understanding Broker-Dealer Fees" (April 2015).

Here is another twist if you are working with a Registered Investment Advisor (RIA). The RIA may pay its advisers salaries that are not tied to sales. If you ask such an adviser the questions listed above, you'll find out how the RIA earns money. The law requires RIAs to disclose direct and indirect compensation they receive in the RIA's "Form ADV Part 2A" or "Brochure."

RIAs typically charge a fee that is based on assets that has to be disclosed in advance in a contract, described in the Brochure, and reported on the brokerage statement. Since I'm a fan of fee transparency, I like to see RIAs provide a bill showing how the fee was calculated each time a fee deduction is made; not all RIAs follow this practice, however.

One more wrinkle: Your adviser may be paying someone for referring you to him. RIAs must report that conflict of interest in their Brochures.

* * *

You are hiring a financial adviser to help manage your money and to grow your asset base. To feel comfortable with this relationship, ideally you are operating in a conflict-free environment. In September 2014, I wrote about a few of the most visible conflicts that could exist between you and your advisers. Knowledge will help you manage the relationship. Read on to learn some strategies for avoiding conflicted advisers.

DISCLOSURE DOCUMENTS AND QUESTIONS CAN HELP DETERMINE IF A FINANCIAL ADVISER HAS A CONFLICT

Originally published September 7, 2014; updated 2017

Most people have no idea whether there are conflicts of interest in the relationship between them and their financial advisers. This column might help.

An interesting case was reported by the U.S. Securities and Exchange Commission (SEC) that gives a good example of the type of conflict of interest that may arise between a financial firm and its clients.

The case had to do with a Houston-based firm that sold mutual funds to its clients, with a payment coming back to the firm from another party.

Let me paint the picture: The firm had an arrangement with a registered broker-dealer (BD). The BD would pay from 2 to 12 basis points as "eligible shareholder servicing fees on eligible NTF mutual funds" based on varying levels of NTF assets. NTF stands for "no transaction fee," meaning that when an order to buy or sell is entered, there is no charge to the client.

Effectively, the clients were buying funds for which they were not charged a transaction fee. However, the firm managing the client's money was getting paid to put the clients in those funds.

That's a conflict of interest.

Why? The payment arrangement creates an incentive for the firm to favor those mutual funds over others.

Even more important, the firm had a chance to let its clients know the arrangement but did not. Those payments were not disclosed, asserted the SEC, even though clients were told that the firm "may receive compensation" from the broker.

Payments actually were being received by the firm from the BD. Hence, as the release stated, "Unbeknownst to investors, [the firm] had an incentive to recommend these funds to clients over other investment opportunities and generate additional revenue for the firm."

According to Marshall S. Sprung of the SEC Enforcement Division: "Payments to investment advisers for recommending certain types of investments may taint their ability to provide impartial advice to their clients. By failing to fully disclose its agreements with the BD, [the Houston firm] deprived its clients of important information they were entitled to receive."

In a 2012 case, two Portland, Oregon, firms had a revenue-sharing agreement for a particular category of mutual fund. Once again, the SEC found that to be a conflict of interest.

"Payments to investment advisers for recommending certain types of investments may corrupt their ability to provide impartial advice to their clients," said Bruce Karpati, chief of the SEC Enforcement Division's Asset Management Unit, quoting from a 2012 release. "[The firm] kept their clients in the dark about this and other conflicts of interest that investors are entitled to know about and advisers must disclose."

These are two examples of conflicts. I'm certain we will see more enforcement actions as time goes on. Regulators want to ensure that clients are fully informed of potential conflicts, especially since consumers may be unaware of these particular types of arrangements.

One way to protect yourself is to ask the firm you are working with for a full explanation of any incentive to recommend a particular investment or course of action. You'll run across sales incentives for financial advisers to sell a particular product or service, sales contests, referral fees, and so on.

Disclosure documents are your first line of protection, but there is nothing better than good old-fashioned face-to-face questioning. Just ask: What incentives do you have to recommend a particular product or service over another? You'll want to hear that there are none. That's a conflict-free environment.

*   *   *

While I wrote the next column in August 2015, the concept of "Personal Risk" is timeless. Assessing risk tolerance should be the first part of the discussion between you and your adviser. You are bringing your financial wants and desires to your adviser in the hope of guidance and advice to achieve your goals. An effective financial adviser will recognize the level of risk your portfolio can handle and will structure a portfolio that works for you.

"PERSONAL RISK" MUST TAKE NO. 1 PRIORITY

Originally published August 30, 2015

People tend to focus on which investments to choose before they understand enough about themselves. Risk-averse retirees, especially those who have little interest in the financial markets, need to assess their "personal risk"—my term—before even thinking about which investments they should buy.

An example came from "Jordan."

Jordan explained that he was risk-averse. He wanted to know what types of investments he should be making "considering the market." At the time, the stock market had just experienced six consecutive declines (August 2015).

After probing, I advised Jordan that before picking investments, he needed to ask himself about his own personal risk.

Personal risk has nothing to do with a risk-assessment questionnaire. It has to do with something much more important, as it leads to an understanding of whether a retiree will run out of money.

Here is the question Jordan has to ask himself: Do you need to access your savings to pay your bills?

Jordan's answer was yes, as his Social Security retirement benefits were insufficient to cover his needs.

Let's stop here for a second.

If someone had no need to access savings for living expenses in retirement, he or she would have a low personal-risk profile. These are individuals who have income from Social Security (and pensions) in amounts that are sufficient to cover their living expenses. In the best situations, these income streams are inflation-adjusted to cover rising expenses.

Anyone who needs to access savings to pay for living expenses has a high personal-risk profile. If that's you, it's best not to choose investments of any kind until you know just how much you will need to withdraw from your savings to pay the bills.

In Jordan's case, he had $1.5 million in savings, which seemed like plenty of money until the expenses come into the equation: Jordan needed to withdraw $150,000 to cover his yearly living expenses above and beyond his Social Security retirement benefit.

Now Jordan's question became: "I have $1.5 million to invest; I need to withdraw $150,000 each year after taxes. I need that withdrawal to increase yearly to cover rising costs caused by inflation as time goes on, and I would like to leave a legacy for my children. I am a novice investor. I don't want to lose money. How should I invest?"

Framing the question this way opened up a different issue altogether, as it is meant to do.

The standard risk questionnaire leads to asset-allocation decisions and investment selection. The personal-risk assessment tees up decisions that preserve a lifestyle, determines the demands that will be made of the retirement nest egg, and sets the stage for organizing a personal portfolio to manage.

With this approach to risk, issues surface that have to be addressed as quickly as possible. In Jordan's case, he will need to lower expenses. Also, he will not be able to avoid some research and learning. Too much is at risk, and it's not just the volatile stock market.

* * *

Life is full of transitions. Are you wondering if it's time to change financial advisers? In the next column from November 2010, an adviser and his client had drifted apart. I suggested giving the adviser some specific questions to address before making a change. While a new adviser might be necessary when someone is approaching retirement, that's not always the case. Open communication is the key to a successful relationship with your adviser.

IS IT TIME TO CHANGE ADVISERS?

Originally published November 14, 2010; updated 2017

Readers "Liz" and "Phil" had been working with a financial adviser who was regulated as an investment adviser. (The investment adviser provided discretionary management services for an asset-based fee.)

They were quite happy until recently, when they became concerned about the risk they were assuming in the portfolio and lack of communication with the adviser.

Indeed, survey data tells us that investors are most likely to change advisers based on a communication failure. For example, according to Spectrem Group's surveys, 57 percent of affluent investors would change financial advisers who did not return phone calls in a timely manner (2017 "Advisor Relationships and Changing Advice Requirements"). When Spectrem surveyed high net-worth investors about why they switched advisers, the most common answer (24 percent) was that their advisers were not proactive in contacting them (2015 "Why Investors Switch Advisors").

Instead of second-guessing specific investment choices, I asked the couple to step back for a minute and take a broader view. How had they stated their investment objectives for the portfolio? What was the adviser's strategy for meeting those objectives?

After we talked a bit, it became apparent that something had changed since the couple had retained the adviser. They were retiring earlier than planned. They would need income from their investments sooner than expected.

Instead of focusing on the individual investments that Liz and Phil saw as problems, I suggested that they have a conversation with their adviser about goals and strategies. The closer retirement date was an important piece of information. They needed to discuss that with him and see whether he would initiate appropriate changes in the risk level of the portfolio.

Because implementing your investment policy is your adviser's job, your job is to communicate with the adviser about changes in your life that might affect that policy.

With that in mind, I counseled Liz and Phil to bring up their new retirement time line with their adviser and give him a chance to respond appropriately.

Here's the script I gave them: "We have some changes in our circumstances that we need to discuss. They might affect our investment objectives and how you manage our portfolio."

You want the financial adviser to come up with answers. You want him or her to take responsibility.

I advised Liz and Phil to listen carefully to see how the adviser addressed the new circumstances, which called for a change in the investment policy.

At this point in our conversation, Liz and Phil expressed concerns that their adviser might not understand their situation; they weren't sure he or she had enough experience with people approaching retirement.

Of course, if the adviser is inexperienced, the couple will need to make a change. But first, they need to find out whether that is indeed the case.

Liz and Phil should engage the adviser on that point: "Tell us how you handle the other pre-retirees in our situation whom you work with. How do you go from a growth portfolio to an income-generating portfolio? Please give us an example of how you would handle our needs based on other clients of yours."

That brings us to roles.

Once you and your adviser set the investment policy for your portfolio, your role as a client is to communicate any changes in circumstances that might call for a change of direction.

With a discretionary investment adviser, delivering on the investment objectives is the adviser's role. You don't want to find yourself giving him or her specific buy or sell instructions. That's the adviser's job.

Financial Advisers

Part 2: Be a Skeptic

ARE YOU CURIOUS:

- How can you avoid making a mistake in choosing a financial adviser?

- Is your adviser's input helping you to make better decisions?

- Should you attend a seminar that promises a "free meal and free advice?"

SECTION PREVIEW:

When dealing with your investments, you must approach financial decision making with a healthy dose of skepticism. After all, there are many optimists in the financial services industry, and their optimism about an investment or strategy can be infectious. Then there are those few (very few) less-than-honest folks who are attracted to the industry because that's where the money is. In this section, I'll share some regulators' concerns, which will help you avoid potential setbacks. And we'll discuss how someone can make a mistake in choosing an adviser.

INSIDER'S PERSPECTIVE:

Finding the right adviser to work with can be challenging, especially if it's the special kind of advice people need when they transition into retirement. If you've watched movies like *The Wolf of Wall Street, The Big Short, Boiler Room,* or the 1987 Michael Douglas classic *Wall Street,* you might have a skewed opinion of financial advisers. A 2016 poll by the American Association of Individual Investors (AAII) offers insights.

When asked, "How much do you trust the financial services industry to do what is in the best interest of its clients?" the responses were not positive (37 percent mistrust a lot; 28 percent mistrust a little; only 2 percent trust a lot; and 15 percent trust a little; the remainder neither trust nor distrust).

As an industry insider, I can tell you that searching for the right (right-for-you) adviser who can properly manage your retirement portfolio is not as easy as asking a few friends for recommendations. In this section of the book, I'll share some insights and cautions from experts and regulators.

*   *   *

I like to think of the relationship between an adviser and a client as a partnership. Both parties should be working toward the same goal of financial security and financial freedom in retirement. The next column from May 2013 is about the search for a financial adviser.

STRUGGLE TO FIND RETIREMENT ADVICE

Originally published May 26, 2013

Picking a financial adviser is a challenge sometimes, particularly if you are looking to invest for retirement. *Wall Street Journal* writer Robert Powell points out the difficulties in "How a Pick for a Financial Adviser Can Go Wrong" (May 19, 2013).

It's an interesting topic for me, since I see the struggle from the outside in (through the eyes of the readers of my column) and from the inside out (when potential clients contact my firm for help with their retirement investing).

Powell makes some very good points, in part by using a health-care example.

"Let's say you have a health problem and you visit two or three internists. Chances are good you would receive a similar diagnosis and treatment from each doctor," writes Powell.

"But let's say you take a financial problem, or your retirement goals, to two or three financial advisers. New studies show that you're unlikely to get the same, or even similar, recommendations about what investment products to buy or what strategy to pursue. And that could make a big difference in your financial future."

So true. If you look at training materials for advisers, you'll see that providing retirement investment advice is not as easy as you might think. A lot more is involved than selling a product to a customer.

Citing a Cambridge, Massachusetts, market-research firm, Powell says that "retirement-savings recommendations vary greatly based on the type of firm for which a financial adviser works." Citing another firm's study, he says that "advisers in different channels use not only different products but also different strategies to generate retirement income for their clients." And some advisers "use the same investment strategy for both building and tapping a nest egg."

Financial advice for retirement is not uniform. Different advisers sell different financial products and services depending on the types of firms they work for. Those who don't focus on retirement investing may not change their methodology whether the client is a retiree who needs income or a youthful investor accumulating a nest egg.

In this set of circumstances, how do you find good advice about retirement investing?

Retirement is all about you and your needs, desires, and circumstances and how those needs may evolve over a long period, perhaps 20, 30, or 40 years or longer. Your unique situation needs to be understood before an investment program can be developed. It's best that you do the homework before seeking investment help so that you can guide the process.

The single most important piece of information is your cash flow. By cash flow, I mean money that comes into the household (pension and Social Security) and money that goes out of the household (living expenses, gifting, etc.). When you understand your current cash flow, you'll know how much money you'll need to withdraw from your investments to pay for living expenses.

Armed with your personal cash flow, you'll be in a better position to start defining your investment goals. You'll know the amount you need to withdraw from your investments this year. To preserve your lifestyle, you'll need to withdraw more in the future to offset inflation or adjust for higher taxes. In addition, you may want to leave a legacy for your children.

Your investment program should be set up to accomplish those objectives. The firm you choose to work with should be experienced in doing this for other people who are in circumstances similar to yours. There are lots of fine firms that can help.

* * *

The next column, published November 2016, takes the conversation about retirement advice a step further, describing how to put safe withdrawal rates into context when dealing with a financial adviser.

HOW ADVISERS CAN AFFECT
WITHDRAWAL RATES

Originally published November 13, 2016; updated 2017

When I was having lunch with a client the other day, he suggested that I continue with the subject of safe withdrawal rates: how much someone can safely withdraw from his or her investments without running out of money.

His point was stated this way: "Julie, don't assume that column readers who are approaching retirement know how to assess the financial advice they are getting at this critical decision-making time of life."

The role of the adviser can be influential. Indeed, "households do not make decisions in a vacuum. . . . One particularly important source of inputs comes from financial advisers," according to "The Market for Financial Advice: An Audit Study" (2012), coauthored by Sendhil Mullainathan of Harvard University, Markus Noeth of University of Hamburg, and Antoinette Schoar, the Michael M. Koerner (1949) Professor of Entrepreneurial Finance.

In an October 27, 2016 column Schoar wrote for the *Wall Street Journal* on the Department of Labor's new fiduciary rule, she made these additional points:

First, "[M]uch research shows that a large fraction of the population is poorly prepared to make these financial decisions by themselves."

Second, "Typically, when faced with complex and important decisions we rely on trusted experts for advice. Sick people turn to doctors, those accused of crimes seek the help of lawyers, and the list goes on. These cases all have a common feature: The expert adviser must abide by a strict code of conduct that puts the interest of the client first. Surprisingly, the same is not always true for financial experts who advise people on their retirement savings."

Third, "By the time you learn whether a retirement strategy was the right choice, it is usually too late to change it."

In determining safe portfolio withdrawal rates, it is important to do a self-audit of cash flows, longevity, inflation, taxes, and the like. This will lay the groundwork for a plan of action, but it also is a guide for assessing a financial adviser or the recommendation of a product such as a retirement income annuity or even a lump-sum distribution from a pension plan. An adviser who recommends a course of action without first fully understanding your circumstances and needs may not be prepared to provide the best solutions.

In addition, there is the quality of advice. In Professor Schoar's words: "[T]he majority of brokers are not paid on the basis of the quality of their advice, but rather on the fee income they generate from their clients. To resort to a medical analogy, this is equivalent to simply prohibiting doctors from recommending drugs that kill you, while not actually requiring they prescribe the best drugs to cure your disease.

"The world we live in asks us to make an abundance of financial decisions every day. These range from the inane, such as whether to risk a parking ticket when you stop for one minute to drop off your dry-cleaning; to the highly complex, such as which funds and investment products to pick for your retirement savings.

"All of these decisions require risk-return tradeoffs. Unfortunately, while people have many opportunities in life to perfect their strategy concerning parking tickets, the same is not true for the complex and all-important decisions of how to invest retirement savings."

How do you know if the adviser's input can help you make better decisions for yourself in the critical period before you retire?

Although it may seem simplistic, this is the bottom line: Be skeptical.

Advisers are not all equally equipped to handle retirement investing; methodology, strategy, and experience with down market periods in particular are essential. There has to be a special respect for the vulnerable early stages of a retirement portfolio when a sharp downward move in the market can cause irreparable damage. The adviser has to have experience working with clients like you.

Interview a number of advisers to assess their expertise. Hire the adviser whose self-interest is aligned with yours; if incentives drive an adviser to provide recommendations that are self-serving, go elsewhere.

We will continue to see a lot more media attention paid to self-interest and the fiduciary standard for retirement plans as we get closer to the implementation of the Department of Labor's (DOL) new rules in the Spring of 2017.

[2017 update: A final DOL rule is still not implemented as of this writing; however, we expect further developments to occur during 2018 and 2019. Source: https://www.federalregister.gov/documents/2017/11/29/2017-25760/18-month-extension-of-transition-period-and-delay-of-applicability-dates-best-interest-contract]

* * *

In the next column published in October 2007, regulators caution investors about optimistic sales presentations. Protect yourself from fraud by educating yourself.

REGULATORS CAUTION:
BE PREPARED TO BE SOLD

Originally published October 7, 2007

You've seen the ads, and you've received the invitations in the mail: "FREE seminar, FREE meal, FREE advice."

Who would pass up a free meal and a chance to learn how to do the following: "Eliminate taxes on Social Security. Eliminate investment fees. Eliminate market losses. Make your money absolutely safe. Reduce your taxes. Increase your spendable income. Get market-linked returns without market risk. Significantly increase the value of your IRA. Never run out of money. Understand reverse mortgages, trusts, and long-term-care insurance."

A particularly enticing ad—one of my favorites—even promises not to be a sales presentation.

Should you attend such a seminar? If you're tempted, be sure to arm yourself in advance.

Here are some valuable tips provided by the North American Securities Administrators Association (NASAA).

Check out strangers touting strange deals. Trusting strangers is a mistake anyone can make when it comes to his or her personal finances. Say no to any investment professional who presses you to make an immediate decision, giving you no opportunity to check out the salesperson, the firm, and the investment opportunity itself.

Stay in charge of your money. Beware of anyone who suggests investing your money in something you don't understand or who urges that you leave everything in his or her hands.

Watch out for salespeople who prey on your fears. Con artists know that you worry about either outliving your savings or seeing all of your financial resources vanish overnight as the result of a catastrophic event such as a costly hospitalization. Fear can cloud your good judgment.

Don't make a tragedy worse with rash financial decisions. The death or hospitalization of a spouse has many sad consequences; financial fraud shouldn't be one of them. If you find yourself suddenly in charge of your own finances, get the facts before you make any decisions.

Monitor your investments and ask tough questions. Don't compound the mistake of trusting an unscrupulous investment professional by failing to keep an eye on the progress of your investment. Insist on regular written reports. Look for signs of excessive or unauthorized trading of your funds.

Look for trouble retrieving your principal or cashing out profits. If a stockbroker, financial planner, or other individual with whom you have invested stalls when you want to pull out your principal or profits, you have uncovered someone who wants to cheat you. Some kinds of investments have certain periods when you cannot withdraw the funds, but you must be made aware of these kinds of restrictions before you invest.

Don't let embarrassment or fear keep you from reporting investment fraud or abuse. Criminals know that you may hesitate to report that you have been victimized in financial schemes out of embarrassment or fear. Criminals prey on your sensitivities and in fact count on those fears preventing or delaying the point at which authorities are notified of a scam. Every day that you delay reporting fraud or abuse is one more day that the criminal is spending your money and finding new victims.

For more tips, go to nasaa.org and search "seniors."

To see other ads, read "Protecting Senior Investors: Report of Examinations of Securities Firms Providing "Free Lunch" Sales Seminars," which you can find online at sec.gov (search for "free lunch" and refer to Appendix A).

* * *

The next column I wrote in late 2009 offers the AARP's point of view on invitations to free-dinner sales presentations as well as some that I cover in one of my books; the points made then still apply.

THERE STILL IS NO SUCH THING
AS A FREE LUNCH

Originally published November 22, 2009; updated 2017

This intriguing offer appears on an invitation to a free gourmet-meal seminar:

> "A hidden asset most seniors don't know exists
>
> Previously only available to large institutions
>
> Double-digit returns for the past 16 years
>
> No volatility
>
> Major risk factors removed"

The sample invitation accompanies a report titled "Protecting Older Investors: 2009 Free Lunch Seminar Report" issued by the American Association of Retired Persons (AARP). The report reviews the results of an AARP-sponsored national survey conducted from August 19, 2009, through September 3, 2009, by International Communications Research.

Although regulators have been monitoring free-lunch sales presentations over the years, there still is great concern that seniors can be influenced to buy a product or service they may not need when they attend such seminars. As Andres Castillo of the AARP puts it: "Unfortunately, a lot of people think they are getting information when in fact, they are being pushed into investing in products that may not be right for them."

Millions of family decision makers age 55 and older—nearly 6 million—attended such seminars within the last three years, according to the AARP, and people 65 and older were twice as likely to attend the seminars as were those age 55 to 64. The invitation comes in the mail most of the time, followed by phone, and by e-mail.

Among those who attended such a seminar, 78 percent saw the event as "mainly an opportunity to learn more about financial issues." Only

21 percent expected that the seminar would be "mainly an opportunity to buy financial products."

Of course, we know from Securities and Exchange Commission examinations of financial firms that the motivation behind such seminars is to sell something, usually not when people are eating but at a one-on-one presentation afterward. "That's when the real hard sell happens," Castillo said.

The irony is that 61 percent of those surveyed who attended such seminars reported that they were "very concerned" about financial scams and another 26 percent were "somewhat concerned."

You have to wonder what draws seniors into such suspect circumstances.

In preparing to write a book in 2009 (*Retirement Survival Guide: How to Make Smart Financial Decisions in Good Times and Bad*, updated and rereleased in 2017), I reviewed the common products that were presented at such seminars, some of which required the attendees to read contracts and prospectuses that were hundreds of pages long. I also reviewed studies of the influence tactics used at such seminars to get people to buy something so that the meal would not only pay for itself but leave a nice profit for the salesperson.

When you understand how easily one can be influenced and how difficult it is to separate promise from fact when one is subjected to multiple sales tactics, you have to wonder why anyone would attend such a seminar, especially when seeking information about how to invest prudently and safely for retirement.

If you are interested in educating yourself about how someone can trigger a desire to buy something, I'll send you the chapter of *Retirement Survival Guide* that reviews the persuasion techniques used in such circumstances. Once you are aware of them, you'll be able to recognize and avoid them.

If you still want to buy something from a stranger who bought you dinner, be alert.

But if you want to know how I feel about such sales environments, you ask yourself: Is this the best way to engage a financial adviser?

*   *   *

If the regulators invite you to a free dinner presentation, that's another matter. The next column discusses an event sponsored by FINRA in April 2015.

FINANCIAL REGULATORS HOLD A
FREE DINNER PRESENTATION

Originally published April 26, 2015

If you read this column regularly, you've developed a healthy skepticism about financial products and services. The last thing you'll want to do is accept an invitation to a free-dinner presentation to listen to a sales pitch.

Let me tell you about one free-dinner presentation you'll want to attend. Next Tuesday, May 5 (2015), FINRA (the Financial Industry Regulatory Authority) will present "What Every Investor Needs to Know: Smart Investing in Today's Environment" at the Stamford (CT) Marriott at 5:30 pm. FINRA is an independent nongovernmental regulator for all securities firms doing business with the public in the United States. Unlike other free-dinner presentations, there's nothing for sale other than good, solid advice from an unbiased source, one that I turn to often when writing this column.

The goal here is to showcase FINRA's many educational resources and leave the attendees better equipped to recognize fraud, assess and possibly avoid overly complex financial products, and ultimately make wiser investment decisions.

It's no secret that people sometimes base decisions on emotion rather than logic. [Then] FINRA Chairman and CEO Rick Ketchum and Senior Vice President Gerri Walsh will talk about the emotional biases that can keep investors from making smarter decisions.

Ketchum and Walsh also will discuss how to recognize and avoid fraud and offer some guidance on specific products, such as more complex structured products, nontraded real estate investment trusts (often called private REITs), and variable and equity-indexed annuities.

Although the presentation will be valuable to all, it usually draws people age 55 to 65, explained Walsh, in part because that demographic often has accumulated sizable retirement savings and other assets.

Low yields are a particular concern for this age group.

"Low interest rates mean that fixed-income investments no longer pay the yields they paid before the financial crises hit several years ago," said Walsh. "We know that many Americans are still feeling pinched, and we're concerned they might be taking on additional risk by chasing yield."

If you attend the event, you'll get a chance to meet Connecticut Congressman Jim Himes, who will comment on proposals to protect investors. "I have worked hard to make our financial regulatory system better and safer for all investors, from the seasoned professional to the recent graduates and retirees that are working to build their savings," said Himes. "I am pleased to be joining the FINRA investor education forum in Stamford to help equip all of my constituents with the knowledge and tools they need to make sound investment decisions."

Here is one more bit of good news: As of last week (April 2015), there is a new FINRA service for seniors that you need to know about. Now you can call FINRA directly if you feel you need help with an investment question or problem or to get help with FINRA tools and resources. The new program is called the Securities Helpline for Seniors, and it is free. You can call 844-57-HELPS (844-574-3577) between 9 a.m. and 5 p.m. (EST) Monday through Friday to speak with a FINRA representative. I gave it a try today (no, they did not ask my age). The representative was both friendly and competent, and the overall experience met my expectations. For more information, go to http://www.finra.org and search "helpline for seniors."

The IRS Isn't Calling: Scams and Shams

ARE YOU CURIOUS:

- How can you protect yourself from identity theft?

- What can you do to guard your personal information?

- What steps can you take if you or a loved one become victims of a scam?

SECTION PREVIEW:

From time to time, readers of the column reach out to me with questions and concerns about security and the other side of the coin: scams. In this section, I share with you incidents to be aware of and knowledge that will help you avoid being scammed. Although that is sometimes impossible (for example, as a result of the Equifax data breach that occurred in 2017), it is important to know what you can do to protect your identity and guard yourself from attacks.

Scams and shams are nothing new—150 years ago, you would have had to look out for snake oil salesmen while nearly 100 years ago, Charles Ponzi himself was enticing investors with high returns, fueled with other people's money. With the advent of computers, the ease of creating authentic-seeming emails, financial statements, caller-IDs, letterhead, and so on has made it easier to defraud and harder to detect malicious behavior. Therefore, it is as important as ever to know what the thieves are up to and how to protect yourself from their malicious intentions. I hope that all of my readers are able to avoid these issues, but if not, my columns offer advice on steps to protect you from further losses.

*   *   *

You cannot read the newspaper or turn on the TV without hearing about yet another data breach or financial scam. Criminals are using technology to take advantage of unprotected and unsuspecting people. I begin this section with the following column from November 2016 to help establish just how widespread and sophisticated scams are now. Read on to learn how to stay one step ahead of the scam artist and maybe even help stop the scams.

ARRESTS SHED NEW LIGHT ON IRS SCAM

Originally published November 20, 2016; updated 2017

What would you do if you got a call from the Internal Revenue Service telling you that you underpaid your taxes and that as a result a jail cell was waiting for you? What if the agent offered some good news: If you paid the outstanding balance right away, the matter would be resolved in your favor?

At this point, it might cross your mind that the call could be a hoax. You check your caller ID. It confirms the caller as the IRS and the phone number as 800-829-1040.

If you are not familiar with spoofing, you might be convinced. Spoofers take control of your caller ID and transmit a false identity such as the IRS or the local police department or anything that helps them take advantage of trusting people.

As reported by the U.S. Department of Justice (DOJ) a few weeks ago, an IRS impostor scam worked on an 85-year-old victim from San Diego. She followed the impostor's instructions to go to a local drugstore to buy $12,300 worth of debit-like cards and then give the impostors the PIN numbers associated with the cards. (I'm sure you've seen these "prepaid stored-value cards" on stands in local stores.)

A Rochester, New Hampshire, resident paid approximately $3,980 to IRS impostors; they threatened to arrest the victim if he did not pay fines and fees for alleged tax violations. The victim's caller ID showed the caller as "U.S. Government" with a 202 area code.

IRS impostors repeatedly called a Hayward, California, victim over a period of 20 days. The impostors told the victim to buy 276 stored-value cards totaling about $136,000, which he did.

These scams were all part of a very well-orchestrated transnational fraud that ended up costing tens of thousands of U.S. residents hundreds of millions of dollars, according to a DOJ press release on October 27, 2016, available by searching justice.gov for "Indian Call Center Scam").

The fraudsters were caught. Twenty were arrested in the United States, and 32 individuals and five call centers in India were charged. The overseas fraudsters used Voice over Internet Protocol devices to make countless long-distance phone calls over an Internet connection.

According to the DOJ release, the sophisticated fraudulent scheme was organized by conspirators and call centers in India. They obtained their victims' personal information from data brokers. The call-center operators impersonated officials from the IRS or U.S. Citizenship and Immigration Services, threatening "arrest, imprisonment, fines or deportation."

When the victims agreed to make payments, the call-center operators turned to a network of coconspirators who laundered the funds as quickly as possible by using prepaid debit cards. Stolen identities were used to register the cards and transfer money by "criminal associates using fake names and fraudulent identifications."

It's reassuring that transnational frauds can be stopped. According to [then] Assistant Attorney General Leslie Caldwell, the DOJ is "prosecuting the individuals behind these impersonation and telefraud schemes, who seek to profit by exploiting some of the most vulnerable members of our communities."

It's important to know that anyone can be victimized. To protect yourself and elderly family members and friends, you need to spread this message from [then] Executive Associate Director Peter T. Edge of U.S. Immigration and Customs Enforcement's Homeland Security Investigations: "U.S. government agencies do not make these types of calls, and if you receive one, contact law enforcement to report the suspected scam before you make a payment."

By the way, if, after reading this column, you think you may be a victim of this particular scheme, contact the Federal Trade Commission at ftc.gov and click "File a Consumer Complaint."

If you want to know more about telefraud scams or preventing identity theft, go to the scam websites of the IRS and the Federal Trade Commission (FTC). For IRS tax scams, go to irs.gov and search for "tax scams consumer alerts." For FTC phone scams, go to ftc.gov and search for "How to Handle an Unexpected Sales Call." For FTC material on identity theft, go to www.consumer.ftc.gov and search "Recovering from Identity Theft." ▪

*   *   *

Next, I'll share a personal experience with a phishing scam. As you'll see from the next column, the activity was intense and the message was ostensibly about fraud prevention. As the April 2006 column shows, some ne'er-do-wells disguise themselves as helpers.

SCAM ARTISTS USE "PHISHING" TO GET PERSONAL INFORMATION

Originally published April 23, 2006

Here's an e-mail that caught my attention. "You have added John Smith to your Chase account."

Well, that was news to me, since I do not know a John Smith and did not add him to my account.

The e-mail looked legitimate enough, instructing me to contact the bank directly, namely, to get in touch with customer service at a secure website, with a URL that looked official but was fraudulent nonetheless. It was not sent by Chase.

According to a Chase spokesperson, Chase will not send you an e-mail of this sort.

"Phishing has become very sophisticated and it's increasingly harder to distinguish legitimate requests for information from fraudulent phishing," says Claudia Bourne Farrell, [then] spokesperson for the Federal Trade Commission. Phishing is a form of Internet scamming in which the attackers try to trick consumers into divulging sensitive personal information, according to McAfee, Inc., a software provider.

"We advise consumers who receive emails asking for personal identifying information never to click on the link," says Farrell. "They should close the email and contact the organization the way they usually do."

That first e-mail arrived on Monday, April 10 (2006). There is more to the story. The phishing attempt was still in play.

On Tuesday, at 9:34 a.m., I received an identical e-mail. Then, at 11:53 a.m., I received the following e-mail from "Chase Security Service," which again was fraudulent:

"Technical services of the Chase Bank are carrying out planned software upgrade. We earnestly ask you to visit the following link to start the procedure of confirmation on customer data. To get started, please click the link below: [directing me to another official-looking URL].

"This instruction has been sent to all bank customers and is obligatory to follow. We apologize for any inconvenience this may cause and appreciate your assistance in helping us maintain the integrity of the entire Chase system."

At 12:30 p.m. the same day, I got an e-mail from "Chase Online Banking" asking me to update my online records by linking to a secure website.

The next e-mail arrived at 1:08 p.m. from "Chase Security Service," the exact same e-mail I received earlier that day.

At 1:34 p.m., I received another e-mail from "Chase Online Banking," again asking me to update my online records and linking to the same site.

At 2:44, I received another e-mail from "Chase Security Service" identical to the earlier e-mails.

Then, on Friday, April 21, I received another e-mail from "Chase Security Department" on the subject of "Fraud Prevention Measures":

"Due to recent fraudulent activities on some of JPMorgan Chase online accounts, we are launching a new security system to make JPMorgan Chase online accounts more secure and safe. Before we can activate it we will be checking all JPMorgan Chase online accounts to confirm the authenticity of the holder. We will require a confirmation that your account has not been stolen or hacked. Your account has not been suspended or frozen. To confirm your account status please LOGIN. . . . If you find any type of suspicious activities please contact us immediately. Please include in your message your account number, your account name and the unauthorized transfer date and time."

None of these e-mails came from Chase. They came from felons who wanted personal information that they could sell or use themselves to steal funds or identities.

Chase is very much aware of these fraudulent schemes and takes great pains to notify its customers about what they should do. Go to

Chase.com to see additional samples of fraudulent e-mails and advice on how to avoid being scammed.

The spokesperson from Chase explained that phishers target the customers of large companies and send out millions of e-mails, hoping to reach a Chase customer who is trusting enough to reply to the e-mail.

Any time you receive an e-mail from an official-looking source (even the IRS), do not respond. Instead, contact the source directly by the phone number on your card or statement.

You also have to be careful when you log on to an official site. According to an April 17, 2006, alert posted to the Internet Crime Complaint Center, the FBI has been alerted to a newly discovered vulnerability of a popular web browser that hijacks you to a fraudulent site. The attacker displays the address bar of the legitimate website while actually displaying a phishing web page. Go to ic3.gov/media/2006/060417.htm for more information.

If that's not enough to keep you worried, there is a new scheme that holds your files hostage by installing malicious software, such as Cryzip on your computer, according to the FBI. When run, Cryzip searches the hard drive for files it can zip and encrypt and hold hostage. To get access to your files, you need a password that will cost you $300.

"Use spam filters and other security measures to keep trash out of your email," says Farrell. File a complaint and find consumer information from the FTC at 1-877-FTCHelp.

To protect yourself, go to ic3.gov/preventiontips.aspx for a list of Internet frauds and prevention tips. Another excellent site is onguardonline.gov. ▓

*   *   *

The next column from February 2014 is about a mail scam that came with congratulations.

CONGRATULATIONS, YOU WON A MILLION DOLLARS

Originally published February 9, 2014

A reader of this column—I'll call her Eva—contacted me about a letter she received in the mail congratulating her on winning $1 million. When she called the phone number listed in the letter as directed, she was told that all she had to do to claim the prize was mail in a cashier's check or money order for $2,000 as a processing fee. She did, but the $1 million has yet to arrive.

This type of fraudulent scheme is not unknown to law enforcement.

Each year, thousands of people complain to the Federal Trade Commission about fraudulent contests and sweepstakes. The FTC warns that legitimate contests don't require winners to pay a fee to process the winnings.

Here is a twist to the story.

Two years later, Eva was still receiving letters notifying her of more winnings. She still believed that she was due the announced prize money, which she was eager to receive to help her family.

Then Eva received a phone call from a person whom I'll call Ed, who said he was with the FBI. He advised Eva that the authorities were pursuing criminals who were perpetrating fraudulent prize schemes on unsuspecting retirees.

Eva was shattered.

She sat down at her kitchen table and collected all the prize notifications she had received as well as receipts for all the money she had mailed in to claim the prizes—more than $100,000 in all—with no winnings to compensate.

Ed went into action. He advised Eva to change her phone number and resist the urge to send in any more money in the hopes of winning prize money.

He offered to help her extricate herself from potential harm by notifying credit bureaus and the authorities. He and a team of agents would take care of everything for $50,000.

Now Eva was alarmed. Who was Ed?

There are laws to protect people from fraudulent promotions. The Deceptive Mail Prevention and Enforcement Act prohibits companies from claiming that you're a winner unless you've actually won a prize. Also, there are laws prohibiting the impersonation of an FBI agent, according to an FBI spokeswoman.

Government agencies—including the FBI—never send e-mails or call people to threaten arrest, ask for money, or request personal information, explained Jaclyn M. Falkowski, director of communications for the Office of the Attorney General of Connecticut.

It is important to realize that if you have to pay to receive your prize, it's not a prize at all. Also, the FTC says that people should be aware that scammers use a "variation of an official or nationally recognized name to give you confidence in their offers. Don't be deceived by these 'look-alikes.' It's illegal for a promoter to misrepresent an affiliation with—or an endorsement by—a government agency or other well-known organization." Be alert to any toll-free 800 number that directs you to dial a pay-per-call 900 number, which can run up very high charges.

One more point: Don't give your checking account or credit card account number over the phone in response to a sweepstakes promotion. It's a surefire way to get scammed in the future, warns the FTC.

If you are scammed like Eva, what can you do?

Act immediately, said Falkowski. Place a fraud alert or credit freeze on your credit report, contact any financial institutions for which you provided information, and be "extra wary" of all future solicitations, as scammers sometimes will share personal information from their victims with other scammers. (Go to consumer.ftc.gov for information on how to do this.)

Report the fraud to your local police department and file a complaint with the FTC (ftc.gov), the Internet Crime Complaint Center (IC3) (for Internet scams: ic3.gov), and your state's office of the attorney general, explained Falkowski. You'll find a list of state attorneys general through the National Association of Attorneys General at naag.org.

Before you react to a call, letter, or e-mail congratulating you on winning a prize, do yourself a favor by reading the FTC's information-packed press releases on their website consumer.ftc.gov, by searching for both "prize scams" and "government impostor scams." ▨

*   *   *

Many of the scams and schemes I have spoken about so far are perpetuated by anonymous faces and names in far away lands. But not every scam artist is anonymous. Acquaintances can and do take advantage of unsuspecting and trusting investors. Hopefully these case studies from September 2012 will help you stay safe and aware. And remember . . . no investment is risk free.

EVEN THOSE YOU KNOW CAN DEFRAUD

Originally published September 2, 2012

Investors can be lured into fraudulent schemes by miscreants. See if you could be taken in by reading these case studies posted by the SEC's Office of Investor Education and Advocacy on Investor.gov. The names are fictional.

SEC Case Study 1

Robert loves the Internet. He belongs to all the social networking sites, and his extensive network is a source of pride. He is linked to everyone.

Recently, he began to get messages from a friend of a friend about a new biotech stock. This friend was sharing his insider information that the biotech company was about to get government approval for one of its drugs, and its stock was going to skyrocket. According to the friend, the stock, currently selling at $1.50 a share, could go as high as $25 per share. The friend urged everyone to get in quickly, because once the FDA announced its decision the following week, it would be too late.

A buying frenzy began. Robert knew of three other friends who also bought the stock. Robert took out a loan to buy 1,000 shares of the stock and dreamed of what he was going to do with the profits. As the friend predicted, the stock began rising. In two days, it had reached $5 per share. Robert was sure a new car was his.

But just as quickly, the stock fell to $1 per share, resulting in losses for recent investors. What happened? Why wasn't Robert rich? He was a victim of a "pump and dump" scheme. How does it work?

- The promoters claim to have "infallible" information about an impending positive development for the company.

- In reality, it is the stock promoters who stand to gain by selling their shares after the stock price is "pumped" up.

- Once these fraudsters "dump" their shares and stop hyping the stock, the price typically falls, and investors lose their money.

Lessons learned:

- Do your own research. Never buy from a stock tip without thoroughly researching the stock. Use the SEC's EDGAR database to read the company's latest filings.

- If it sounds too good to be true, it probably is.

- All investments carry risks; no stock is a sure thing.

SEC Case Study 2

Aiesha lives in Brooklyn, New York, and is active in her church. Last June, she was approached by a fellow church member about an investment opportunity that he said was too good to miss.

The man said he was a successful money manager and represented GTF Enterprises Inc., a firm comprising "extremely knowledgeable strategists with years of experience working with top financial firms on Wall Street." Aiesha wasn't sure what strategists did, but she figured they had to be smart and important.

Aiesha also was told that:

- GTF practices "sound and careful" investing in options, futures, commodities, and other investment products.

- Investments are risk-free—GTF assumes all of the trading risks.

- GTE guarantees investors will earn between four percent and 20 percent per quarter.

She initially invests $5,000. Each quarter, she receives account statements showing high returns. Based on the account statements and pressure from other church members, she withdraws all the money from her savings account and invests it with GTF.

But if it sounds too good to be true, it usually is. Soon she learns that she has lost her entire life savings. She is a victim of affinity fraud, a type of scam that preys upon members of groups such as religious people, ethnic communities, the elderly, or professional groups.

Lessons learned:

- Don't be taken in by people just because they are a member of your group or seem to have the group's support.

- Check out the investment professional. Had Aiesha done this, she would have learned that the man who approached her was not a money manager and was not registered with the SEC, New York State's securities regulator, or FINRA, and that GTF "strategists" did not have years of Wall Street experience.

- Be extremely leery of any investment that is said to have no risks; no investment is risk-free.

- Don't fall for investments that promise spectacular profits or guaranteed returns.

For more, go to investor.gov/investing-basics/avoiding-fraud/case-studies.

If you find yourself in a situation in which you may have fallen for a fraud, you can contact the SEC's Office of Investor Education and Advocacy, which is manned with "investor assistance specialists" who can address questions and complaints. The telephone number is 800-SEC-0330. ▪

* * *

Now, let me warn you about scams that target children in this next column from October 2011, updated for 2017.

CHILDREN CAN BE VICTIMS OF
IDENTITY THEFT TOO

Originally published October 23, 2011; updated 2017

Parents may not realize that even babies can be victims of identity theft.

In fact, children are more likely to have their identities stolen than adults are. According to Carnegie Mellon CyLab's (cylab.cmu.edu) recent report on child identity theft, "unused social security numbers are uniquely valuable as thieves can pair them with any name and birth date."

The stolen Social Security numbers are used for "illegal immigration (e.g. to obtain false IDs for employment), organized crime (e.g. to engage in financial fraud) and friends and family (e.g. to circumvent bad credit ratings, etc.)."

According to Cylab, "one reason that minor social security numbers are so valuable is that there is currently no process or organization, like an employee or creditor, to check what name and birth date is officially attached to that social security number. As long as an identity thief has a social security number with a clean history, the thief can attach any name and date of birth to it."

To read the report, "Child Identity Theft: New Evidence Indicates Identity Thieves Are Targeting Children for Unused Social Security Numbers," go to cylab.cmu.edu.

Once there is a breach, it may go unnoticed. Traditional credit reports don't do the job in uncovering theft, since thieves don't typically use the child's name, only his or her Social Security number.

To raise your awareness of the issues at hand, take this quiz, which is provided courtesy of National Foundation for Credit Counseling (NFCC). The NFCC is the nation's largest financial counseling organization.

1. True or false? Children are at low risk for identity theft.

False—Anyone with a Social Security number assigned to him or her is at risk for identity theft. Because Social Security numbers are commonly assigned to children at a very young age, even newborn children are at risk for identity theft. In fact, children are 51 times more likely to be a victim of identity theft than is an adult.

2. True or false? Parents don't need to check for identity theft until a child is 16.

False—The longer child identity theft builds up on a child's record, the longer and more complex the case can be to resolve. Parents should check their children's Social Security numbers for identity theft starting when they're young so that they can identify signs of fraud and work to clean up their record. If you wait until a child is older, the fraud could affect the child's ability to get a job, apply for school loans, or get a mobile phone or apartment.

3. True or false? A child's credit record is wiped clean when he or she turns 18.

False—When a child becomes of age (frequently prior to age 18) and starts applying for accounts that review a credit history, the child is held responsible for debts and accounts attached to his or her Social Security number regardless of whether the child opened the accounts. This means that child identity theft has a real impact on a child's future—from getting a job to applying for student loans.

4. True or false? Receiving preapproved credit offers for your child in the mail is a sign of child identity theft.

True—One of the first signals that a child may be a victim of identity theft is receiving preapproved credit offers in the mail. If your child ever receives offers like this, you need to investigate further to see if your child is a victim.

5. True or false? The most common causes of child identity theft are friends and family using a child's Social Security number and criminals selling valuable child Social Security numbers on the black market.

True—Criminals find child Social Security numbers to be extremely valuable because the crime of child identity theft can be difficult to detect. In addition, friends and family using a child's Social Security number (called "friendly fraud") is a leading cause of child identity theft.

6. True or false? A child can be a victim of identity theft prior to birth.

True—When Social Security numbers are assigned to children, there is no way to check and see if they have been used by criminals, or by mistake by other adults, to establish a history for the SSN.

7. True or false? You can request a credit report to check for signs of child identity theft.

False—A regular credit report can detect only 1 percent of child identity theft. This is because credit reports check for a full match of name, birthday, and Social Security number, but child identity theft is most commonly a result of someone using *just* a child's Social Security number and attaching it to a new name and birth date.

If you want to check to be sure that a child's identity has not been compromised, AllClear ID provides parents with a means of doing so. The free service is available at allclearid.com/child. [2017 update: AllClear ID is a technology leader in the consumer and corporate identity market.]

* * *

The next column published in August 2009 discusses debt relief scams and sets out cautions provided by the Federal Trade Commission.

BE WARY OF DEBT RELIEF CLAIMS

Originally published August 9, 2009

In financial distress and getting ready to respond to "Are you in debt? We can help" ads on the radio and TV? Getting calls at home with offers to settle your debts for 10 cents on the dollar?

If you talk to people in the know, they'll tell you to stay clear of these debt settlement services because they may be costly, may be harmful to your credit score, and may lead to bigger financial problems down the road—and some may be out-and-out frauds.

"Consumers don't understand what they are getting into," explained Gail Cunningham, vice president of public relations for the National Foundation for Credit Counseling, "and they might turn up worse off than they began."

These debt relief companies may instruct consumers to cut off communications with their creditors, said Cunningham. Some even give you change of address labels to use when mail comes in from a creditor. The address change forwards all future correspondence to the debt settlement company, leaving the consumer in the dark about progress or the lack of it. The company may even provide the consumer with a script to read if the creditor calls, Cunningham explained.

This can go on for months, Cunningham continued. Then collections begin, possibly including garnishment of wages and a suit for judgment against the debt. All along the consumer is unaware because all the mail from the creditor is bypassing him or her and going to the debt settlement company.

Many of these services collect their fees up front before delivery of services (for example, $4,500 on a $30,000 debt), during which time no money goes to creditors. Interest and penalties are piling up, and your credit score is dropping, which affects your future ability to borrow, all without your knowledge.

You also may be told that you can settle your debt without any negative impact on your credit or that the credit bureau will remove negative information about you after you settle your debts. The Federal Trade Commission warns that this is not the case. By law, creditors must provide information about delinquencies to credit-reporting agencies, and this will affect your credit report negatively.

That's why the FTC warns that you should stay clear of anyone who claims the following:

- Creditors don't sue consumers if they don't pay their credit card debts.

- Nothing negative will appear on your credit report if you use their services.

- They can have negative information deleted from your credit report.

Cunningham recommends using a debt settlement service only after ruling out other options for all these reasons and one more: If you want to negotiate a settlement of your debt by offering a lower amount than what you owe, which is what debt settlement is all about, you can do that yourself, and it won't cost you anything.

Here are some tips:

- Continue to make your minimum payments.

- When you call your creditor, ask for the debt settlement department.

- Advise the creditor that you would like to pay 100 percent of what you owe but cannot, stating the reason. Don't try to hide anything. Creditors know more about your finances and credit than you do.

- Negotiate with the creditor. The creditor will work with you because it wants to get paid. See if you can work out a deal: Offer to pay one-half or more of the debt in exchange for a settlement.

- Be prepared for a serious hit to your credit score.

Connecticut takes a hard line against those who mislead consumers. At a news conference earlier in the year, [then] State Attorney General Richard Blumenthal commented on proposed legislation to fight fraudulent practices: "Rescue predators pitch a variety of financial snake oil—promises to stop foreclosures and save homes, reduce mortgages and erase credit card debt, eliminate back tax obligations and rehabilitate bad credit histories. Most charge up-front or advance fees—only deepening debt. Debt reducers promise homeowners help but deliver only hardship. They leave consumers out of cash and out of luck—and even out of their homes. As economic woes worsen, financial bottom-feeders become more prevalent and pernicious."

When the subprime mortgage loan business dried up, said State Senator Bob Duff, D–Norwalk, a lot of people from those operations started becoming debt reducers. The new law, which goes into effect in October, requires debt negotiators to be licensed. They must provide a written contract to the debtor that spells out a detailed list of services, and the debtor can cancel the contract within a three-day period. The law also prohibits the debt negotiator from charging for services until they are performed.

Bottom line: "Don't fall for false promises," Duff said. "Do your homework before signing on to debt management services."

The FTC can be reached at 1-877-FTC-HELP (1-877-382-4357). To locate nonprofit credit counseling agencies, go to nfcc.org, a website maintained by the National Foundation for Credit Counseling. ▪

*　*　*

Identity theft has become a problem, most recently with the Equifax data breach that affected more than 143 million Americans in 2017. The next column, which was originally published in 2014 and updated in 2017, discusses earlier breaches. What you need to do if your identity has been compromised remains the same.

WAYS TO FIGHT IDENTITY THEFT

Originally published February 2, 2014; updated 2017

Since the Fall (2013), when Target and Neiman Marcus reported unauthorized access to payment card data, the possibility of identity theft has been on the minds of consumers. (In 2017, Equifax, a credit-reporting agency, also was compromised, exposing 143 Americans' personal information [source: equifaxsecurity2017.com].)

Thieves steal personal information such as your name and address, Social Security number, and date of birth to commit fraud by, for example, getting a loan in your name.

The first line of defense is to be informed. The best source for information on how to protect yourself is the Federal Trade Commission, a federal agency whose mission is consumer protection and law enforcement.

The FTC website (consumer.ftc.gov) provides a series of action steps for those whose identity has been compromised as well as preventive measures you can take to protect yourself.

Next, contact one of the three national credit-reporting companies: Equifax (equifax.com, 866-349-5191), Experian (experian.com, 888-397-3742), and TransUnion (transunion.com, 800-680-7289).

If your identity has been stolen, you'll want to place an "initial fraud alert" on your credit file to prevent new accounts being opened in your name, according to TransUnion spokesman Cliff O'Neal.

The fraud alert is intended to raise a cautionary flag for creditors to make sure they are dealing with you instead of a scammer. The initial alert lasts for "at least" 90 days but can be renewed. An alert with one bureau will trigger alerts with the other two. There is no charge for placing an alert.

To get an "extended alert" for seven years, you'll need to provide an identity-theft report after filing a report with a law enforcement agency.

To read more about fraud alerts, visit identitytheft.gov. You should also request that a credit bureau send you a credit report. Under the Fair Credit Reporting Act, everyone is entitled to receive one free report every 12 months. You'll want to review each and every item on the report to make certain fraudsters aren't using your identity to borrow money in your name. You can request a free report at annualcreditreport.com.

If you have not been a victim but would like some protection, ask a credit bureau for a "security freeze," which puts a complete block on your credit report indefinitely, that is, until you ask that the freeze be lifted either permanently or temporarily. If you request a freeze with one credit bureau, you'll also need to contact the others, since a freeze is not shared among them.

If you intend to apply for credit during the freeze period, you'll have to communicate with the credit bureaus to lift the freeze temporarily so that your legitimate creditors can access information. You can do this online.

Bureaus may charge a modest fee for a freeze depending on the state you live in. For example, in California the initial request fee is $10 ($0 if you are 65 or older); lift requests are $10 each if you are under 65 and $5 each if you are 65 or older. Connecticut charges $10 for the initial request if you are under 62; it is free for those 62 or older. Lift requests are also $10 in Connecticut if you are under 62; no charge if 62 or older. New York's initial request is free, but it costs $5 for subsequent requests. There is no fee if you are an identity-theft victim; there is no cost to remove a freeze.

You can find a list of all states and all fees charged on the TransUnion website (go to transunion.com and search "Credit Freeze Fees"). You also may consider signing up for monitoring services with one of the credit bureaus. For example, TransUnion provides monitoring for $19.95 a month, which includes identity-theft insurance that covers certain expenses during the time you take corrective action as a result of identity theft. According to their websites, Equifax charges $16.95 a month and Experian charges $9.99 for basic protection and $19.99

for premium level. [2017 update: As a result of the cybersecurity incident, Equifax offered all U.S. consumers identity theft protection and credit file monitoring through TrustedID Premier at no charge to the consumer.]

Another step is to opt out of credit offers that are based on your credit record. You can do that by going to optoutprescreen.com or by calling 888-5-OPT-OUT (888-567-8688). You can choose to opt out for five years or permanently.

You also can opt out of mail lists produced by the Direct Marketing Association by registering at DMAchoice.org. There is a $2 processing fee for this service. To reduce telemarketing calls, register with the National Do Not Call Registry at donotcall.gov or call 1-888-382-1222.

More than 17.6 million Americans were victims of identity theft in 2014, up from 11.7 million from January 2006 through June 2008, according to the Bureau of Justice Statistics. [2017 update: For more current statistics, go to bjs.gov. Search for "identity theft."] ▪

*   *   *

You would expect it to be relatively easy to obtain a report that contains all your personal financial information. The reality is quite the opposite. As with all the columns in this section, there are scams to look out for even with something as simple as requesting a report. The next column from September 2016 provides detailed steps to follow to review your credit and to achieve some peace of mind.

DO'S AND DON'TS OF GETTING
YOUR CREDIT REPORT

Originally published September 4, 2016; updated 2017

We've all seen advertisements for "free" credit reports. A reader of this column wants guidance: "I would appreciate if you could let me know how I safely could obtain my three credit scores from the three main credit bureaus, such as Experian, without paying for them. In the near future I plan to be making some purchases, which I believe, after reading your most recent column, will be impacted by my credit scores."

There is a federal law called the Fair Credit Reporting Act (FCRA) that governs credit reporting. That's where the free-credit-report requirement comes from: You have a right to a free report every 12 months upon request.

Most people are aware that there are three national credit-reporting companies: Equifax, Experian, and TransUnion. You would think that a person could contact any one of them to get a free credit report, but that is not the case. Instead, you'll need to contact annualcreditreport.com online, or by mail (Central Source LLC, P.O. Box 105283, Atlanta, GA 30348-5283). This resource was set up by the three credit-reporting companies to handle requests for free annual credit reports.

No matter which approach you use (online, or mail), you'll need to provide the following information: name, current address (and possibly previous addresses), date of birth, and Social Security number. Usually, if you go the online route, you'll be able to get your credit report right away. You'll have to wait about 15 days if you order the report by mail.

Should you use other sources? The question is, Why would you want to? There are impostor websites that could compromise your identity, according to the Federal Trade Commission, the nation's consumer protection agency.

The FTC wants you to know the following: "Other websites that claim to offer 'free credit reports,' 'free credit scores' or 'free credit monitoring' are not part of the legally mandated free annual credit report program. In some cases, the 'free' product comes with strings attached." This quote is from "Free Credit Reports," which can be found by going to consumer.ftc.gov and clicking "Get Your Free Credit Report."

"For example, some sites sign you up for a supposedly 'free' service that converts to one you have to pay for after a trial period. If you don't cancel during the trial period, you may be unwittingly agreeing to let the company start charging fees to your credit card."

Be careful when you go to log in to annualcreditreport.com. The FTC warns that there are impostors that "purposely misspell annual-creditreport.com in the hope that you will mistype the name of the official site. Some of these impostor sites direct you to other sites that try to sell you something or collect your personal information."

By the way, if you receive an e-mail from annualcreditreport.com (or if you see a pop-up ad, or get a phone call from someone claiming to be from annualcreditreport.com or any of the three nationwide credit-reporting companies), do not reply or click on any link in the message. "It's probably a scam," according to the FTC. If you receive an e-mail like this, you'll want to forward it to the FTC at spam@uce.gov.

Why Bother Checking Your Credit Report?

Credit reports are used by banks, finance companies, and others that are trying to decide whether you have the financial wherewithal to pay interest on a timely basis and repay a loan when it comes due. They include your address, employer, debts, bankruptcies, lawsuits, and creditors.

Check the data in your report periodically for two reasons. First, if you need to apply for credit, you'll want to make sure that your data is accurate; errors do occur. Second is to detect identity theft. If a fraudster steals your identity and applies for credit in your name, you'll notice it on your report, especially if the accounts go unpaid.

To learn how to correct errors on your credit report or to better understand how to improve your credit, read the FTC's guide titled "Building a Better Credit Report," which you can find online, consumer. ftc.gov/articles/pdf-0032-building-a-better-credit-report.pdf.

Financial Literacy Starts Early

ARE YOU CURIOUS:

- How should you teach children the tenets of saving and the responsible use of credit?

- What is the true cost of college and what do you need to know about the "value" of a particular college?

- Will you have to pay the full "sticker price" for college?

SECTION PREVIEW:

This section includes advice about must-have conversations with children and young adults about their financial futures, including the importance of saving and avoiding mistakes when borrowing money. We'll talk about the importance of including children in the decision to fund their college educations and explore some tools that can help determine whether a college is a good value, that is, whether it is worth the cost of attendance. We'll also explore tools that can help you figure out the "net price" of college, how to make college more affordable, and how to file loan applications.

INSIDER'S PERSPECTIVE:

The National Financial Educator's Council asked over 1,000 people aged 18–24 "What high school-level course would benefit your life the most?" 51.4 percent said, "Money management." When FINRA's National Financial Capability Study asked student loan holders "If you could go through the process of taking out loans to pay for your education all over again, would you take the same actions or make a change?" Fifty-three percent said they would do things differently. Until we can make financial literacy a required high school course, there is much that we as role models can do to ensure that young adults are prepared to launch into full independence.

*   *   *

I selected the first column of the section to set the stage for the importance of financial literacy today: many Millennials find themselves with overwhelming levels of debt that could have been avoided had they been educated about the relationship between cost and value. The need was such that in 2014 the Treasury Department created the President's Advisory Council on Financial Capability for Young Americans, which I discuss in the next column. The council completed the term in 2015.

PREPARING YOUNG AMERICANS
FOR THEIR FINANCIAL FUTURE

Originally published April 13, 2014; updated 2017

Considering that April is Financial Literacy Month, there is no better time to shine a light on the need for education, especially for young Americans.

The U.S. Treasury reported on April 10 (2014) that there is a "lack of research on the efficacy of financial education, especially for young elementary and middle school children." However, there are a number of government and private initiatives under development.

At the highest levels, President Barack Obama created the President's Advisory Council on Financial Capability for Young Americans. The council met for the first time on March 10, 2014, in Washington, D.C., at the Treasury Department.

[Then] Treasury Secretary Jack Lew set the tone. He said that President Obama established the council to advise him on "an issue of profound importance to the future of our economy: the financial capability of America's young people."

He explained, "Whether it is teenagers deciding how to spend their first paycheck, college students making crucial decisions about how to repay their student loans or new parents trying to save for a child's education and their own retirement—helping young Americans build a sound financial foundation is not only important for their futures, it can also strengthen our economy for generations to come." You can find a webcast of Secretary Lew's comments at treas.yorkcast.com/webcast/Play/96be254b59c14a59a2e9654af37f760d1d.

The council's aim is to encourage building the financial capability of young people at an early stage in schools, families, communities, and the workplace and through the use of technology.

Importantly from my perspective, the council will "identify and test promising and tested approaches for increasing planning, saving, and investing for retirement by young people; and promote the importance of starting to plan and act early for financial success broadly among Americans through public awareness campaigns or other means."

My personal belief is that young adults can reap great benefits if they are educated when they start to make financial decisions on their own.

When college students start to receive credit card offers in the mail, they need to be prepared to reject them or to pay bills in full as they come in. Before students borrow money to pay tuition, they need to understand their repayment obligations and evaluate whether there are better, lower-cost alternatives to fund their education. They also must consider the bigger-picture question: Will the education lead to a good job?

Those who don't explore these basic questions can wind up with too much debt or engage in costly borrowing behaviors.

According to a recently released study, close to half (46 percent) of Millennials were concerned that they had too much debt. Forty-three percent engaged in costly nonbank forms of borrowing in the last five years, such as pawnshops and payday lenders. The study, which is titled "The Financial Capability of Young Adults—A Generational View," was released last month (March 2014) by the FINRA Investor Education Foundation. It concluded that Millennials "display low levels of financial literacy, engage in problematic financial behaviors and express concerns about their debt."

"Many Millennials began their adult lives in the midst of the worst economic downturn in generations, and our survey reveals just how deeply and broadly the Great Recession has marked the financial lives of this generation of Americans," said FINRA Foundation President Gerri Walsh. "Unfortunately, far too many Millennials trying to cope with these economic conditions have low levels of financial literacy and are wrestling with concerns about their debt."

For more information on the study, see usfinancialcapability.org.

[2017 update: You can find the Council's final 2015 report at treasury.gov.] ▦

*   *   *

The next column from September 2013 discussed how to teach children about financial independence. Because of the impact that a college education can have on income, there are a number of decisions that children need help making well before they enroll. For that reason, in this section, I'm sharing a number of columns to help locate and finance a valuable college experience. Here is a preview of what's coming:

- *"Preparing Young Americans for their Financial Future" addresses this question: Will the education lead to a good job?*

- *"Involve Youngsters in College Funding Talks" puts current numbers on published prices for schools, and discusses sources of funding, such as grants and scholarships.*

- *"Figuring Out the True Cost of College" provides a framework for thinking about how to pay for college: past (savings), present (current wages), and future obligations (loans).*

- *"Sort Through the Value of Potential College Choices" walks you through an essential tool called the College Scorecard to arrive at schools worth considering.*

- *"A College Degree is a Good Investment" shines a light on how important education can be to future income.*

TEACH CHILDREN THE IMPORTANCE OF SAVING

Originally published September 15, 2013

Survey data tells us that people are worried about the financial capabilities of their children and grandchildren. Educational costs are a concern because some retirees are helping their grandchildren pay for college. Adult children are moving in with their parents. Jobs are hard to find.

None of this is news, of course, but it raises doubts about how well we are doing as parents when it comes to teaching children about work and money. It also raises the question: With the benefit of hindsight, is there anything you would do differently if you had the chance for a do-over in your life?

What do you know about money now that you wish you knew when you were younger?

Here are some thoughts:

First, everyone makes hundreds of financial decisions regularly, ranging from what groceries to buy, to whether to take a long drive, to what beverage to drink. Although your circumstances may dictate your income, you decide what to spend and what to save. As a result, you may have more control over your financial destiny than you think, and it might pay to spend some time making financial literacy a priority early in life.

Second, parents need to understand that buying things for their children may make them feel good about themselves, but it does not make a child a better person. Children will not remember you as a good parent because you indulged them with toys and gifts. They may learn to be self-indulgent. However, spending time with children to create good memories costs nothing.

Third, children are a significant long-term financial commitment that may last well beyond the age at which they should be independent. Nowadays, you have to be prepared to have them move back home after college. "Good parents" will keep the door open to help children in need at any point in their lifetimes. Is the opposite true? Do "bad parents" produce self-reliant children? Or is there a happy medium where children learn financial values?

Fourth, it's natural for young families to focus their energies primarily on the present needs of their members. If you do that, time will fly by. Before you know it, your children will be grown and on their own, and you'll need to start thinking about your own needs and resources. But will you be sufficiently on track in securing your own financial future?

Fifth, money is a natural part of everyone's life. It's just a tool, and everyone needs to know how to use it. Only with hindsight do people know that it's not enough to save what's left over after paying the monthly bills. It's smarter to envision the future and set priorities to save money over a lifetime. Then there will be no regrets about not starting early enough.

Sixth, when surveyed, people say that they regret saving too little and starting too late. The most effective way to save for retirement is to save consistently each month over a lifetime. The earlier the start, the higher the payoff. The amounts do not have to be large, however.

Even $100 a month saved over a 35-year period can turn into a sizable nest egg. A 30-year-old who invests that amount in a solid balanced fund can reasonably expect to approach a million dollars by the time she retires. The total investment over that time is only $42,000. The power behind those numbers is the math of compounding.

Seventh, investors make mistakes when markets decline by losing heart and selling out when they should be continuing their investment program. Fear should not dictate investment decisions.

*   *   *

The next column, also published in 2013, and updated for 2017, highlights the importance of including children in the decision to fund their college education. I wrote about what you need to know generally, and provided links to a number of resources that will put in stark numbers the costs of various college decisions.

INVOLVE YOUNGSTERS IN
COLLEGE FUNDING TALKS

Originally published September 29, 2013; updated 2017

Did you know that families whose children will go to college at some point are better prepared if they include their children in funding conversations? So concludes Fidelity's seventh annual College Savings Indicator study, which was conducted by the independent research firm Research Data Technology.

Ninety-three percent of families that included their children in those conversations at a young age (under 10) started saving for college. Among those who reported not talking with their children about college at all, only 58 percent started saving for college.

The families that engaged their children are on to something.

The major factor in making college affordable, as with any other major expense, is planning. The sooner you start, the better.

What do you need to know?

First, you have pricing options. A private college will cost more than a public in-state college. A commuter will save money compared with an on-campus student.

If you add together tuition, room and board, fees, books, supplies, transportation, and other expenses, the average cost of earning a bachelor's degree from a private college is about $50,000 per year, compared with about $25,000 for an in-state public college, according to the 2017–2018 College Board's Annual Survey of Colleges.

Second (this may surprise you), you don't need to pay the full price. The actual cost the average family really pays (called the "net price" by the College Board) can be substantially less than the sticker price.

The sticker price for tuition and fees for a four-year public college is $9,970 (2017), according to the College Board, but the net price is only $4,410 (2017). For a private four-year college, the sticker price is $34,740 (2017), but the net price is just $14,530 (2017). These are figures for full-time, first-time students in 2017–2018.

Third, "grant aid" makes up the difference between sticker price and net price. Grant aid is money awarded on the basis of financial need or academic achievement—grants and scholarships from different sources, such as federal and state government, private sources, and colleges themselves—and does not have to be repaid. In 2017–2018, more than 70 percent of full-time college students received grant aid.

You can see why parents need to start preparing college-bound children in more ways than one, and they need to start early, ideally before the children reach age 10.

You don't want the alternative, which is leaving things until a child reaches age 17, when college road trips begin in earnest. Procrastinating can lead to last minute Band-Aids such as loans. It also can lead to decisions that are based on personal preferences (campus location or size of the student body) instead of value.

To get started, parents should think about what they expect the child to get out of college. To get a degree? To reach the next level of socialization? To prepare for a fulfilling and successful career?

This process will help the child crystallize goals and career possibilities while identifying strengths and interests that will open up grant opportunities. Most important, the child can experience firsthand how preparation can lead to success; that is a valuable life lesson.

Here are some helpful tools to use in the process.

To learn more about college costs, go to trends.collegeboard.org/college-pricing/figures-tables/average-estimated-undergraduate-budgets-2017–18. For information on grants and scholarships, go to collegeboard.org and search for "The Basics on Grants and Scholarships." On the same website, you can find a good resource for college funding by searching for "Things You Need to Know About Net Price." To figure net price, use the calculator at studentnpc.collegeboard.org.

Make a stop at Fidelity's College Savings Resource Center at fidelity.com/college, where you'll find a wealth of information on cost, planning, funding, and saving. As Keith Bernhardt, vice president of college planning at Fidelity, says, preparation is the key. ▪

*   *   *

We all know that the full cost of college has skyrocketed well ahead of just about any metric for inflation. But did you know that some families pay the "sticker price" and some don't? In the next column (September 2015, updated for 2017), I go through essential resources for parents and students who don't want to incur debt to pay for college.

FIGURING OUT THE TRUE COST OF COLLEGE

Originally published September 6, 2015; updated 2017

Since September is National College Savings Month, let's talk about kids and college.

In some families, the parents cover the entire cost of college. In others, the college student pays 100 percent by working his way through school and possibly taking out loans (you have to ask yourself whether this student might have a better appreciation for the educational experience). In still others—and this is the most prevalent—paying for college is a joint effort between parents and students.

According to Sallie Mae's 2017 National Study of College Students and Parents, "How America Pays for College," the largest share is covered by scholarships and grants (35 percent of the cost). Parents pay 31 percent (down from 36 percent in 2015). Nineteen percent is supplied by student borrowing, and eight percent by parent borrowing. Eleven percent comes from the student's income and savings. Relatives and friends contribute 4 percent. To see the study, go to SallieMae.com/HowAmericaPaysForCollege.

In a 2017 survey published by Discover (investorrelations.discover.com, search "Parents Prioritize Academics Over Cost When Considering Their Child's College"), 74 percent of the parents surveyed are planning to help pay for college (down from 81 percent in 2013). Twenty-six percent are not worried about having enough money to pay for college. Twenty-nine percent say most of the money required to pay for college will come from student loans.

Just how much will college cost? Lots if the cost continues to increase faster than the rate of inflation.

Fidelity, the financial services corporation, has a college savings calculator online at fidelity.com/misc/college-savings/college_savings.html. You insert your child's age, what percent of the cost that you want to be covered by savings, how much you've already saved, and what you intend to save each month going forward. The planner will give you the annual cost and calculate the savings required to reach the amount needed for a four-year college stint.

For example, for a one-year-old born in 2016, college would begin in 2034 and end in 2038. For a private college, the Fidelity calculator indicates an annual cost of $45,370 in today's (2017) dollars, based on the national average for four-year private colleges.

Say you have $5,000 tucked away for your one-year old. According to the calculator, that would cover only three percent of your child's private four-year tuition. [2017 update: The calculation is based on the following assumptions for the 2016–2017 academic year: average total annual charges at a four-year private college of $45,370; you are saving no additional amounts on a monthly basis; you intend to pay for all of your child's college from savings. So, this is simply how much $5,000 will grow in the 17 years until your child is ready for college, based on the rates of return and asset allocations Fidelity has assumed for the calculator.]

You can bring coverage up to 60 percent by saving an additional $500 a month to the original $5,000 savings balance, according to the calculator.

What are the parents of college-bound children to do if they are short?

I turned to Mark Kantrowitz for some answers. Kantrowitz is a nationally recognized expert on student financial aid. His website (edvisors. com) is a valuable resource for both students and parents and includes tip sheets on Student Loans, Planning for College, Making College More Affordable, Scholarships, Filling the FAFSA, and Education Tax Benefits.

Kantrowitz suggests that parents think in three's. Realize that you won't be paying for college all at once, he explains: "Plan on ⅓ of the cost coming from past savings, another ⅓ coming from current income, and the final ⅓ coming from future income from loans."

For more wisdom, check out Kantrowitz's book *Twisdoms about Paying for College*.

"Twisdom" is a funny word, but it has a serious meaning. It's a short but sweet tweetlike rule of thumb that even the most short-attention-span student will enjoy.

Kari Emerson, my 20-something editorial assistant who pays great attention to detail, loved these insights. She said, "Twisdoms are easy to wrap my head around and easy to process and remember (especially compared to the other long, data-intensive resources on college savings that are out there)."

Who can argue with that? Here are some examples:

"It is cheaper to save than to borrow."

"Save a fifth of your income for the last fifth of your life."

"Live like a student while you are in school so that you don't have to live like a student after you graduate."

"Every dollar you borrow will cost about two dollars by the time you repay the debt."

"Budget before you borrow."

"Students who drop out of college are four times more likely to default on their student loans than are students who graduate from college."

Let me add a final thought: How about going to a college that replaces loans with grants? According to Sandra Block of Kiplinger, those schools are Yale, Vanderbilt, Davidson, Princeton, Harvard, Amherst, Bowdoin, Pomona, Swarthmore, and the University of Pennsylvania. To read Block's 2015 story, "10 Colleges That Don't Require Student Loans," go to kiplinger.com/slideshow/college/T014-S003-colleges-that-won-t-make-you-take-student-loans/index.html.

*   *   *

The next column is about College Scorecard, which is a terrific resource that may provide numbers that surprise you. Obviously, it's incredibly tough to get into Harvard, but did you know that it is, on average, pretty afford-able? Plus, with a high graduation rate and a low loan default rate, you can have some assurance of good value for your dollar. The site, run by the U.S. Department of Education, can help you to make more informed value choices when selecting schools to target.

SORT THROUGH THE VALUE OF POTENTIAL COLLEGE CHOICES

Originally published June 22, 2014; updated 2017

If you have a high-school student in the family who is going to be borrowing money to pay for college, consider choosing a college that is a good value.

How can you get information about affordability and value?

The place to start is the College Scorecard, a free site run by the U.S. Department of Education that you can find at collegescorecard.ed.gov/

The Scorecard was first made available online in early 2013; the data here is updated through 2017.

The site has information about almost 4,000 colleges that you can research one by one. You also can search based on programs/degrees, location, size, name of the college, type of school, specialized mission, and religious affiliation.

When I downloaded the list, first I screened for four-year bachelor-degree colleges, which gave me over 2,000 institutions. I sorted by average annual cost (also called net price), an exercise I highly recommend to parents of high schoolers who are getting ready for college.

The net price is "what undergraduate students pay after grants and scholarships (financial aid you don't have to pay back) are subtracted from the institution's cost of attendance."

If you compare the net price with the sticker price, you'll get an idea of how much grant and scholarship money is actually being applied to matriculating students. The Department of Education pulls data used to calculate average net price from IPEDS (the Integrated Postsecondary Education Data System), which is the annual report institutions file with the Department of Education. For more information about IPEDS, go to nces.ed.gov/ipeds.

More than one-half of the list cost under $20,000 a year, 302 were under $10,000, and 53 were under $5,000.

It may surprise some that Harvard's average net price is listed at only $17,882 per year. If you look up Harvard's College Scorecard, you'll see that the graduation rate is a strong 98 percent and that 70 percent of graduates who borrowed are paying down their debt within three years of leaving school and have less than one percent default rate, compared with a national average of 46 percent and 11.5 percent national average. The median earnings of former students who received federal financial aid is $90,900 compared to a national average of $34,300.

If you go back up the page to costs, you can click through to a "net price calculator" that will take you to Harvard's website. There you can see the sticker price —$69,600 a year—paid in full by some.

If you enter your personal financial information, you also can see the scholarship money that you might be able to claim if you were accepted.

Another way to use the College Scorecard is to search by degree and major, occupation, size of the student body, degrees offered (certificate, associate's degree, bachelor's degree), and location (ZIP code, state, region) and campus setting (city, suburb/town, rural area).

I searched for certificate programs for "culinary arts and related services" in the state of Kansas, finding 13 options that ranged from 309 students to 11,610 students. One had an average net price of $3,161 a year for an institution with a graduation rate of 26 percent and a cohort loan default rate of 9.6 percent. Another had an average net price of $15,094 per year with a 22 percent graduation rate and a 10 percent loan default rate, which is lower than the national average of 11.5 percent.

In searching New York, I found the Culinary Institute of America with an average net price of $30,321 per year, a graduation rate of 73 percent, and a loan default rate of 7.1 percent.

Of course, these numbers alone won't lead you to a decision, but they can give you perspective. You can judge whether the college is a good deal for you and open your eyes to good values outside of your local sphere.

If your goal is to prepare for the career of your choice while not over-paying for your education, College Scorecard is worth your time.

While the cost of college has skyrocketed, a college degree remains a reliable indicator of future earnings potential. In the next column, written in 2018, I discuss how to pay for college. While you should absolutely discuss with your children the value proposition of a certain college, if college is something your children are prepared to tackle, they can expect to have that recognized in future pay for the rest of their lives.

A COLLEGE DEGREE IS A GOOD INVESTMENT

Originally published January 28, 2018

If you have a junior in high school in your family, you may be planning to visit some college campuses over Spring break. As college education is still one of the best investments you can make, it's not too soon to think about paying for college.

College graduates earn almost twice as much as those who end their formal education at high school. And, the gap between high school drop outs and those who earn advanced degrees is even greater.

Based on the most recent Bureau of Labor Statistics data (3rd quarter 2017), the median income was only $27,144 for those who did not graduate from high school. Contrast that with a median income of $76,440 for those who earned an advanced degree.

The median income of graduates with bachelor's degrees (but no advanced degree) was $60,528 compared with $37,128 for high school graduates.

Paying for College

Finding the money to make the investment in a college education can be a challenge, but that should not stop you for two reasons.

First, there are new ways to save for college that are completely tax free. The 529 college savings plan offers tax-free savings opportunities to students and gifting opportunities for parents and grandparents.

Second, the true cost of college may be lower than you think. Before abandoning hope of a college education, look beyond the published "sticker" price.

Costs

If you are like many people, you may think that you need more than $200,000 to pay for a college education. You may be surprised to learn that this does not have to be the case.

Based on data from the National Center for Education Statistics (NCES), about 17.5 million students are enrolled in undergraduate college programs in the United States. About 7 out of 10 high school graduates went on to college (2 or 4 year programs) after graduation, according to NCES' most recent data (2016).

Most pay less than $12,090 a year for a college education—that's the published price for tuition and fees for the 2017/2018 school year at four-year colleges, according to the College Board ("Trends in College Pricing" [trends.collegeboard.org/college-pricing]).

If you carve out private colleges, the cost is even less: For the 2017–18 school year, the national average published cost of tuition and fees at four-year in-state public colleges was $9,970 a year, according to the College Board. Room and board averaged $10,800 at public colleges on a national basis for the 2017–2018 school year.

There are regional differences. For example, New England four-year public college tuition and fees were higher, averaging $12,990.

Paying for College

It is also very important to understand that very few students actually pay the full cost of going to college.

The truth of the matter is that most students receive some sort of financial assistance.

Financial Aid

More than 90 percent of students enrolled in private four-year colleges full time and more than 84 percent of public college students receive some form of financial aid, according to the most recent (2014–2015 school year) NCES study. While a new study is expected in early 2018, financial aid has been and continues to be a significant source of college funding.

Students enrolled in the 2017–2017 school year received $125.4 billion in grand aid (undergraduate and graduate), according to a study commissioned by the College Board titled "Trends in Student Aid."

Loans

In addition, students took advantage of $106.5 billion that was made available to them through various types of loans, according to the College Board. Work-study programs accounted for an additional $803 million of the available funding.

For further information on college costs and financial aid, you'll find College Board an excellent resource. You can call them at 212-713-8000 or visit their website at CollegeBoard.com. ▨

* * *

To make certain that your applications for aid and loans are given their proper due, be sure to read the next column for information on deadlines and a long list of common mistakes that applicants make that you can avoid.

APPLYING FOR A STUDENT LOAN
NOT AS EASY AS IT APPEARS

Originally published December 7, 2014; updated 2017

If you have a child who is applying for student loans, you'll want to get involved. The playing field is much too complicated for a 17- or 18-year-old to navigate alone. (Also, your financials will come into play unless your child is no longer your dependent.)

First of all, nothing is easy. Even deadlines can be complicated, there being three types: federal (June 30), state (they vary), and college (they vary as well). For a list of deadlines, go to https://fafsa.ed.gov/deadlines.htm, which is the U.S. Department of Education site for applying for a federal loan. The FAFSA application seems simple enough. The official website (https://fafsa.ed.gov/) makes it seem easy, telling the applicant that the application can be completed in an hour. There are five sections in the application: Student Demographics, School Selection, Dependency Status, Parent Demographics, and Financial Information. Then you sign and submit the application. What could be simpler?

Nonetheless, people make mistakes in filling out the FAFSA. Here are some of the most common, adapted from Mark Kantrowitz's book *Filing the FAFSA: The Edvisor's Guide to Completing the Free Application for Federal Student Aid*, which you can download for free at http://www.edvisors.com/fafsa/book/direct/.

One of the most common errors is to transpose digits when entering a Social Security number. "It is surprising how often applicants will swap two adjacent digits in their Social Security number or telephone number or have a typo in their names," according to Kantrowitz.

Here are 16 prevalent errors, adapted from the guide:

1. Avoiding the FAFSA altogether because of its complexity.

2. Transposing digits or letters (see above).

3. Including an extra zero, especially in dollar amounts, or duplicating a digit. Writing $500,000 instead of $50,000 or $511,000 instead of $51,000 can affect the expected family contribution (EFC).

4. Filing the FAFSA too late. Watch the deadlines. "Some award aid on a first-come, first-served basis until the money runs out," Kantrowitz said.

5. Filing the wrong year's FAFSA.

6. Using the wrong Social Security number, for example, using the Social Security number of a sibling or using the student's number when the parent's number is requested.

7. Using the student or parent's incorrect legal name. The name must match the name on the Social Security card. If the card shows a maiden name, use that name on the FAFSA. Later, correct the name with the Social Security Administration (ssa.gov).

8. Using the wrong date of birth.

9. Listing the student or parent's marital status incorrectly.

10. Writing in the wrong address (it must be the permanent home

address). It should match the address on the federal income tax returns.

11. Writing in the wrong federal income tax figure from a specific line on the federal income tax return.

12. Accidentally reporting adjusted gross income (AGI) as the federal income tax.

13. Estimating federal income tax because the 1040 has not been filed.

14. Specifying the wrong type of income tax return (Form 1040 or 1040A or 1040EZ).

15. Including qualified retirement plans and the net worth of the family home; these amounts are not reported as assets on the FAFSA.

16. Failing to report college savings plans of siblings (and the student) as assets of the parent if the custodial parent is the account owner. This includes 529 college savings plans, prepaid tuition plans, and Coverdell Education Savings Accounts.

You can get help from the financial aid office at your college or the college you want to attend. The FAFSA's online help is at fafsa.gov, or you can call 1-800-4-FED-AID (1-800-433-3243), the Federal Student Aid Information Center.

* * *

If you already have a family member with student debt, none of the facts in the next column will be news to you. But if you'd like to avoid being part of the statistics of crippling debt and credit-ruining defaults, consider thinking about the colleges and fields of study that are more likely to result in a student able to graduate with a high chance of paying back his or her loans. While college is about ambitions, I wrote the next column to say that a dose of pragmatism will pay off in many ways.

STUDENT LOAN DEBT IS A
TRILLION-DOLLAR PROBLEM

Originally Published June 15, 2014; updated 2017

The size, scope, and growth of student loan debt is a big deal: This type of debt is the highest form of household debt after mortgages, according to the Federal Reserve Bank of New York's "Quarterly Report on Household Debt and Credit" released in November 2017.

More than 45 million people had federal student loans as of the fourth quarter of 2017 according to Federal Student Aid, an office of the U.S. Department of Education. The total debt outstanding was more than $1.3 trillion.

During the last 30 years, costs have tripled at public four-year colleges, according to the College Board "Trends in College Pricing" 2017 publication. In the twenty years from 1997–1998 to 2017–2018, costs increased 110 percent.

The cause? An increase in enrollment and in tuition, according to the report. During the last 30 years, costs have tripled at public four-year colleges. From 1999–2000 to 2012–2013, costs increased 87 percent.

On a state-by-state level, the average outstanding federal student loan balance ranges from a low of $19,975 (Utah) to a high of $36,367 (New Hampshire). These are averages, of course; some balances are significantly lower and some are significantly higher, especially for students who borrow to pay for both college and graduate school.

Loan defaults are up. Eleven and one-half percent of borrowers entering repayment in 2014 defaulted on their loans, compared with only five percent in 2003, according to the report. A large number have small balances ($4,000 or less) to repay.

It's probably not surprising that more dropouts default than those who complete college. This also is not surprising: A student's major has been linked to the default rate. Some majors just don't prepare one for work, much less good pay. If you think about it, if you are going to borrow to go to school, the first thing on your mind should be your "hire-ability" after you graduate.

Choosing a major on the basis of earnings doesn't do the trick either, according to the report: "Choosing a major with high average earnings does not guarantee favorable outcomes for all students."

The seriousness of defaulting may not be appreciated fully by borrowers. Defaults are reported to credit agencies. That means credit ratings will be affected negatively, which in turn can preclude the ability to make purchases on credit.

Having a high student debt burden also can lead to defaulting on other obligations, such as credit card debt, according to the report. It can deter college students from pursuing graduate study. Although this may be heresy, I believe this is a good thing. From a financial management perspective, smart sequencing demands delaying grad school until college debt is paid off.

There are flexible repayment options available to borrowers that can help when making payments becomes difficult. Do borrowers know about these options?

The Department of Education is testing "new ways to reach 2.5 million borrowers with the greatest risk of encountering payment difficulty, such as borrowers who have left college without completing their education, missed their first loan payment, or defaulted on low balance loans, and get them back on track with their loan payments. The Department will also evaluate these strategies to identify which can be used on a larger scale and which are the most effective."

The bottom line is this: Student loans are one way to pay for education but not the only way. Eighteen-year-olds need guidance before entering into debt and in choosing a college on the basis of a value proposition instead of the size of the campus or whether it is in a large city. ▪

In the previous column, I suggested that pairing college dreams with some pragmatism might save a lot of financial headaches down the road. But how do you know if a career choice is a good one? In the next column, I describe a public site mynextmove.org available for free to all (including adults looking for a career change) that will allow you to see what sorts of knowledge, skills, and abilities are needed to do a particular job, what those jobs pay, and what the demand is in various geographies. You may even find a career suitable to your personality that doesn't require the expense and loans of a four-year college, pays good wages, and is in high demand in your desired area.

CAREER PATH IS A BIG CONSIDERATION WHEN CONTEMPLATING COLLEGE

Originally published June 29, 2014

Before incurring student loan debt, wouldn't it make sense to have a good idea of a career path? There is an abundance of information available to students on careers, and it is 100 percent free, thanks to the U.S. Department of Labor.

If you are interested in careers with a bright outlook—those which "will grow rapidly in the next few years, will have large numbers of openings, or are new and emerging careers"—visit the National Center for O*NET Development at Mynextmove.org.

There you will find a list of 109 careers that are expected to grow rapidly, 173 careers that have current openings, and 152 that are new or emerging careers.

In the first category, you'll find actuaries, geographers, electricians, elevator installers, health-care social workers, interpreters, nurse anesthetists, riggers, stonemasons, and surgeons, to name a few.

In the current openings category, you'll find accountants, bartenders, civil engineers, coaches and scouts, correctional officers and jailers, dental assistants, hairdressers, lawyers, machinists, pathologists, software developers, teachers, tellers, and welders, among others.

In the category of new and emerging careers, you'll find acupuncturists, anesthesiologist assistants, biochemical engineers, business continuity planners, compliance managers, endoscopy technicians, green marketers, intelligence analysts, online merchants, video-game designers, wind-energy project managers, and many more.

If you click on any of the careers, you'll be taken to a detailed description of the job. For example, an actuary's job outlook is bright, with new job opportunities "very likely."

The salary for an actuary is listed at $100,610 per year on average. You can click on "check out my state" to view a map of the nation showing where the opportunities for employment might be.

If you want more detailed location information, you can click the "employment and wages" link for a set of additional maps from the Bureau of Labor Statistics that show metropolitan areas. For example, the Kansas City, Missouri/Kansas, metropolitan area has 480 actuaries who earn an annual mean wage of $125,270. New York City's metropolitan area has 2130 actuaries who make an annual mean wage of $142,980. Another map shows the top-paying states for actuaries (Colorado, New York, Texas, and Idaho).

Back on the career detail page at MyNextMove.org, you also can find the broad industries employing actuaries: Finance and Insurance and Professional, Science, and Technical. There is even a "Find Jobs" link that brings you to current job postings for actuaries in a particular geography. Then go back to see what sort of training is required under "Education." A bachelor's degree or a certificate after college is "usually needed" to be an actuary.

If you click on "Find Training," you can search for schools offering the typical degrees. In Connecticut, Yale University, University of Connecticut, University of New Haven, and Central Connecticut State University offer programs preparatory to being an actuary: actuarial science, applied mathematics, or statistics.

If you click "find certifications," you'll be brought to a list of organizations that provide training and information, such as the American Society of Pension Professionals and Actuaries in Arlington, Virginia (asppa.org/). Work experience is required to gain an actuarial designation, as well as oral or written exams and continuing-education credits.

What do actuaries do? Quoting from the MyNextMove.org website, they "analyze statistical data, such as mortality, accident, sickness, disability, and retirement rates and construct probability tables to forecast risk and liability for payment of future benefits. May ascertain insurance rates required and cash reserves necessary to ensure payment of future benefits." The site also lists what you would do on the job, the knowledge you would need to do the job, the skills and abilities needed, your typical personality traits, and the technology you would use. In addition, you are offered the opportunity to explore similar careers, such as accountants, biostatisticians, and logistics analysts, among others.

The Bureau of Labor Statistics also offers information for an exhaustive list of careers. Search for Occupational Employment Statistics and profiles at bls.gov/.

With all this information so easily available, all students and their parents can address the choice of college with a view to preparing for a good career.

If you put this career information together with the column in this section on how to pick a college on the basis of value and affordability, you can improve your chances of graduating on a fiscally sound footing. ▪

*　*　*

Can generous benefactors who are paying for a student's education take advantage of tax breaks? While the simple answer is yes, I encourage you to read the following column, which will walk you through who can pay for what and qualify for what tax relief. It's a complicated, but potentially rewarding answer.

DO I GET A TAX BREAK IF I PAY EDUCATIONAL EXPENSES?

Originally published March 13, 2016; updated 2017

Here is a letter from a reader in New York:

> "There appear to be three ways to file and get credit for educational expenses: the American opportunity tax credit, the lifetime learning credit, and the standard tuition and fee deductions. What are the pros and cons and requirements of each?"

Tax breaks for education are important to understand, but they are not simple or straightforward. A lot depends on your personal situation.

Here are a few guidelines.

First, there are income caps. You cannot claim a lifetime learning credit (LLC) if you earn $65,000 or more (single filers) or $130,000 or more (joint return). When I use the term "earn," I'm talking about "modified adjusted gross income" (MAGI). Your MAGI is your gross income plus any tax-exempt interest income. Worksheet 3-1 in IRS Publication 970 shows how to calculate MAGI.

The American opportunity tax credit (AOTC) has a slightly higher income cap: $90,000 for single filers and $180,000 for joint filers.

Thus, if your earnings qualify you for the LLC, you also qualify for the AOTC, but you cannot use both credits for the same student (or take the tuition and fees deduction for the same student). The AOTC credit can be as high as $2,500, and the LLC can be up to $2,000. The AOTC is a refundable credit; the LLC is not. (If you don't normally file a tax return and you qualify for a refundable credit, you'll get a check in the mail from the U.S. Treasury.) You can claim both credits on the same tax return, but not for the same student.

Second, the expenses you want to claim for the credit have to be "qualified education expenses," which are generally tuition and fees "required for the student's enrollment or attendance at an eligible educational institution," according to the IRS. The IRS definition of an eligible educational institution is "generally any accredited public, nonprofit, or proprietary (private) college, university, vocational school, or other postsecondary institution."

The LLC applies to postsecondary education or courses to improve job skills. The AOTC is limited to four years of postsecondary education.

Third, the student also must qualify.

The AOTC is more restrictive than the LLC. A student cannot take advantage of the AOTC if any of the following apply:

1. The student had completed the first four years of postsecondary education as of the beginning of the relevant tax year.

2. The student claimed either the AOTC or the Hope Scholarship Tax Credit (replaced by the AOTC) for any four tax years before the relevant tax year.

3. The student enrolled for less than half-time or for less than one academic period at the educational institution.

4. The student was convicted of a federal or state felony for possessing or distributing a controlled substance.

None of these limitations applies to the LLC.

The best way to get an answer on which credit applies to your situation is to go through IRS Form 8863 (IRS.gov; search "Education Credits"), which you would attach to your tax return to claim a credit. You'll also want to study the instructions to the form.

Form 8863 starts you off with the following caution: "Complete a separate Part III on page 2 for each student for whom you're claiming either credit." You'll come back to Part I only after completing Part III for each student.

In Part III, you'll enter information about the student, who can be you the taxpayer, your spouse or a dependent, and the qualified educational institution.

By answering the questions in Part III, you will find out whether the student qualifies for the LLC or the AOTC.

Then you will return to Part I, which is all about you, the taxpayer. By filling out this section, you'll discover whether you qualify for a refundable AOTC. If you don't qualify, you'll go through Part II, which will determine whether you qualify for the nonrefundable LLC (a nonrefundable credit can reduce your tax, but any excess is not refunded to you).

If you don't qualify for the credits, you may qualify for a tax deduction. Deductions are not as valuable as credits. Credits reduce your tax bill dollar for dollar. Deductions reduce your tax bill by a smaller amount (the amount of your income that is subject to tax). Deductions require you to fill out Form 8917 (IRS.gov; search "Tuition and Fees Deduction").

* * *

Part of a child's education in financial literacy must include credit cards, as they are all but a necessity to navigate payments in the internet age. Teenagers have seen people swipe their credit and debit cards thousands of times, but do they really understand what is happening? Do they know about balances and the cost of carrying them? Do they understand what a credit record is, why it is important, and how to get a good one? As a parent, it helps to make the certainty of credit card applications at college a learning moment, an opportunity to teach someone about this important but potentially risky tool.

STUDENTS NEED TO LEARN
CREDIT CARD LESSONS

Originally published January 14, 2018

Do you have children in college? Have you talked with them about how to handle credit? When I wrote about this topic in 2008, students were inundated with credit card offers. According to Benjamin Lawsky, who, as a special assistant to the New York state attorney general, testified before the U.S. House of Representatives' Subcommittee of Financial Institutions and Consumer Credit, "marketers set up tables in high-traffic spots on campus, such as cafeterias, student unions, bookstores, and other campus buildings . . . [and at] campus events including freshman orientation, activity fairs, athletic events, and graduation fairs."

Then came the Credit Card Accountability Responsibility and Disclosure Act of 2009 (the CARD Act). Now, after the passage of the CARD Act, companies cannot sign up individuals under the age of 21 unless they or a cosigner over the age of 21 can demonstrate the ability to make payments on the account, according to Lewis Mandel, Emeritus Professor of Finance, State University of New York at Buffalo.

Marketers offering incentives like pizza can no longer do so while at "an institution of higher education" or even within 1,000 feet of the school. They also may not make such offers "at an event sponsored by or related to" the school. Credit ratings agencies are not prohibited from providing credit information for those under age 21. However, since few of those under 21 qualify for credit cards, their ability to build a credit record is limited.

Still, card offers are being made, and students need to know whether to act on them. You can expect that student credit cards will have less favorable terms than those offered to people who have a credit history; students are higher-risk borrowers.

Further, students, even those over age 21, may not understand that missing a payment or making a late payment not only increases the cost of credit, but also creates a negative credit history, something everyone should work to avoid.

"A bad credit history can make it harder for you to get mortgages, car loans and credit cards in the future," explained Matt Schulz, a senior industry analyst at CreditCards.com, a credit card comparison website.

"If you do get them, crummy credit can also cost you a fortune over the years in the form of higher interest rates and fees. It can also stand in the way of getting a job," explained Schulz.

What can a parent do?

Since going away to college is the first step toward independence, you want to be sure that you respect your child's need for self-sufficiency. But that doesn't mean he or she has to go it alone. There are simply too many serious, long-lasting repercussions.

Communication and planning are key.

First, before your child leaves for school, talk to him or her about the benefits and the detriments of getting a student card. Establishing a credit history is a benefit. So is learning the discipline of paying bills on time to avoid a negative history.

Second, research options together with your child. Look online at CreditCards.com (search for "student cards"), WalletHub.com (click on "Credit Cards," then "College Student") or creditkarma.com (go to "Credit Cards," then "Student"). Consider the fees, rates and penalties of different cards, and make a joint decision on the type of card that might make sense.

For example, you might consider prepaid cards or secured cards. Prepaid cards work like debit cards. No credit is extended. You prepay the card, and when the balance is low, you fund it. Secured cards require a cash deposit that acts as the credit line for the account. This allows a credit limit to be established, without risk to the bank.

Third, decide on an acceptable monthly budget and what to do if it isn't followed. Talk about how you would like your child to communicate with you if that happens.

Fourth, determine whether you and your child agree that he or she should not accept credit card offers before reviewing them with you.

Fifth, agree on how the two of you should check in with each other. Will you talk each month about finances, perhaps setting a date in advance? Will you encourage your child to let you know about challenges before they become problems?

In the beginning, your child will benefit from some gentle guidance. You don't want him or her to be adrift in a financial morass that could have been avoided with a little planning and care. Financial literacy calls for learning a new skill, and it is not reasonable to expect a child to go on this financial journey alone.

For information on the impact of the CARD Act, read the Consumer Financial Protection Bureau's report (the Card Act Report), which you can find at www.consumerfinance.gov. ▪

SECTION 8

Estate Planning

ARE YOU CURIOUS:

- When is the time right to discuss estate planning with your family?

- What should you do if you (or your spouse) suddenly become incapacitated?

- How can you prepare beneficiaries to manage an inheritance?

SECTION PREVIEW:

Estate planning is not just for the extremely wealthy who have "country estates." In this section, I have included columns that address questions such as: What happens if you have no will? What happens if you are incapacitated? What happens to your retirement plan when you die? I also cover tips on finding the right professionals as well as communicating your plans to your family members.

INSIDER'S PERSPECTIVE:

The 2016 Estate Planning Awareness Survey from Wealth Counsel reported on people's perceptions of estate planning. It found that "nearly half of all respondents believe that estate planning is only for the ultra rich and most people don't need it." That's not the case, as you'll discover in this section. For one, incapacity planning is important. For another, investment planning must be integrated with estate and incapacity planning. When we talk about estate and incapacity planning, we're talking about issues that need to be addressed to protect people as they go through life.

*   *   *

I kick off this section with a column on wills, as a will is the foundational document that will guide the disposal of your estate. In essence, if you want your wishes for your property, your children, your heirs, and even your burial to be followed, the best way to do it is to have a clear plan.

WILLS: WHO NEEDS THEM?

Originally published February 26, 2017

Sometimes it's beneficial to be in the minority: Only 42 percent of U.S. adults have wills, according to a recent survey conducted by Princeton Survey Research Associates International.

If you are not part of this select group, which includes only 20 percent of Millennials but 81 percent of people age 72 and up, the state you live in will determine the distribution of your estate when you pass away. That result may not be desirable.

For example, in my home state (Connecticut), if you have no will and are married but have no children, your in-laws receive a large share of your deceased spouse's estate. You, the surviving spouse, receive the first $100,000 plus three-quarters of your spouse's estate. Your in-laws receive the remainder. Thus, if your spouse has an estate of $500,000, you receive $100,000 plus $300,000 (three-fourths of $400,000). Your spouse's parents receive $100,000.

How many married couples without children would write their wills to achieve that result? I'm guessing not many.

Further, married or not, if you do have children, the probate court will determine your children's guardians. If you have a house, the court must appoint an administrator and hold a hearing before it can be sold.

Avoiding surprises is one very good reason to call a lawyer to do an estate plan even if you are a 25- or 30-year-old just embarking on a career and even if your biggest asset is your personality.

A well-crafted estate plan will include lifetime documents that go into effect in case of an incapacity—you run into a tree when you go skiing, someone T-bones your car, or you trip over a misplaced object. Incapacity can be temporary or permanent at any age.

Planning for incapacity through health-care directives, powers of attorney, and revocable living trusts is important regardless of your age. If you are a high earner or have significant savings or if you anticipate a sizable inheritance, estate tax and privacy considerations also need to be considered. Charitable interests and caring for siblings, parents, or children who may not be able to care for themselves also are part of the estate-planning exercise irrespective of age.

Although everyone needs an estate plan, younger adults may benefit from an attorney who is closer in age to them than to their parents, advises attorney Dan Fitzgerald of Cummings & Lockwood LLC, a Millennial with 11 years of practice under his belt.

Fitzgerald brings a fresh perspective that is based on his experience with young adults who are due to inherit wealth or have been financially successful at a young age.

For example, he points out that Millennials may have assets that previous generations did not have. "On top of the usual assets such as a home, cash, life insurance, retirement accounts, etc., Millennials have assets that are less tangible, such as the value derived from Facebook or Instagram accounts or an investment in a crowdfunding campaign," Fitzgerald explained. "These new modern digital assets, often governed by user agreements, need to be addressed in an estate plan to avoid unnecessary costs or disputes."

Another issue is marriage, which in previous generations was a trigger for estate planning. Now young adults are staying single longer, perhaps living together, and delaying marriage; only about 27 percent of Millennials are married.

Single Millennials require extra attention, Fitzgerald explained. They need to consider nontraditional estate-planning agreements such as co-tenancy agreements for nonmarried individuals who are cohabitating. Those documents need to account for the new definitions of marriage, such as same-sex marriage and domestic partnerships, for insurance purposes.

One final point: Many times, young adults don't realize they own assets that may push them into estate tax territory. Add a life insurance death benefit to the value of your house and you may have an estate that is potentially free from estate taxes on the federal level but taxable on the state level. With proper planning, the life insurance death benefit can be removed from your taxable estate.

No matter whether you consider yourself wealthy or poor, young or old, an estate plan can save real money and emotional grief, explained Fitzgerald.

* * *

While most think of estate planning in terms of what happens when you die, planning for what happens when you are unable to make decisions is just as important. To plan for that possibility, you may want to consider using a power of attorney in the event that you become unable to make the decisions for yourself. Read the next column to find out what a POA can and cannot do.

UNIFORM POA LAWS FOCUS ON INCAPACITY

Originally published July 3, 2016; updated 2017

What happens if a loved one becomes incapacitated after an accident or a disabling illness? Who pays the bills, does the banking, balances the checkbook, and takes on the financial responsibilities of everyday life?

To prevent uncertainty, you can take action in advance to appoint someone to step into your shoes if the need arises. One method is a power of attorney (POA) that is "durable," meaning that it's effective even if you later become incapacitated.

A POA is a legal document that gives authority to someone to act on your behalf. That someone is your "agent." You are the "principal."

In the POA document, you give the agent specific authority to act for you. For example: "I, Sam Smith, do hereby appoint Jan Jones my agent to act in my name, place, and stead in any way which I myself could do, if I were personally present, with respect to the following matters."

The POA goes on to list the matters over which the agent has authority and power to take action. Some examples are real estate transactions, banking transactions, handling insurance policies, making decisions on retirement plans, and taxes. Other possibilities are creating, amending, or revoking a living trust; creating or changing a beneficiary designation on an IRA; and even making a gift.

POAs are creatures of state law, which means two things: (1) specific rules must be followed for the POA to be valid, and (2) rules for POAs vary by state. In some states, the POA becomes invalid if the principal becomes incapacitated unless the POA contains special language providing for continuation.

Since our society is mobile, it would be nice if POA laws were consistent across all the states, especially when it comes to POAs that survive the principal's incapacity. That way, the POA would be valuable as an inexpensive way to have someone act for you "in the same way wealthier people use revocable, inter-vivos trusts," according to Benjamin Orzeske, chief counsel at the Uniform Law Commission (ULC), also known as the National Conference of Commissioners on Uniform State Laws (uniformlaws.org).

Established in 1892, the ULC studies different laws and drafts "uniform" legislation for the states to consider for adoption.

In 2006, the ULC tackled the issue of durable POAs when it released the Uniform Power of Attorney Act (UPOAA). That seems like old news, but it isn't. For example, Connecticut, my home state, adopted the UPOAA last year; the new laws were to become effective on Friday, July 1, 2016. However, on May 27, 2016, the effective date was delayed until October 1, 2016.

Other states that have adopted the UPOAA are Alabama, Arkansas, Colorado, Hawaii, Idaho, Iowa, Maine, Maryland, Montana, Nebraska, Nevada, New Mexico, Ohio, Pennsylvania, South Carolina, Utah, Virginia, Washington, West Virginia, and Wisconsin. (As of 2017, UPOAA had also been enacted in Wyoming, Texas, North Carolina, New Hampshire, Georgia, and introduced in Mississippi and the District of Columbia.)

The UPOAA offers some distinct societal benefits, according to Orzeske:

First, the POA is effective by default even if the principal becomes incapacitated at a future date. No special language is needed.

Second, safeguards are built in to protect an incapacitated principal from potential financial abuse. Also, there are statutory remedies to ensure that agents are held responsible for reimbursement of the principal's accounts.

Third, third persons (such as banks) are required to accept a POA unless a specific exception applies.

Fourth, there are clearer guidelines for agents.

Fifth, if the agent resigns, he or she must give notice to the principal. If the principal is incapacitated, notice is to be given to the person responsible for the principal's care.

Sixth, an agent who acts with care, competence, and diligence for the best interest of the principal is not liable solely because the agent also benefits from the act or has conflicting interests, which may be the case when the principal and the agent are members of the same family. Also, the principal may include an exoneration clause for the benefit of the agent.

For the lawyers: The UPOAA replaced the Durable Power of Attorney Act of 1979 (amended in 1987) and augmented the POA previously incorporated into the Uniform Probate code in 1969.

*   *   *

Let's face it, when seeking estate planning professional advice you are at a disadvantage in judging expertise. In the next column, I offer some tips on how to narrow the field and get to someone who is a good fit for you and your personal circumstances.

HOW TO FIND A LAWYER WHO CAN HANDLE ESTATE PLANNING

Originally published June 12, 2016; updated 2017

In my practice and through this column, people ask me how to find an attorney who can do estate planning for them. Finding an attorney is easy. The hard part is finding one who will be best suited for you. That is, you'll want to assure yourself that you hire a competent attorney who fits your personality, can meet your objectives, and is free from conflicts of interest.

Before beginning the search, you should know that some lawyers segment their practices by wealth. That happens either by design or by accident.

The smallest estates don't require tax planning. The primary concern may be how and to whom assets are distributed. You won't need someone who is an expert at transfer taxes (estate, gift, and generation-skipping taxes).

Tax planning becomes important with estates that will trigger a state or federal estate tax. [In 2017 the federal exemption was $5.49 million and was scheduled to increase to $5.6 million with the annual inflation adjustment. However, the new tax law effective 2018 doubled the exemption, but also changed the measure of inflation adjustment used. It is expected that the exemption will be $11.18 million, but that has not yet been confirmed by the IRS. Further, on 1/1/2026, the exemption will revert back to pre-2018 law, with the result that it will be reduced by 50 percent.]

Between $10 million and $15 million, people want to know how to take advantage of the lifetime gifting exemption and their annual exclusions (2018 update: $15,000 per recipient), according to estate-planning attorney David A. Handler of Kirkland & Ellis LLP of Chicago. Gifts reduce your taxable estate and the potential estate tax.

Above $15 million, which is Handler's primary focus, clients engage in proactive estate planning. Among other things, they may look into establishing foundations and setting up trusts that benefit charities and enable gift tax-free and estate tax-free transfers of wealth to heirs.

When you are ready, here are some questions to ask:

Experience: "What is your experience and background in estate taxes and planning?" You are looking for 10 years of experience or more unless you're willing to have the lawyer learn on your dime.

Clients: "What types of clients do you normally work with?" Look for assets, situations, ages, and needs similar to yours. A lawyer whose practice is built around hundreds of small clients will have a different focus from that of a lawyer who specializes in large estates.

Referral fees: If you were referred by a financial adviser or accountant, simply ask, "Are you getting paid a referral fee from the person who told me to call you?" (There also may be a reciprocal referral arrangement between lawyers; no money changes hands.)

Life insurance: Since insurance trusts have to be funded with life insurance policies, you need to know if the lawyer sells insurance. If the answer is yes, tell the lawyer that you won't be buying insurance from him or anyone who would share commissions with him for a sale. Why? You want independent advice from someone who has no incentive to sell you something, says Handler.

Fees: Ask about fees. Attorneys should be able to estimate the time it will take them to prepare a plan or offer you a fixed fee for the project.

References: It's always a good practice to ask the attorney to arrange for one or more references from clients who are in circumstances similar to yours. Find out whether the attorney returns phone calls, answers questions, and coordinates with other advisers.

Fiduciary relationships: Some lawyers volunteer to serve as trustees or executors, and many times consumers (grieving widows in particular) don't realize the potential for conflict.

If a lawyer drafting the trust also serves as a trustee, how can she represent the beneficiaries in the event of a dispute? A will may have ambiguities that can be challenged, or the will may be declared invalid. Handler asks: If the lawyer drafting a will is the executor, who is he representing other than himself?

Where can you find lawyers to interview? Start with the trusts and estates section of your local bar association or the American Bar Association (www.americanbar.org) to find an attorney in your community.

One final piece of advice: Remember that you are the client. The lawyer works for you. If you don't feel comfortable in an interview, you won't be comfortable as a client, and neither will your children or heirs who may inherit the relationship. ▪

* * *

One oddity of IRAs many are not aware of is that when you inherit an IRA, no matter how old you are, you must take distributions from the IRA. In the case of a child as the inheritor, this could be an interesting cash flow stream that, if properly invested, could come in very handy in supplementing income for a lifetime. Read on to see numbers showing the power of time and compounding.

RMDS FOR THREE-YEAR-OLDS:
THE BENEFITS OF STRETCHING AN IRA

Originally published January 4, 2015; updated 2017

If you have children or grandchildren, think about naming them as the beneficiaries of some of your traditional IRAs (individual retirement accounts). Inherited IRAs are a perfect way for youthful beneficiaries to benefit from lifelong cash flow. Handled correctly, they can be "stretched" to grow capital, continue tax deferral, and create wealth. But they also can be squandered easily when beneficiaries cash them out for consumer purchases, unaware of the huge opportunities they can offer.

Let me give you an example.

Jack, age 74, is the owner of a traditional IRA, and his granddaughter Jackie, age 2, is his one and only beneficiary. Say Jack died in 2017. At that age, his required minimum distribution (RMD) would have been $4,201, based on his $100,000 December 31, 2016, IRA balance. His RMD is calculated from IRS tables that you can look up in Appendix B of IRS Publication 590-B. Different tables apply depending on whether you are the owner of the IRA (Table III) or the beneficiary (Table I). Table II is for married owners whose owner-spouses are more than 10 years younger than they are (and sole beneficiaries of the IRA). Note that Tables I and II use the term "life expectancy," whereas Table III uses the term "distribution period."

For an IRA owner age 74, the Uniform Lifetime Table (Table III in Appendix B) shows a "distribution period" of 23.8 years; thus, $100,000 divided by 23.8 gets you the result ($4,201).

Since Jack died in 2017, Jackie will start taking her RMDs as a beneficiary in 2018 on the basis of her age, not Jack's. That switch to Jackie's age also changes the divisor, in this case to 79.7.

To make the math easier, assume that the inherited IRA's value was $100,000 at the end of 2017. Using Jackie's divisor of 79.7

(Table I for Use by Beneficiaries), her RMD would be $1,254, a fraction of Jack's RMD.

As a beneficiary in the following year, Jackie's divisor decreases by one. That is, instead of 79.7, the divisor becomes 78.7; the next year, the divisor becomes 77.7, and so on.

Using Brentmark Retirement Distributions Planner software (brentmark.com), I ran a few different return scenarios and limited the withdrawals so that nothing more than the RMD was withdrawn each year. I assumed that Jackie lived into her early eighties.

Because a two-year-old has a very long investment time horizon, I used an 8 percent return. At that rate, the $100,000 that Jackie inherited paid out $7 million over her lifetime. Although she started out with modest yearly withdrawals, as a result of long-term compounding, by the time Jackie reached retirement age, her RMDs were around $150,000 a year, increasing yearly. By age 70, her withdrawal was $225,000; it was $330,000 by age 75 and $486,000 by age 80. These withdrawals are taxable as income earned, somewhat like a pension check.

With just a 3-percentage-point differential (5 percent rate of return), the inherited IRA distributed substantially less over Jackie's life: only $1.2 million. Jackie's annual RMD started off at a low of around $1,200 and continued to increase yearly up to $56,000 by age 81. Even at this lower return, stretching the inherited IRA has a far better financial outcome than withdrawing the $100,000 IRA that Jackie inherited at Jack's death, paying income taxes on the withdrawal, and spending the rest.

Every time we talk about RMDs and IRAs, I will caution you to get tax advice before taking any actions. This is an area of tax law that keeps certified public accountants (CPAs) and lawyers busy year-round.

If you would like some additional resources, check out Vanguard (vanguard.com) and Fidelity (fidelity.com), both of which offer accurate information that you may find a tad easier to follow than IRS Publications 590-A and B. ▪

*   *   *

While we have talked about the importance of having a will earlier in this section, some assets may pass on to heirs outside of your will. An example is a 401(k) beneficiary designation. It is important to understand these types of directives and keep them up to date. This is discussed in the next column.

BE AWARE OF HOW ASSETS PASS TO HEIRS

Originally published March 18, 2012; updated 2017

Proper drafting of your will is only one step in the process of protecting your heirs from surprises.

You also need to be aware of how assets pass to heirs. Let me illustrate.

Your will provides that all of your assets go to your only child, Sonny. Your only asset is a 401(k) plan.

When you started participating in the plan 10 years ago, you filled out a 401(k) beneficiary designation naming your wife, Sonny's mother, as the sole beneficiary. You haven't made any changes since then even though you got divorced in 2005.

Who gets your 401(k) at your death? Your former wife. Unless there is an express provision in the 401(k) plan document that a beneficiary designation is revoked upon divorce (or a similar revocation provision), your former wife will receive the 401(k) upon your death, according to attorney Victoria Zerjav [then with] Kelley Drye & Warren LLP of Stamford, Connecticut.

Why? The beneficiary designation, not your will, directs what happens to your 401(k) at your death.

What does Sonny get? Nothing, since you have no assets passing by will.

You can think of a will as a catchall. A will controls property you own at your death that is not passed to beneficiaries through some other means. One example of such a transfer (called a "nonprobate" or "nontestamentary" transfer) is a 401(k) beneficiary designation. Another is a transfer-on-death account.

Your retirement plan may contain provisions that control what happens at death even *without* a beneficiary designation.

If you participate in a 401(k) or another retirement plan, you'll want to check the plan document, advised Bob Kaplan, [then] vice president and national training consultant for ING U.S.

Under the Employee Retirement Income Security Act (ERISA) (the law that governs 401(k)s), the spouse is automatically the beneficiary of the participant's 401(k) account, according to Mark Johnson, founder of ERISA Benefits Consulting Inc.

The participant can name someone other than the spouse as long as the spouse provides written consent. Some plans provide that only 50 percent of the account balance goes automatically to the spouse and the participant can name anyone else he or she wants to receive the remainder, Kaplan explained.

The default in 401(k) plan documents is usually in the following order: spouse, children, parents, siblings, and estate. Defaults come into play if you don't fill out a beneficiary designation.

In the case of divorce, some (but not all) beneficiary designation forms automatically revoke the election, Kaplan explained. However, some will not presume that there is an intent to revoke (some people may want to leave their ex as the beneficiary).

Getting back to the example above, suppose you remarried in 2006 but did not update your beneficiary designation.

Does wife number one or wife number two get the account?

If a participant remarries, the new spouse is the spouse and will assume all beneficiary rights, explained Kaplan.

"The reason that wife number two gets it over number one is because under ERISA, the spouse is the beneficiary unless the spouse waives his or her benefit," said ERISA attorney Ary Rosenbaum of the Long Island–based The Rosenbaum Law Firm P.C. Even if the second spouse signs a prenuptial agreement waiving his or her benefit, it is not considered a valid waiver under ERISA because the waiver must be completed after the marriage, Rosenbaum explained.

Of course, all these concerns can be minimized by simply updating the beneficiary form when life-changing events occur, such as marriage, divorce, or the birth of a child, suggested Kaplan.

Now is the time to review your holdings to determine how each asset would pass to a beneficiary or heir. Then do a flowchart to see what happens in the event of your death: who gets what and by what means. What passes through the will? What passes outside of the will? With that knowledge, you'll be able to do some contextual planning and avoid surprises. ▨

*   *   *

Let's discuss what happens to a 401(k) in the event of the owner's death and what to look for to ensure that the asset passes to the right beneficiary with the fewest complications. In the next column, you'll notice that special rules apply.

WHAT HAPPENS TO YOUR 401(K)
IN THE EVENT OF DEATH?

Originally published November 7, 2004

Your 401(k) plan is an asset. What will happen to that asset when you die? Who has the right to access the 401(k)? What steps do they have to take? Can they continue the 401(k), or do they have to close it out? Are there any tax consequences? Are there any tax-planning opportunities? Are there any time limits? Does the participant's age at death make a difference? If the participant is married, does that make a difference? What happens if a loan is outstanding at death? What about unvested employer contributions?

A 401(k) plan is governed by law and by the 401(k) plan document. Death will trigger a distribution from the plan to the beneficiary, and that in turn will trigger income taxes. The distribution does not have to be immediate, however.

Let's go through what happens at the death of a participant.

When a 401(k) participant dies, someone has to contact the 401(k) plan administrator to notify the plan of the death. The beneficiary should not wait to be contacted by the plan.

Usually, a family member or the executor of the participant's estate will make the call. Sometimes people identify themselves as the beneficiary, send in a death certificate, and wait. That's not enough. According to the U.S. Department of Labor, claims must be made in writing, and the sooner a claim is made, the better to start the period during which that claim must be processed.

The processing of a death claim may be done relatively quickly, but payment may be delayed. The timing of payments is set out in the plan document.

Processing also can be delayed. By law, the plan must tell you, the beneficiary, whether you will receive the benefits requested within

90 days after you file a claim. If the plan needs more time to determine your request, you must be notified within that 90-day period.

If your beneficiary claim is denied, you normally will be notified in writing; if you don't hear within the 90 days, you can assume it's been denied. In that case, you need to appeal the denial by following the plan's procedure for denials.

Before a distribution can be approved, the plan administrator needs to review documentation to ensure that the distribution is being made properly. The administrator will ask for a certified copy of the death certificate and will look up the beneficiary designation form.

Now let's turn to the plan participants. The plan participant normally fills out a beneficiary designation form when you enroll in the plan. (It is always wise to keep a copy of the form in a safe place together with your will or give a copy of the form to your lawyer.)

Normally, the beneficiary designation form will govern who gets the 401(k), but there is an exception. If the deceased participant was married and the beneficiary form designates someone other than the spouse, the administrator will not honor the directive unless the spouse consented to waive his or her rights to the 401(k).

The spousal waiver usually appears on the bottom of the beneficiary designation form.

If the administrator cannot locate a beneficiary designation (and the beneficiary cannot find a copy), the administrator will turn to the plan document to determine who is entitled to the 401(k).

In the absence of an effective beneficiary designation form, your spouse will get 100 percent of the 401(k). If there is no spouse, the plan document can provide any number of possibilities, and so it is a good idea to read it.

You can get one from your human resources contact. You'll find this information in condensed form in the summary plan description you receive when you enroll in the plan.

Some plans provide that when there is no spouse and no beneficiary designation, your 401(k) will be paid to your estate. That works for the plan, but it puts your heirs at a disadvantage, because the tax deferral benefits of your 401(k) normally may be lost if the 401(k) goes to your estate.

*　*　*

In the next column, let's turn to IRAs. What happens when an owner dies after the age of 70½?

WHAT YOU NEED TO KNOW ABOUT IRAS IN THE EVENT OF THE DEATH OF THE OWNER

Originally published January 11, 2015; updated 2017

Many times, couples name each other as the sole beneficiaries of their IRAs (Individual Retirement Accounts). Let's talk about what can trigger an IRS penalty if action is not timely in the event of the death of a spouse.

There are two types of IRS-mandated withdrawals from traditional IRAs. One is a withdrawal that the owner of the IRA needs to take if he or she is over age 70½—I'll call that an owner's RMD (required minimum distribution). Remember, we're talking about traditional IRAs, not Roth IRAs. Roth IRAs do not have owner RMDs.

The second is the withdrawal required of the beneficiary, the person who inherits the IRA—let's call that a "beneficiary's RMD." Both traditional and Roth IRAs have beneficiary RMDs.

In this column, let's talk about the owner's RMDs.

Say the husband owns a large traditional IRA and he is 75 when he dies in 2017. His widow must check to see if he satisfied his 2017 RMDs before 2017 ends. If the RMDs were not fully withdrawn by the husband in the year of death (2017 in this example), his widow (as the sole beneficiary in this example) has to direct the IRA custodian to make the withdrawal before Dec. 31, 2017.

The wife needs to submit a beneficiary claim form to the custodian of the IRA along with a death certificate. Some custodians make things easy; some don't. As an example, American Funds includes a provision in the claim form that takes care of the final RMD. "If claiming in the year of death and the RMD for the deceased owner was not satisfied, it will be removed proportionately from your account prior to any movement of assets." The RMD is sent to the beneficiary and is taxable to her as income.

If the widow does not take the RMD before the end of 2017, she will owe an extra tax when she files her 2017 tax return. The tax is the IRS's penalty on missed RMDs—a whopping 50 percent of the amount that should have been withdrawn but wasn't. For example, if the husband's remaining RMD is $50,000, the penalty is $25,000.

The IRS will know how much should have been withdrawn from IRS Form 5498, according to attorney Michelle L. Ward, JD, LLM, CSEP of Keebler and Associates LLP of Green Bay, Wis.

IRA custodians are required to provide IRA owners (and the IRS) with IRS Form 5498 each January based on the previous Dec. 31 value of the IRA. So, in this example, the IRS will have a copy of the 2017 Form 5498, as will the IRA owner.

Box 12a of the form shows the date by which the RMD must be withdrawn to avoid the excise tax (Dec. 31, 2015, in this case). Box 12b shows the amount of the RMD. However, the custodian has the option of leaving the box blank and offering to calculate your RMD for you in a separate statement by Feb. 1.

Box 11 shows whether an RMD is due for the tax year, but instructions for the form warn that even if the box is not checked, an RMD may be required.

The IRS knows how much was actually withdrawn from an IRA during a calendar year. Custodians report withdrawals on IRS Form 1099-R, according to Ward. Your tax adviser reports the missing RMD on Part IX of IRS Form 5329 (Additional Taxes Qualified Plans (Including IRAs)), which is attached to your Form 1040. The first line in Part IX is the RMD ($50,000 in our example). The next line is the amount actually distributed to you in 2017 (0). For the third line, you subtract the second from the first ($50,000-0 = $50,000). The last line is the additional tax: "Enter 50 percent of (the third line)."

The extra tax ($25,000) carries over to line 59 of Form 1040 (additional tax on IRAs).

That tax will be added to the total the widow owes in taxes in the year of her spouse's death.

It's best to notify your CPA (certified public accountant) or tax adviser immediately upon losing a spouse so that he or she can review RMDs with you—and help with tax filings should the final RMD be late. There is a way to request the IRS waive the 50 percent penalty for good reason, such as death within the last few weeks of December.

As always, let me caution you: Before taking any action as a beneficiary of an IRA, be sure to review your particular situation with your tax adviser. ▩

*   *   *

I included the next column here to highlight the need for communication with your family to ensure everyone understands your intentions. You may be gone, but you can save your loved ones additional grief by planning ahead.

TAKE TIME TO DISCUSS ESTATE PLAN WITH FAMILY

Originally published December 23, 2007

Should you ever talk to your adult children about your finances or your estate plan?

On the basis of my experience as a money manager, arbitrator, and mediator and previously as a lawyer on Wall Street, I can tell you when it is essential to do this:

- Situations that open you up to undue influence
- Situations that cut you off from your family

The worst cases are those which combine the two: A widowed individual is gradually cut off from his or her family by one of the children, a new spouse, or a trusted adviser.

The problem is that people who are under influence may not realize it, or if they do, they may not be able to do anything about it.

If they are infirm, they may even depend on that person for their care and find themselves in a Rasputin-like grip, powerless to change the dynamic.

Or they may be controlled by the voice from the grave. All too often one spouse tells the other, "Our adviser has taken care of us for a long time. If anything happens to me, just rely on him. Nobody else." The tragedy here is that a lot of things can change over 1, 5, 15, or 20 years. The size of the estate can multiply. Family situations change. Grandchildren come in to the picture. Tax laws change.

Although I have many examples I can share, here is one that involves a blended family.

In a late-in-life second marriage, a wealthy Florida doctor in his seventies, whom I'll call Rodney, marries a woman in her fifties whom he meets on a trip to Europe.

Rodney has two sons and six grandchildren, and his wife has two children of her own. The wife understands that she will inherit the home and that the rest of his assets will go to his children and grandchildren.

Rodney's health soon starts to decline, and his new wife steps into the role of caretaker. Rodney's friends call to check in on him, but he is usually unavailable to talk, either having a meal at the time or taking a nap, they are told.

They leave messages, don't hear back, and eventually stop calling.

Rodney's sons make efforts to see him. Many times they have trouble reaching him. Visits are awkward, since they have no private time with their dad.

The wife takes over the finances even though she has no experience making financial decisions. She starts interacting with Rodney's broker and establishes a relationship with Rodney's attorney.

Even though the children are concerned, they do nothing in order to give their dad the dignity he deserves.

Dad feels forgotten by his friends and family, unaware that they have been frustrated in their efforts to connect with him.

This is a disaster waiting to happen.

SECTION 9

Giving and Gifting

ARE YOU CURIOUS:

- How can you make gifts to your children that start them on the path to retirement security?

- Have you thought about leaving a legacy to your family or charity?

- What laws apply to gifting or charitable donations?

SECTION PREVIEW:

This section discusses buying stocks for young children, how a parent can set up an IRA for a minor, and helping children benefit from the advantages of Roth IRAs. We will also explore the concept of setting up a family foundation and discuss donor-advised funds as ways to give to charity and instill a philanthropic way of thinking for your family.

INSIDER'S PERSPECTIVE:

In my experience working with the wealthy, I often see families that have a culture of giving and gifting. Parents and grandparents often want to encourage learning through gifts that educate, such as gifts of stock or the gift of a college education. They may want to teach their children and grandchildren about the nobility and power of charitable activities. Knowing the options that are available for transferring wealth with little or no tax ramifications is essential.

*   *   *

How can parents and grandparents instill a love of learning through a gift? While a gift of cash is practical, have you considered the idea that a share of stock has the potential to increase in value, pay dividends, and possibly lead to knowledge and awareness of the financial markets that will benefit a child for a lifetime? Read on for some suggestions on how to implement this idea.

STOCKS FOR BABIES?

Originally Published May 1, 2014; updated 2017

"Mary," a brand-new grandmother, wants to buy a stock for her grandson, "Jeff." The question is: Which stock?

I asked Mary about her goal. Did she want the biggest potential gainer for some time far in the future, to help with college tuition, perhaps? Or was she thinking of using stock ownership to teach Jeff about investing when he got older? Did she want to build the stock position every year? And so on.

If the goal is simply to make money, the most efficient and diversified approach would be to buy a stock index fund. The oldest index fund for individual investors is the Vanguard 500 Index Fund (VFINX). You'll want to look at Vanguard's website at vanguard.com. Vanguard is the world's largest mutual fund company.

You'll also want to check out the SPDR S&P 500 ETF Trust (SPY), which is the most frequently traded exchange-traded fund, as well as iShares Core S&P 500 ETF (IVV).

If Mary wants to develop an interest and love of investing in Jeff, she might want to buy a stock that has two important characteristics: (1) The company's products need to be recognizable: products that Jeff will experience and relate to as a child; and (2) The company has to be known for longevity and safety. After all, the goal is to hold the stock for a very long time.

Since I make my living as a professional money manager, I have a policy of avoiding stock names in my column. This is the one and only time I'm making an exception, and I have to disclose that I do own the stocks I will be talking about next.

I'm sure you can think of a few stocks that fit the characteristics I mentioned: Coca-Cola (KO) and McDonald's (MCD) come to mind. These are stocks that are components of the S&P 500 Dividend

Aristocrats Index, which includes stocks that have increased their dividends for the last 25 consecutive years.

Another that may not be so obvious is Procter & Gamble. P&G has been in business for 180 years, and I think it's pretty safe to say that it will continue to be in business when Jeff turns 20 or 30 or even 90. The company has raised its dividend for the last 61 years (through 2017), which is significant to me.

Studies show that stocks with rising dividends outperform others over time. A 40-year (1972 to 2013) study reported by the American Association of Individual Investors, citing Ned Davis Research and Oppenheimer Funds, concluded that stocks with rising dividends rose 4,312 percent on a cumulative basis over that 40-year period. Compare that with stocks that cut dividends; they lost 5 percent during the same period.

P&G's products are household names. While Jeff was still in diapers, perhaps his mom was buying Pampers or Luvs. When Jeff is old enough to brush his teeth, he may be using Crest toothpaste. He may use Ivory soap and Pantene shampoo. His mom may use Olay Lotion.

When I asked Ian Gendler, executive director of research for Value Line (a provider of independent research), for a quick reaction to Mary's question, he said: "Without having the luxury of time to do some in-depth research, two stocks immediately came to mind that I would recommend for a 20-year holding period: Berkshire Hathaway (BRK.B) and General Mills (GIS). Both own and operate market-leading businesses in industries with high barriers to entry. No matter the economic climate or advances in technology, I am confident that Berkshire's insurance operations, railroad, and utilities will be in demand. The same goes for General Mills' cereals and other offerings." Good ideas indeed.

I encouraged Mary to do some research before deciding what to buy. There will be plenty of good options to choose from.

Start your research online at morningstar.com, a provider of independent investment research. Explore the website of the American

Association of Individual Investors (AAII.com). AAII is a nonprofit organization whose purpose is to educate individual investors. At valueline.com, you'll find complimentary reports and rankings. You'll find the top ten stocks by index weight chosen for the S&P 500 Dividend Aristocrats Index on the S&P Dow Jones Indices website at us.spindices.com. For a 2017 list, see Appendix B.

One final word. From my perspective, there is nothing better than a gift that educates. When a grandparent starts a child off with a small investment in a company that the child can understand as a user of the company's products and an owner of the company, that child can flourish as an investor later in life.

*   *   *

Do you agree that you should save for your retirement throughout your entire working life? If so, what if your child begins to earn money as young as 12? It turns out that if the child earns money in any given year, he or she is eligible to contribute to a retirement account. The next column walks you through a few scenarios for how you can help your child get started on a lifetime habit of saving.

CAN A 12-YEAR-OLD HAVE AN IRA?

Originally published March 23, 2014; updated 2017

Can a mother open an IRA (individual retirement account) for her 12-year-old son who earns money mowing lawns, shoveling snow, and doing other odd jobs?

After reading my columns on the benefits of Roth IRAs, "Emily" wants to know if she can set up one for her 12-year-old son, "Luke."

The answer is yes, and there is no better way to get Luke on the road to building retirement wealth slowly but surely, something he will need to do considering four facts:

1. People are living longer, increasing the risk of outliving one's money.

2. Social Security retirement benefits are potentially vulnerable in light of the federal debt.

3. Investing small amounts of money over long periods builds wealth through the math of compounding.

4. A Roth IRA allows growth to occur free from the drag of taxes during the investment period and when one is withdrawing money after retirement.

How can someone in Emily's position make it happen? Does she need Luke to focus on a future 50 years from now instead of using his earnings to go to the movies with his friends?

Hardly.

As long as Luke has earnings, a parent, grandparent, aunt, uncle, family member, or anyone else who cares about Luke's future can make a gift to a Roth IRA set up for him by an adult. (However, note that not all IRA custodians accommodate IRAs for minors.)

Say Luke earned $500 during a tax year when the maximum allowed to be contributed to a Roth IRA is $5,500, as it is now (in 2017 and 2018).

Emily can "gift" $500 to Luke's Roth. That's the amount he is eligible to contribute to the IRA on the basis of his earnings. (The maximum is the lesser of $5,500 or 100 percent of earnings. In this case, $500 is 100 percent of his earnings.)

Emily is comfortable making the gift, but she also would like Luke to learn the importance of saving for the future. Therefore, instead of funding the entire $500, she decides to offer Luke a matching program. For every dollar Luke contributes to the IRA, she will contribute $5. Again, based on Luke's earnings of $500, the maximum total contribution is limited to $500.

That way, Luke can have his spending money and help fund his IRA at the same time. The Internal Revenue Service does not care that the cash that goes into the IRA came from a gift. It just wants to make sure that Luke actually earned the money that has been contributed to his IRA.

By the way, Emily will want to help Luke create a file that records Luke's annual earnings and contributions.

There are no gift tax consequences in this scenario. Keep in mind, however, that if Emily's gift puts her total gifting to Luke over $14,000 for the year (2017), she will need to file a gift tax return [2017 update: $14,000 is the annual gift tax exclusion amount for 2017, rising to $15,000 in 2018]. For more information on gift taxes, read instructions for Form 709, United State s Gift (and Generation-Skipping Transfer) Tax Return. Another resource is the IRS's "Frequently Asked Questions on Gift Taxes," which is available at irs.gov and search for "gift tax."

Don't confuse the annual gifting exclusion with the annual IRA limit, which is the lesser of 1) $5,500 for someone under age 50 ($6,500 for those age 50 or older) and 2) 100 percent of earned income.

To actually set up a Roth IRA for a minor child who has earned income, you'll need to locate an IRA custodian that accepts minor accounts.

Here are a few that offer both traditional and Roth IRAs to minors: Schwab, E*TRADE, and TD Ameritrade. If you go online to these organizations and search for IRAs for minors or custodial IRAs, you'll find information on how to proceed.

Schwab calls a minor's IRA a Custodial IRA. The account minimum is $100. You can find the application at schwab.com and search for "custodial IRA for children," or you can call 866-855-5635.

E*TRADE's (us.etrade.com) program is called IRA for Minors. There is no minimum. Find the application on their website by searching "IRA for Minors" and click "Get Application," or you can call 877-921-2434.

TD Ameritrade's program is called Minor Individual Retirement Account, and you can find it online at invest.tdameritrade.com and click "Open New Account" (fill out your personal information and then click on "all account types" below the box with "Most common account types," and there you will be able to select "Minor Roth IRA"). You also can call 800-276-8746. As with E*TRADE, there is no minimum to open an IRA.

One more thing: When Emily sets up the Roth for Luke, she is the "custodian" and Luke is the "account owner."

When Luke reaches the age of majority (18 in most states), he will obtain full control of the IRA and the custodian will fall away, explained Mark Luscombe, principal analyst at Wolters Kluwer Tax and Accounting. ▪

*   *   *

The next column, written in 1999 and updated in 2017, continues the subject of Roth IRAs for kids. A key message is how a small stock market investment can benefit from time.

The returns mentioned in the column have been achieved historically—the secret is taking advantage of a long investment horizon.

Gifting, even to minor children, may take the form of Roth IRA contributions if they earn money. This will not only be tax advantaged for your child, but can lead to educational moments that he or she can pass on to his or her own children.

HOLIDAY GIVING

Originally published December 19, 1999; updated 2017

As the holiday season approaches, think about funding a Roth IRA for your children if they have earnings.

A parent or legal guardian may establish a Roth for a child and fund it up to the maximum permitted by law (check for current contribution limits at irs.gov). The actual dollar amount you can put aside will depend on your situation. Here are a few examples.

Your daughter, "Janie," is 12 years old. Janie baby-sits for the neighbor's children. This year she makes $500. Based on Janie's earnings, the maximum Roth contribution she can make is $500.

Your son, "John," is 22 years old. John makes $10,000 this year. Based on John's earnings and age, he can put a maximum of $5,500 into his Roth.

There are two big advantages to gifting a Roth to a child.

First, this is money earmarked for retirement that Janie and John cannot access without paying a penalty. If it is invested for growth in stocks or stock mutual funds, this money can grow and compound over and over before your children start to take any of it out.

The second issue is taxes. There aren't any.

The Roth is not tax-deferred. It is tax-free. In contrast to a traditional IRA, the IRA owner (Janie or John) will not get a tax bill from Uncle Sam when they take out Roth money in retirement (more than 5 years from the establishment of the Roth). Also, unlike a Uniform Gift to Minor's Act account you can set up for your children, neither you nor your child pays any taxes at all. In a Roth, you can sell holdings for a gain without paying a capital gains tax. You can earn interest and dividends without paying an income tax.

To give you an idea of how significant these two advantages can be, let's say you give Janie $500 a year until she is 18 to fund her Roth, for a total investment of $3,500 [$500 a year for 7 years].

[2017 update: We're working with a very long investment horizon of 53 years (from age 12 through 65). For historical context, consider all 55 year holding periods in the stock market from 1927 through 2016. Following the investment pattern described in this column, here are the returns for large company stocks: 13 percent (best); 11 percent (median); and 9 percent (worst). Shortening the holding period to 40 year holding periods, the best drops to 12 percent, but the median and worst remain at 11 percent and 9 percent.]

Let's say Janie adds no money of her own at any time, even after she starts earning a paycheck. If she holds on to her Roth through good markets and bad and her investments average a 10 percent return per year, at the age of 65 (53 years from age 12) she will have half a million dollars in her Roth.

With luck (a particularly favorable market), she might achieve a 12 percent average annual return. Then, at age 65 Janie would have a $1 million Roth, all of which is tax free.

How can an investment of $500 a year for seven years (over a holding period of 53 years) grow to a million dollars? When sound investments are made and taxes do not eat away at returns, time works its magic. That's compounding.

Janie will be able to continue to hold on to the Roth for as long as she likes. In contrast to a traditional IRA, there is no requirement to start withdrawing her money after she reaches the age of 70½. Janie can withdraw any time after age 59½ without any penalties, and anything she withdraws will not be taxed.

Are 10 and 12 percent returns reasonable?

Ten and 12 percent are not unreasonable long-term expectations for a diversified portfolio of stocks. I stress the words "long-term" and "diversified." For a $500 investment, you might consider stock mutual funds as an investment for Janie's Roth.

How do you get started?

Call your mutual fund company, broker, or financial adviser. Confirm that they can offer a Roth for a minor (not all Roth custodian agreements allow parents or guardians to sign on behalf of a child). Ask for a Roth application and an investment recommendation. Choose your investments, fill out the application, and send in your check. It's as easy as that.

If you are considering a Roth for yourself, remember that you need to qualify. To be eligible for making a $5,500 annual contribution, there are income limits. (Check irs.gov for the current limits.) Because these limits are based on modified adjusted gross income, make sure you check with your accountant before disqualifying yourself.

* * *

Let's discuss giving to charity through a DAF or donor advised fund. Keep in mind that a DAF is somewhat like a mutual fund for charitable giving— you pay someone else to administer what can be fairly small sums of money (as little as $5,000), yet you still have the opportunity to have your gifts benefit the causes you support. In the next column, you'll find a number of resources to aid your research into whether this solution is right for you.

DO YOUR HOMEWORK ON DONOR-ADVISED FUNDS

Originally published March 26, 2017; updated 2018

If you are charitably inclined, you may have come across donor-advised funds. DAFs are sponsored and administered by public charities, such as community foundations and charitable institutions set up by major financial firms such as Vanguard and Fidelity.

The idea is that you can use a DAF for your charitable gifting in an administratively easy fashion.

You set up an account with your favorite DAF sponsor. You send in a donation, which is an irrevocable gift—you give up control over the funds. You get a tax deduction for that donation (within tax limits). The sponsor of the DAF now owns the money.

The sponsoring charity keeps it invested until you are ready to make donations to specific charities. When you are ready, you "tell" the DAF sponsor to send gifts to your charities of choice. However, the DAF is donor-*advised*, not donor-controlled (in contrast to foundations). As a result, you are making "recommendations" to the DAF sponsor on where to send money.

For that reason, one of the most important things to do when choosing a DAF sponsor is to understand its grant-making policy and grant-making restrictions. "The challenging part is to match your charitable gifting desires to a compatible DAF sponsor," explained Eileen Heisman, president and CEO of the National Philanthropic Trust (NPT).

Grants to charities from DAFs exceeded $15.5 billion in 2016 [2018 update], according to NPT. The average size of a DAF acount was about $299,000 [2018 update], but DAFs can be as small as $5,000 (the minimum for Fidelity Charitable or Schwab Charitable) or $25,000 (the minimum for Vanguard Charitable).

You could have a DAF with millions of dollars as well, according to Heisman.

To get a handle on DAFs, I would start with NPT's most current donor-advised fund report, which you can find at nptrust.org/daf-report/. Take a look at recommended reading as well at nptrust.org/philanthropic-resources/recommended-reading/.

That will give you a good start.

Then you'll want to dive into details. The best way to do that is to compare and contrast some offerings. For example, you'll want to know the fees that apply (setup fees, annual administrative and maintenance fees, other fees, and the cost of investments). You'll want to explore grant recommendation minimums, timing, and amounts as well as the basics, such as how to open an account, how tax deductions work, and whether you can donate stock or other assets or just cash. Don't forget legacy options: what happens to your DAF after your death.

To do further research, read Vanguard Charitable's "Policies and Guidelines" at Vanguardcharitable.org, search "Policies and guidelines," then click to download. Compare it with Fidelity's (Fidelitycharitable. org and search "donor advised."); then click "What is a Donor-Advised Fund?" NPT's (Nptrust.org and mouseover "What We Offer;" then click "Donor-Advised Funds"), and Schwab's (schwabcharitable.com), then check "Program Policies" at the bottom of the home screen.

When I asked Heisman why DAFs are so popular now even though they have been around since the 1930s, she shared this insight: DAFs used to be the domain of development officers when everything was paper-based. When financial institutions entered the scene, they saw DAFs as an opportunity to reach the mass market through technology. Now a donor can go online to set up a DAF and make grant recommendations. Fast-forward to today: There are thousands of financial advisers, and they often are the catalysts for creating DAFs.

Here is Heisman's recommendation: "Do your homework when you pick a sponsor. Make sure you pick one that is a good match to your profile as a donor."

According to NPT sourcing the Urban Institute, there are an estimated 1.6 million registered public charities in the United States. The number of DAFs increased by 6.5 percent in 2016 from 2015, reaching 284,965.

*   *   *

For those of you with substantial assets that they desire to donate to charity, you may want to consider setting up a private foundation. In the next column from 2014 (updated 2017), I provide resources that will help you to decide how to structure your charitable giving program.

FEELING CHARITABLE? HERE ARE SOME GUIDELINES TO GIVING

Originally Published June 1, 2014; updated 2017

If you believe you can make a difference in the lives of others, you may be thinking about volunteering your time to charitable causes or making gifts to a charity.

The "vast majority" of high-net-worth individuals and families do, according to the "2016 US Trust Study of High Net Worth Philanthropy." Almost 91 percent of those surveyed give to charity, and almost 5 out of 10 volunteer.

Why do people give to charity?

Most (94 percent) give because they "believe their gift can make a difference," according to the study. Donors report feeling personally fulfilled when they engage in charitable activity. Only about 1 out of 3 make gifts to charity primarily because of the tax benefits.

For people who want to have a more direct impact on a person in need, private foundations are worth consideration. There are close to 80,000 private foundations, according to the Indiana University Lilly Family School of Philanthropy.

The Barbara and Stephen Miller Foundation intervenes at "crisis points" when people find themselves on the verge of becoming homeless. Something as simple as a car breaking down can cause a person to be unable to pay a utility bill. The foundation steps forward with a grant of less than $1,000. That's made a difference in the lives of 109 people the foundation has helped in two years.

A private foundation usually is funded by a family or corporation. Its primary activity is giving away money to other charities, but private foundations are able to give to individuals in need as well. The IRS publication to read is "Disaster Relief: Providing Assistance Through Charitable Organizations," which is available at irs.gov/pub/irs-pdf/p3833.pdf.

These individuals cannot be relatives or friends. Such gifts are not permitted under self-dealing rules and trigger an excise tax. You'll want to read more on that topic in IRS Publication 557, "Tax-Exempt Status for Your Organization." Another resource is "Life Cycle of a Private Foundation," which you can find at irs.gov.

Foundation Source, the nation's largest provider of support services for private foundations and the winner of the Best Philanthropy Offering at the inaugural Family Wealth Report Awards 2014, provides 10 reasons to consider setting up a foundation.

Here are a few to consider:

1. Get a current tax deduction in the year in which you make a contribution to your foundation. However, you can make grants from the foundation to your charitable causes over time. You are required to distribute 5 percent of the assets of the foundation yearly.

2. Leave a lasting legacy: Foundations last beyond the donor's lifetime, as the assets of the foundation can grow because of earnings and additional gifting. As a result, your grants to your charitable causes can be far greater than the amounts you donate to your foundation.

3. Family involvement: Through your foundation, you can establish a tradition of charitable giving with your children and grandchildren.

For more information, Foundation Source provides a wealth of resources for those who want to learn more about setting up and running a private foundation at foundationsource.com.

For a copy of the current Foundation Source material on private foundations, go to foundationsource.com. Search for "annual report." [2017 update: called the "Private Foundation Investment Performance Report," www.foundationsource.com/resources/library/2017-private-foundation-investment-performance-report/.]

For information on tax deductions, you'll want to read IRS Publication 526, "Charitable Contributions," which is available at irs. gov. Gifts to charities are tax-deductible if you itemize deductions on Schedule A of your tax return (IRS Form 1040). As explained in IRS Topic 506, "Charitable Contributions," to be deductible, charitable contributions must be made to qualified organizations, never to individuals except that you can affect individuals directly through a private foundation. ▪

*　*　*

In the next column, I discuss some of the differences between foundations and donor advised funds and offer resources for further research.

WHEN IS A FOUNDATION A BETTER OPTION THAN A DAF?

Originally published April 2, 2017

Donor-advised funds (DAFs) can be funded with low minimums (for example, $5,000). A private foundation is another vehicle for charitable causes.

For a number of reasons, the dollar amount that it takes to set up and manage your own private foundation is higher. My rule of thumb is this: Consider a private foundation if you start with, say, a $500,000 donation, but only if you intend to add more either during your lifetime or through your will.

Some would consider that dollar amount too low, and indeed it would be except for the advent of foundation administrators such as Foundation Source, the nation's largest provider of comprehensive support services for private foundations. Although this is not an endorsement, I have had clients use Foundation Source, and so I am familiar with its services.

In my personal experience, the motivation to set up a foundation instead of donating through a DAF has to do with family dynamics and the desire to be in charge of your own charitable entity.

I see two types of situations that seem to favor foundations over DAFs: (1) wealthy individuals and families who want their children and grandchildren involved in a very meaningful way—somewhat like running a family business—with the goal of supporting the family's lifelong charitable causes and (2) wealthy, charitably inclined individuals and couples who have no heirs. In either case, the motivation is to use wealth to benefit charitable causes now and beyond the lifetimes of the donors, in fact, in perpetuity.

The focus on perpetuity can be persuasive. With a DAF, your "advisory privileges" can end at a point in time, depending on the DAF (for example, after one or two generations). When that happens, the money held in the DAF can revert to the DAF's sponsor.

The assets you donate to the foundation are within your control when it comes to how you invest and where you custody those assets as well as how much you give to charity. (Once you donate to the foundation or a DAF, the money belongs to it, not to you.)

The foundation is required to give away 5 percent of its assets each year. Normally, there is no comparable requirement for DAFs, but one may be imposed by a particular DAF-sponsoring organization.

It is possible to fund a foundation with a wider array of assets than DAFs, such as real estate, stock options, art, and privately held stock, with the understanding that the deduction usually is done on a cost basis instead of market price.

If the donation is cash or qualified appreciated stocks (publicly traded and not restricted), the deduction for a foundation (and a DAF) is at market value. For example, a stock with a cost basis of $10 per share and a market value of $100 per share qualifies for a deduction of $100 per share. The donation caps out at 20 percent of your adjusted gross income (AGI) but can be carried over for five years (DAFs have a 30 percent cap). To get a much better understanding of taxation, an excellent resource is "The Nuts and Bolts of Private Foundations (for Estate Planners)," a presentation by attorney Alan F. Rothschild, Jr., of Page, Scrantom, Sprouse, Tucker & Ford P.C. of Columbus, Georgia. (The paper was presented at the Heckerling Institute conference in 2017. For a copy, e-mail lwr@psstf.com.)

Unlike DAFs, the foundation can reimburse you for expenses you incur to run the foundation, including your visits to charities, legal and accounting fees, and the cost of family members who work for the foundation.

You can do more creative gifting with a foundation than with a DAF. A Foundation Source publication states, "Foundations may grant directly to individuals, support international organizations, establish scholarship and award programs, run their own charitable programs, make loans, loan guarantees, and even donate to for-profit businesses when the funds are used for a charitable purpose."

This column only touches on some of the important distinctions. You'll definitely want to know more. Here are two additional sources of information.

An excellent resource is "Private Foundations: What You Need To Know" (AdlerColvin.com; click "Resources" then "Select Practice Area" and click "Private Foundations;" scroll to select the memo), with general information of interest to all and special interest to my California readers, by attorney Erik Dryburgh of Adler & Colvin of San Francisco.

On Foundation Source's website (foundationsource.com), you'll find numerous references, including "Tax Benefits of Creating a Private Foundation" and "Private Foundation and Donor-Advised Funds: A Side-by-Side Comparison."

Epilogue

Sharing Wisdom

G IFTS OF MONEY HAVE TANGIBLE VALUE, BUT WHAT ABOUT gifts of knowledge? In this final column of the book, I share the wisdom of a gentleman who wrote to me about how his generation was influenced by the legacies of frugality, thriftiness, and education instilled in him by his parents. Wisdom: There is no more valuable gift that a person can give to another. "Sam" said it well: *"No secrets; you just have to set ideals and ethics, learn from those before you, and don't be dumb."*

SAM'S SIX LESSONS

Originally published November 19, 2015

Every now and then, I get a letter from a reader that I must share with you (with his permission). I'll call him "Sam." His letter is priceless:

My parents were high-school graduates, blue-collar, FDR Democrats—married 63-plus years before they passed away. My dad was a machinist his whole life (except for World War II). The most he ever made was about $8.50 an hour, and that was after all of us kids (five of us) had left home. My mom was a stay-at-home mom and frugal shopper extraordinaire. After Dad's retirement they lived solely on Social Security, albeit in a paid-off home and a relatively cheap economy in [the Midwest].

We were raised in a small town in a kind of "Mayberry" upbringing that revolved around family, school, church, and social organizations. By today's definitions, we would have probably been considered lower income (or less), but we never thought of ourselves as such. Our parents were prime examples of frugality and thriftiness. Even though they were "only" high-school graduates, education was primary in the home, and it was just expected that each of us would go to college. All five of us did; however, our parents did not and could not afford to help us out, so we all financed college on our own way. Here we are 73 years after their marriage, and this is how their five children have fared:

My oldest brother: Two years of college, flunked out, joined Seabees, Vietnam vet. Started own remodeling company, married a teacher. Married 45 years, both retired. Net worth $1.5 million—investments and real estate. . . Reside in [the Midwest] part of the year, in the [South] for four months in winter and travel extensively in RV. Two sons—one college degree, both working and married.

Myself: Went to undergraduate college on ROTC scholarship, then got two master's degrees, Vietnam vet, got flying training in Air Force. Retired airline pilot. Married 42 years to teacher. Both of us retired. Net worth about $3 million—I took a lump-sum retirement prior to company going into bankruptcy. Also small teacher's pension. . . Travel extensively. Two daughters—both with degrees, one has master's, both working (one lives [overseas]) and one married.

Sister: Went to college on loans and worked part time. Retired teacher married 27 years (second marriage after first husband died) to a retired teacher. Have two teacher's pensions, plus additional net worth about $1 million—mostly in real estate and investments. Two sons—one college degree, both working, one married.

Younger brother: Went to college on scholarships, loans, and working. College graduate with some post-grad credits. Still working—executive in high-tech manufacturing. Married 34 years to a teacher. Net worth $1 million in real estate and investments.

Two daughters and a son—all three with degrees, all working, one daughter married.

Youngest brother: Went to college on a full scholarship for academics and need. College degree, worked as executive in consulting industry, now retired. Married 30 years to a college-trained counselor, but she was strictly the "CEO of the family" while he worked up the corporate ladder. Net worth $20 million. Two sons, both with degrees, both working, neither married. So what is the "secret" of our success? The fact of the matter is that there is no secret:

1. Get that college degree—lots of ways to finance it, but get a degree. Get the degree in an employable field—a "gender studies" degree is admirable, but how does that translate into a job? Education is key—not only in the field you will work, but in educating yourself about money and investing.

2. Find a good spouse and stay married—divorce is financially devastating. The five of us have been married a total of 178 years.

3. Start investing early in your working life. We all did that. I started putting into a 401(k) when it was first offered by my company in 1984. Time and consistency are your allies.

4. Six of us have or will have pensions from our employers during retirement—unfortunately, that is a benefit that is quickly vanishing from the employment landscape.

5. Live within your means—don't "try to keep up with the Joneses." One of my favorite quotes is from Lee Eisenberg's book *The Number*: "Want what you have, not have what you want." We all buy automobiles, no leases. The youngest brother did lease a car once a number of years ago and vowed never again. We drive our cars for

years; no new cars every three years for us. My sister just traded in a 20-year-old, 240,000-mile van a few weeks ago. Her and her husband were going to pay cash for the new car, but got a 1.5 percent interest rate. They figured they could make more keeping the money invested, so took the loan. All of us do such transactions.

6. Be as financially savvy as possible. The five of us have had a family "mutual fund" since 1991. We each put in money each month, and it gets invested in individual stocks. It keeps us all connected, we learn from each other, and currently it finances the yearly "meetings" we have. Each summer since about 1989, we have gotten together as a family for at least a week—great times and memories.

In looking to the future, what we achieved is not impossible—maybe just a bit harder in today's economy. Of my parents' 11 grandchildren, five are married. Of those 16 in the next generation, 12 have college degrees, all 16 are employed in well-paying jobs, and the five married couples all have their own homes. None of the 12 college graduates has any college debt. All have followed our example and invested money toward retirement, although all are eventually destined to inherit various sums of money.

No secrets; you just have to set ideals and ethics, learn from those before you, and don't be dumb.

*   *   *

What a great letter. Don't hesitate to share your thoughts and advice with me anytime. Email me at readers@juliejason.com. While responding to all letters is not always possible, I do read them and welcome your views.

Appendices

Appendix A

	S&P 500 Dividend Aristocrats Class of 2009	
#	Ticker	Company
1	MMM	3M Company
2	ABT	Abbott Labs
3	AFL	AFLAC, Inc.
4	APD	Air Products & Chemicals
5	ADM	Archer-Daniels-Midland
6	ADP	Automatic Data Processing, Inc.
7	AVY	Avery Dennison Corp.
8	BCR	Bard (C .R.), Inc.
9	BBT	BB&T Corporation
10	BDX	Becton, Dickinson
11	BMS	Bemis Co.
12	CTL	Century Telephone
13	CB	Chubb Corp.
14	CINF	Cincinnati Financial
15	CLX	Clorox Co.
16	KO	Coca Cola Co.
17	ED	Consolidated Edison
18	DOV	Dover Corp.
19	EMR	Emerson Electric
20	XOM	Exxon Mobil Corp.
21	FDO	Family Dollar Stores
22	GCI	Gannett Co.
23	GE	General Electric
24	GWW	Grainger (W.W.), Inc.
25	TEG	Integrys Energy Group, Inc.

		S&P 500 Dividend Aristocrats Class of 2009
26	JNJ	Johnson & Johnson
27	JCI	Johnson Controls
28	KMB	Kimberly-Clark
29	LM	Legg Mason
30	LEG	Leggett & Platt
31	LLY	Lilly (Eli) & Co.
32	LOW	Lowe's Co.
33	MTB	M&T Bank Corp.
34	MCD	McDonald's Corp.
35	MHP	McGraw-Hill
36	PEP	Pepsi Co, Inc.
37	PFE	Pfizer, Inc.
38	PBI	Pitney-Bowes
39	PPG	PPG Industries
40	PG	Procter & Gamble
41	STR	Questar Corp.
42	ROH	Rohm & Haas
43	SHW	Sherwin-Williams
44	SIAL	Sigma-Aldrich
45	SWK	Stanley Works
46	STT	State Street Corp.
47	SVU	Supervalu, Inc.
48	TGT	Target Corp.
49	USB	U.S. Bancorp
50	VFC	V.F. Corp.
51	WAG	Walgreen Co.
52	WMT	Wal-Mart Stores

Appendix B

#	Ticker	Company
		**S&P 500 Dividend Aristocrats Class of 2017**
1	MMM	3M Co.
2	ABT	Abbott Laboratories
3	ABBV	AbbVie, Inc.
4	AFL	AFLAC, Inc.
5	APD	Air Products & Chemicals, Inc.
6	ADM	Archer-Daniels-Midland Co.
7	T	AT&T, Inc.
8	ADP	Automatic Data Processing
9	BCR	Bard C.R., Inc.
10	BDX	Becton Dickinson & Co.
11	BF.B	Brown-Forman Corp B
12	CAH	Cardinal Health, Inc.
13	CVX	Chevron Corporation
14	CINF	Cincinnati Financial Corporation
15	CTAS	Cintas Corporation
16	CLX	Clorox Co.
17	KO	Coca-Cola Co.
18	CL	Colgate-Palmolive Co.
19	ED	Consolidated Edison, Inc.
20	DOV	Dover Corporation
21	ECL	Ecolab, Inc.
22	EMR	Emerson Electric Co.
23	XOM	Exxon Mobil Corp.
24	FRT	Federal Realty Investment Trust

		S&P 500 Dividend Aristocrats Class of 2017	
25	BEN	Franklin Resources, Inc.	
26	GD	General Dynamics	
27	GPC	Genuine Parts Co.	
28	GWW	Grainger W.W., Inc.	
29	HRL	Hormel Foods Corporation	
30	ITW	Illinois Tool Works, Inc.	
31	JNJ	Johnson & Johnson	
32	KMB	Kimberly-Clark	
33	LEG	Leggett & Platt	
34	LOW	Lowe's Cos, Inc.	
35	MKC	McCormick & Co.	
36	MCD	McDonald's Corporation	
37	MDT	Medtronic PLC	
38	NUE	Nucor Corporation	
39	PNR	Pentair PLC	
40	PEP	PepsiCo, Inc.	
41	PPG	PPG Industries, Inc.	
42	PG	Procter & Gamble	
43	SPGI	S&P Global	
44	SHW	Sherwin-Williams Co.	
45	SWK	Stanley Black & Decker	
46	SYY	Sysco Corporation	
47	TROW	T Rowe Price Group, Inc.	
48	TGT	Target Corporation	
49	VFC	VF Corporation	
50	WBA	Walgreens Boots Alliance, Inc.	
51	WMT	Wal-Mart Stores	

Appendix C

		Bulls and Bears		
Bull or Bear	Start Date	End Date	Months	S&P % Change
Bull	8/1/1921	9/7/1929	97.2	394.9%
Bear	9/7/1929	6/1/1932	32.8	−86.2%
Bull	6/1/1932	7/18/1933	13.6	177.3%
Bear	7/18/1933	3/14/1935	19.8	−33.9%
Bull	3/14/1935	3/6/1937	23.7	131.8%
Bear	3/6/1937	3/31/1938	12.8	−54.5%
Bull	3/31/1938	11/9/1938	7.3	62.2%
Bear	11/9/1938	4/28/1942	41.6	−45.8%
Bull	4/28/1942	5/29/1946	49.0	157.7%
Bear	5/29/1946	5/17/1947	11.6	−28.8%
Bull	5/17/1947	6/15/1948	13.0	24.4%
Bear	6/15/1948	6/13/1949	12.0	−20.6%
Bull	6/13/1949	8/2/1956	85.7	267.1%
Bear	8/2/1956	10/22/1957	14.7	−21.6%
Bull	10/22/1957	12/12/1961	49.7	86.4%
Bear	12/12/1961	6/26/1962	6.5	−28.0%
Bull	6/26/196	2 2/9/1966	43.5	79.8%
Bear	2/9/1966	10/7/1966	7.9	−22.2%
Bull	10/7/1966	11/29/1968	25.7	48.0%
Bear	11/29/1968	5/26/1970	17.9	−36.1%
Bull	5/26/1970	1/11/1973	31.5	73.5%
Bear	1/11/1973	10/3/1974	20.7	−48.2%

Bulls and Bears				
Bull or Bear	Start Date	End Date	Months	S&P % Change
Bull	10/3/1974	11/28/1980	73.8	125.6%
Bear	11/28/1980	8/12/1982	20.5	−27.1%
Bull	8/12/1982	8/25/1987	60.4	228.8%
Bear	8/25/1987	12/4/1987	3.3	−33.5%
Bull	12/4/1987	7/16/1990	31.4	64.8%
Bear	7/16/1990	10/11/1990	2.8	−19.9%
Bull	10/11/1990	3/24/2000	113.4	417.0%
Bear	3/24/2000	10/9/2002	30.5	−49.1%
Bull	10/9/2002	10/9/2007	60.0	101.5%
Bear	10/9/2007	3/9/2009	17.0	−56.8%
Bull	3/9/2009	12/31/2017	105.7	295.2%

Bull	Average		52.0	160.9%
	Median		49.0	125.6%
Bear	Average		17.0	−38.3%
	Median		15.8	−33.7%

Source: CFRA S&P DJ Indices. Past performance is no guarantee of future results.

Index